POSITIVE RECOVERY DAILY GUIDE

THRIVE IN RECOVERY

Jason ZW Powers, MD, MAPP

POSITIVE RECOVERY

FLOURISH IN RECOVERY

ISBN: 1492952648
ISBN 13: 9781492952640
Library of Congress Control Number: 2013919223
CreateSpace Independent Publishing Platform,
North Charleston, South Carolina

"This is another must-have book from Dr. Jason Powers. He truly seems to have tapped into the science of happiness with his latest work. This is a powerful daily tool that will enable you to lead a more meaningful and fulfilling life. Best of all, this daily guide is not just for people in recovery from drugs or alcohol. It is useful for anyone desiring relief from helplessness, depression, anxiety, and pessimistic thinking. It can lead to genuine victories over the wrong ways of thinking we are all capable of. I will insist my patients get copies!"
—Mike Leath, MD, Chief Medical Officer, Memorial-Hermann Prevention and Recovery Center

"Dr. Jason Powers has created a practical guide for addiction recovery that differentiates itself from others by employing a selected set of sage theories and principles drawn from his studies in positive psychology to addiction management recovery. His book is the full package. It dispenses an array of practical tools to help move forward toward a better self. This is not 'happiology.' This experience is infused with scientific wisdom."
—Bob Easton, flourishing researcher

"Dr. Jason Powers continues to write with thoughtfulness and rich insight. His book communicates practical, engaging tools to awaken individuals in recovery."
—Bryan M. Davis, MD, DABAM

"People will love how this book mixes scientific data with wonderful quotes from a variety of inspiring sources ranging from literature, science, and the arts. Personally I loved the direct, succinct style of presenting what can be for many a simple, direct process in their lives. This work rolls medicine, science, recovery, and psychology all into some amazing thoughts and tools that anyone can use to enrich his or her life."
—Dr. Don Hauser, MD, President, The Hauser Clinic

"Bravo to Jason Powers for successfully translating and integrating the evidence of the science of positive psychology into practical implementation for addiction recovery. Positive Recovery is Jason's masterpiece and will revolutionize the way addiction is treated."
—Larry Benz, President and CEO, Confluent Health

"In *Positive Recovery Daily Guide*, Dr. Jason Powers offers a simple yet effective way to enhance the happiness of the recovery journey. Using a simple daily approach, Dr. Powers gives the reader a view of SMART (specific, measurable, achievable, relevant, and timed) activities one can do to change one's life. This new book doesn't ask every reader to be a saint but rather to change just a little one day at a time. This is something anyone can do, and it's an achievement every recovering person wants."
—Howard C. Wetsman, MD, FASAM, Chief Medical Officer, Townsend

"Action is an essential tool to long-term, successful recovery. *Positive Recovery Daily Guide* is an action tool that will empower anyone in recovery! These daily strategies are effective, fun, and inspirational. They will boost self-esteem and lead to a happy, joyous, and free recovery."
—Scott F. Basinger, PhD, Founding Executive Director, The Hope and Healing Center Institute; Former Dean, Baylor College of Medicine

"Dr. Powers puts the resilience in recovery! *Positive Recovery Daily Guide* is an invaluable recovery tool that combines the right amount of inspiration and structure to support the newly recovering into long-term resilience."
—Crystal Collier, PhD, LPC-S, Director, Behavioral Health Institute at the Council on Alcohol and Drugs Houston

When I was five years old, my mother always told me that happiness was the key to life. When I went to school, they asked me what I wanted to be when I grew up. I wrote down "happy." Then they told me I didn't understand the assignment, and I told them they didn't understand life.

—John Lennon

Welcome! This book is *your* daily positive recovery guide. Mark the date you begin so you can keep track. Start on day one and go through the book every day for 365 (or 366) days. Then repeat the process year after year.

Positive Interventions

Each day reflected in this book comes with an intentional strategy designed to boost well-being. These strategies are called positive interventions—PIs for short. Benefits of engaging in these enriching activities include improved relationships, strengthened recovery, more balanced emotional health, and much more.

Slow and steady wins the race. When you repetitively apply yourself to making positive contributions to your (and others') well-being, you broaden your skills and build your resources. In turn, these positive strides in wellness are self-reinforcing. They enable you to flourish in your recovery and life.

Often Getting Sober Is Not Enough

Leaving the wretched prison of active addiction is awesome and liberating, but even if you work a great program, there is no guarantee you will truly flourish in recovery. The PIs in this book use new scientific findings and combine those with effective relapse-prevention techniques. The end result is this custom-tailored book specifically geared to help you thrive in recovery.

Each PI in this book is engineered to bring about positive changes and help you flourish in recovery. While some of these PIs have been scientifically validated using the same rigorous standards as medical research, the field of science dedicated to improving well-being (positive psychology) is new. So far, different validated PIs can't fill a calendar year, but I'm not so easily dissuaded. I don't know about you, but I'd rather strive to thrive by applying what we've learned so far than settle for less, waiting around for more empiric PIs. I'd much rather try to flourish and live the best life I can than simply live in order to avoid a relapse.

Get Busy

Any happiness-building PI only works when it's applied—not studied in the abstract. My hope is that you will engage with these PIs and try them yourself. You can't read or think your way to living the best life possible. You gotta get going.

Not a Cure-All

While every day of this guide contains specific strategies to help maintain recovery and enhance well-being, this book is not a self-help cure-all with a euphoric guarantee. You won't love every PI.

Some PIs will speak to you more than others. Some will really resonate, and some might seem dull. However, keep an open mind, and put in the work. Like the character in Dr. Seuss's *Green Eggs and Ham*, you'll never know what you'll like until you try it.

Habit and happiness take time, effort, and repetition. Finding what works for you takes practice and dedication. Who knows? You might find you will adapt in surprising ways. What once seemed silly could end up bringing the most joy.

Most importantly, you should realize that there are no shortcuts in living the best life possible. The PIs outlined in this book are not commandments. They are meant to be both profound and fun.

Get Gritty
Getting out of one's comfort zone is required to leave addiction behind. Be prepared to dig in and use grittiness when the PIs challenge you to push through preconceived notions or just to find the time to get 'em done.

Getting through life's difficulties fosters the admirable and durable character trait of grit—a gift that can carry you through other challenges that life will inevitably present. Grit helps maintain long-term recovery.

Remember that these strategies are meant to significantly add to your life, but they are *not* meant to replace your recovery program or any other form of treatment. These PIs can be used within any recovery fellowship or program, but PIs can only add to, not replace, other effective tools.

I make no guarantees as to the medical or therapeutic information in this book. It's not an alternative to medical or psychological advice from your physician or other health-care provider. If you attend therapy or treatment for any emotional issues whatsoever, please clear these techniques with your physician or other health-care provider. While positive psychology interventions are generally benign, it's better to use prudence here.

PositiveRecovery.com
This website is meant to be a safe online community of like-minded people pursuing the same end—happiness in recovery. There you'll find a portal with resources. This includes a place to keep track of each day's positive intervention.

It's free of charge (although we won't refuse donations to help maintain the site). Check in with us as often as you like to keep track of your recovery, goals, and progress. You'll also be able to journal on the site on those days whose PIs call for that, as well as discover helpful tips, share experiences, and perhaps offer some of your wisdom to others.

Jason ZW Powers, MD, MAPP | vii

Often you'll see a variant of "share with us" at the end of a PI's instructions. This phrase is simply asking you to share your thoughts or entries *if you wish.* Don't feel obliged; it's completely voluntary. The site is not meant to be a form of treatment, so make sure you don't confuse this social media platform for a substitute for therapy.

Happiness

The secret to happiness is not a secret. Happiness is not "all in your head." People cannot simply decide to be happy. It's not that easy. You can increase your overall level of happiness, but it takes intentional practice—repeatedly doing the right things.

Contrary to what you might have heard, happiness isn't waiting for you with the perfect job, fewer pounds, or a better climate. What is happiness, anyway? Have you given that question much thought? If you have, you know defining happiness is not simple.

It's complex, to be sure, but we now know a lot more about happiness (from a scientific perspective) than we've ever known before. We know it's not pleasure. It's not an emotional state of perpetual bliss. Happiness isn't limited to temporary warm and fuzzy emotions. It might include pleasure and other positive emotions, but happiness isn't even possible without occasionally experiencing negative emotions such as sadness, resentment, disappointment, and loneliness. Humans are not made to walk around with permanent smiles on their faces. Trying to force happiness all the time is unnatural and leads to unhappiness.

William James, the father of American psychology, said, "Thinking is for doing." Positive thoughts are important, but you cannot get all that you wish by hoping or thinking. Positive thinking alone is not at all sufficient to bring about the best life possible. While positive recovery leans heavily on building happiness, I appreciate that life is not a fairy tale, and no amount of work can possibly shield everyone from what might come. Pain and fear are not optional in life, but what you do with them is up to you.

Positive Recovery is designed to help you learn effective strategies for managing life's difficulties, such as anxiety, stress, longing, resentment, and self-doubt. I believe that by engaging in the PIs in this guide, you might not feel fantastic all the time, but your authentic state will move steadily toward a more enhanced, thriving, and complete version of your best self.

How Much Happiness Is in Your Hands?
Human beings are born with genetic set points for happiness. Those with high set points (people with a happy disposition) will never become low set pointers (people with a not-so-happy disposition), or vice versa. However, research reveals that it is within an individual's power to live at the highest range of what is possible.

While your genes contribute approximately 40 percent to your overall well-being, genes are not in charge of your destiny. Your set point is more like a set range. High and low set pointers alike benefit from positive interventions. No matter where your set point might be, you can habituate those behaviors that improve and sustain well-being.

Where you focus your attention and how you act are the keys to happiness. People can change their overall levels of well-being! Surprisingly, where people live and how much money they make contribute very little (if at all) to their happiness. To put it simply, apply yourself where you have the power to change things, and leave the rest where it belongs—out of your control.

What Gives?
You might wonder how happiness is related to addiction. After all, isn't this a book to help people thrive *in recovery?* For a more in-depth view on the relationship between happiness and addiction, check out the videos on PositiveRecovery.com. However, also chew on the following:

Addiction Develops Due to Misguided Pursuits of Happiness

Emotionally speaking, addicts generally use addictive substances or engage in addictive behaviors for two primary reasons: to make good feelings feel better (celebrating a promotion, holiday, or accomplishment; getting "high") or to make bad feelings feel less bad (seeking numbness; avoidance; alleviation of anxiety, depression, or pain). In either case, these goals (though misguided and shortsighted) basically define the pursuit of happiness.

This drive to feel good, however, is not sustainable over the long run. Fortunate addicts find their way into recovery, and in doing so, they open themselves up to developing sustainable means of fostering happiness without substances and/or processes. Moving away from misguided pursuits of happiness allows people to examine their choices and live in harmony with integrity.

Develop Positive Habits

Take your time. Be patient. The results will come. Remember, Rome was not built in a day, and hindsight is twenty-twenty. Studies that examine so-called overnight successes reveal that companies and people who achieve greatness do so by repeatedly making small steps. Like the tortoise and the hare demonstrate, incredible feats arise from the repetition of small feats. As cliché as it sounds, the journey of a lifetime starts with just one step. Similarly, thriving in recovery happens one day and literally one choice at a time. Choices become actions, actions become habits, and habits become character. Character makes one's destiny, which leads to one's legacy.

Grow to Progress—Not to Perfect

Growth is your birthright. Remember that recovery is about progress and not perfection. By intentionally directing your attention and behaviors, you make the choices that shape your progress as you forge your destiny. Trials and tribulations are part of life, and you are not a victim of circumstance unless you think you are.

In order to fulfill your potential, you must face new challenges over and over again. Fortunately, you can nurture your building blocks, such as character strengths and mutually supportive relationships. That way, when challenges face you, you're likely to do more than just survive; you're prepared to thrive.

One Day at a Time—One Year at a Time

You will only get out of this (or anything else for that matter) what you put into it. Commit to going through this guide for one calendar year. When you have a year's perspective, judge for yourself. In one year, see whether or not you've experienced an improvement in your overall level of happiness. If you're interested in actually measuring your well-being, you can find links to free, scientifically validated surveys that can measure and help you track everything from happiness to grit on PositiveRecovery.com.

Other People Matter

Christopher Peterson, one of the fathers of positive psychology, often said that other people matter. The reason is simple: research clearly shows that nurturing relationships are the largest contributor to overall well-being. In recovery, others matter a whole lot. They can offer accountability, insight, and support, and all of these contribute to either preventing relapse or intervening quickly should one happen.

Journaling

Journaling is key. Indeed, writing goals down is so important to attaining goals that many claim something simply won't happen if it's not written down. This claim is based on findings that show that people who write down their goals are more likely to achieve them, earn more money, and enjoy more overall success.

Journaling has many other benefits as well, such as enhancing resilience, organizing thoughts, promoting self-awareness, and helping promote insight. On days you choose not to journal, make sure you at least spend some time reflecting on the day's exercise. Create a section in your journal called "Where My Mind Wanders To." Keep track of this section and compare its entries over time to discover your mind's travel habits.

Just Say *Om*

Meditation is key too. It can help you learn more, boost your well-being, and improve your physical and emotional health. Preliminary studies of addicted populations using meditation demonstrate that it can reduce drug and alcohol use and substance abuse—related problems in addicts and alcoholics, as well as decrease psychiatric symptoms such as depression and anxiety.

Additionally, meditation is linked with other psychosocial benefits. It can increase mental clarity, engender more positive relationships, and increase work productivity.

Stress can hurt us physically and emotionally. Relaxation techniques and their emotional signature of contentment help to undo the harmful effects of negative emotions. Learning to cultivate mindfulness during calm periods of life can help you build supplemental emotional resources to be drawn upon during challenging moments. Meditation does not have to be long to be effective. Even brief relaxation practices can decrease the negative effects of stress.

Mindfulness meditation (defined as nonjudgmental awareness of experiences in each present moment) directs attention in positive ways. Mindfulness can improve a variety of psychiatric symptoms, decrease activity in the amygdala (the brain's main fear structure), and enhance relaxing alpha waves in the brain.

Meditation is challenging and can be especially so for addicts. Many serenity seekers state that they struggle with meditating, as they are convinced they aren't doing it right or can't clear their minds. This is a state of paralysis by perfectionism—inactivity brought about by the conviction that meditation should be something it's not. I encourage you to release these perfectionist ideals that hold many back. Allow yourself to engage with the work and learn from your experiences as you go.

Spirituality—Search for the Sacred

For the purpose of engaging with this book and your recovery, personal exploration of your concept of "spirituality" is paramount. You alone have the responsibility and privilege of exploring what you hold sacred or uplifting. Across all major world religions and spiritual, moral, and theological perspectives exists the creed of avoiding harm to others; many also say that we should treat others with the kindness we would like to receive. Yet despite this widely accepted belief structure, many also still struggle with exclusivity, judgment, and intolerance toward others. This judgment prevents people from learning from fellow humans and cuts them off from life-enhancing connections. People risk falling into resentment, arrogance, or ignorance when they judge and prematurely shut out those around them.

Watch

I've discovered and employed one interesting and unusual strategy for improving well-being. The scientific study of happiness teaches us that it is possible to improve well-being by doing what happy people do. Among other things, happy people are grateful, optimistic, and prosocial (they help others). I was not born with a genetically high set-point range for happiness. Even in recovery, my natural perspective was not sunshine and smiles. My mind would automatically identify and point out whatever was wrong or lacking in a situation, place, or person. It can be frustrating to live with such a mind.

After learning about positive psychology, however, I decided to wear a vibrating watch that was set to vibrate five to eight times daily. Whenever this alarm went off, I would practice doing what happy people do. After a lot of diligent practice, my mind began to shift away from anxiety and pessimism toward happiness and hope. Why not give it a shot yourself? For example, when the watch vibrates, you can:

- Focus on something to be grateful for
- Look for new ways to use strengths
- Remind yourself to be present in the moment
- Focus your attention on something good in your environment
- Focus your attention on something good about other people
- Reflect on ways you are growing
- Look for ways to help others and take the focus off yourself
- Remind yourself of the day's assignment
- Savor something in the past, present, and/or future
- Respect happiness and aim to improve it in yourself and others
- Listen to any music playing in the background of your location and try to enjoy it
- Do something for someone else as soon as the alarm goes off

- Go outside and enjoy nature
- Savor a simple pleasure you are experiencing at the moment
- Unplug from all media for three minutes and meditate
- Remind yourself of your personal mission (see Day 5)
- Smile authentically
- Change small talk–dominated conversations to something deeper (if appropriate)
- Take the moment to really listen to others
- Laugh out loud

Within a year of doing this, optimism, gratitude, and peace became the norm for me. I'm still the same (occasionally moody) person with the same imperfect tendencies, but I worked hard to create positive habits, and I have felt what it's like to rewire my brain. Also, I am not alone. So far, many others have told me about their own similar life-changing experiences as a result of either having been trained in leading Positive Recovery groups or by having been 'students.'

I do strongly believe that if you engage in these PIs, you will bear witness to positive transformations in your life—but there is only so much any one approach can do. Please make sure you seek professional help whenever needed.

DAY 1

Goals are dreams with deadlines.

—Diana Hunt

Setting goals is an essential element of effective personal development. You can help yourself achieve what you desire in life and boost your happiness by making SMART goals (S: specific; M: measurable; A: achievable; R: relevant; T: timed). One reason many people do not attain their goals is that they don't make them with these qualities in mind. SMART goal planning helps people conceptualize and achieve valuable and even audacious goals.

Meaningful goals increase your chances of success, but they also improve well-being and life satisfaction. Another simple yet powerful tool to help you achieve your goals is planning specific steps by which to reach them.

Today's PI
Start this year in positive recovery with a goals-related PI.

    1)   List three goals to accomplish in the next year.
    2)   List three things you can do in the next six months to reach each goal.
    3)   List three things you can do in the next three months to reach each goal.
    4)   List three things you can do in the next month to reach each goal.
    5)   List three things you can do in the next week to reach each goal.
    6)   List three things you can do today to reach each goal.

Remember, the greatest feats or accomplishments come about when you choose to release yourself from the self-defeating idea of "impossibility." Dream large! Once you are done, place your list somewhere visible (and safe) at home or at work. Keep track of your progress at PositiveRecovery. com. Read over your goals daily.

Note: you will revisit these goals and make changes along the way.

DAY 2

For the things we have to learn before we can do them,
we learn by doing them.

—Aristotle

An effective technique when you feel low is to fake it until you make it. Research shows that when people imitate how the body naturally behaves when experiencing a certain emotion, they can powerfully influence the production of the thoughts and feelings that usually result from that emotion. The very act of smiling, for instance, can lead to positive emotions; you can feel better simply by flexing the facial muscles that are engaged when smiling and laughing.

It works both ways, too. For example, many slouch while standing or sitting, due to tiredness, boredom, or simply the desire to relax, but slouching can in fact *cause* tiredness, boredom, or even powerlessness. Standing and sitting upright takes effort and focus, especially when bored or tired, but it can have positive and energizing effects. Many healthy things (eating right, exercising, practicing positive recovery, etc.) take effort and self-discipline. The rewards are worth the exertion. Once you start feeling the productive benefits of making healthy choices, those choices become easier to make and are self-reinforcing. Once you get on a winning streak, it's easier to keep going.

Today's PI

Apply yourself to making the next right choice for your overall health, happiness, and recovery. Be brave and industrious. Don't quit before the miracle happens. Practice mindfulness about your small choices, and remember to smile and hold your body in an upright posture. Do the next right thing all day long, and when tired or in doubt, fake it until you make it. At the day's close, journal about your experiences.

DAY 3

We can only be said to be alive in those moments when our hearts are conscious of our treasures.

—Thornton Wilder

One of the best ways to live in the upper reaches of what's possible is to cultivate an attitude of gratitude. Gratitude boost overall well-being, and it is an effective tool to handle difficult situations. Gratitude is so important that you will undergo approximately one different gratitude activity each week within this program. Studies suggest that when people space out gratitude exercises, they increase the benefits of the practice.

Gratitude unlocks the ability to fully enjoy what you treasure in the past (reminiscing), present (savoring), and future (anticipating). Gratitude also prevents you from taking for granted all those wonderful things (small and large) in your life. Actively maintain the gratitude attitude in order to cherish what you have.

Today's PI

For the next three nights, write down three good things that happened to you that day. Explain why these good things happened. Discovering why these good things happened is the most important part. Look for qualities in you that contributed and accept these parts of you that are permanent and pervasive parts of your life experience. Try not to dismiss the good things as luck. Be optimistic about the "why." You will be repeating this exercise throughout the year, as its benefits are significant and sustainable.

DAY 4

———⟡———

*By three methods we may learn wisdom. First, by reflection,
which is noblest. Second, by imitation, which is easiest.
And third by experience, which is the bitterest.*

—Confucius

The third method for developing wisdom is living through hardships and learning from those experiences. Confucius points out that life is hard, but the reward for surviving and persisting through hardships is wisdom. Research reveals that most people who go through trauma come out the other end with posttraumatic growth—a transformative new state of being with deeper insight into and appreciation of life. If you are in recovery, addiction can be the springboard to thriving. Wisdom and happiness cannot arise from hiding in a hole, and positive recovery is not achieved by working diligently to prevent bad things from happening; rather, it is the embodiment of responding well when tragedy does strike. Most elements that elevate a happiness set point are the same tools used to grow after traumatic events: taking responsibility for your life and actions, nurturing relationships, leading with your strengths, finding meaning, practicing optimism, and looking for the good (gratitude, spirituality, and love).

Today's PI

Journal about a trauma or difficulty you've experienced and learned from. Choose a trauma that gives you a sense of resolution, since the object here is to learn how traumas can be enriching. Write down how your worldview changed, how you gained insight into yourself, and how you ended up benefiting as a result of the trauma. What did the experience mean to you in the moment, and what does it mean now? Do those meanings differ from each other? What gratitude can you now find, looking back at the challenging experience?

DAY 5

Of all gifts, good health is the greatest.
Of all wealth, contentment is the greatest.

—Mahabharata

Good health (like wealth) is a state of mind. Your health is good when you have a good relationship with your current state of health, just as wealth is satisfaction with what you have. While perfect health is a great gift, any health is good when appreciated. Deepak Chopra said, "If we are creating ourselves all the time, then it is never too late to begin creating the bodies we want instead of the ones we mistakenly assume we are stuck with."

Today's PI

Focus on your health. Write ten things you can be grateful for regarding the current state of your health. Choose one thing to do today in order to improve your physical health: schedule a doctor's appointment, exercise, make healthy eating choices, floss, prioritize rest, or ensure all your basic needs are met. Whatever you choose to do today, stick to it, and practice it with intentionality.

DAY 6

*Everyone should try to learn before they die
what they are running from, and to, and why.*

—James Thurber

It is time to write your personal mission statement, which is a concise statement that puts your values and your life purpose into words. Here are three examples:

1) I provide insight and direction through connecting with others and helping them reach their financial and lifelong goals.
2) I will leave the world a better place than I found it—even in a small way. I make a difference in the lives of others and the world around me through service.
3) I am a good mother, partner, and role model for others through love, compassion, and listening.

Your personal mission statement is a purposeful promise that helps guide you in fulfilling your life's potential. It is the unique definition of how you choose to live. Today you will literally write it, just as you figuratively author (choose) your choices, habits, character, and destiny. Every person has the responsibility and gift of deciding how to live and what to stand for.

Today's PI

Draft your mission statement. It should be one sentence, so take your time. Keep writing until you get it down to one sentence. Keep it on your desk, by your bed, or on your calendar. Commit it to memory. Your mission statement might grow and change as you mature and develop. You can change it at any time, but always have one.

DAY 7

In the hopes of reaching the moon, men fail to see the flowers that blossom at their feet.

—Albert Schweitzer

The future holds many potential outcomes. Putting off happiness for a future time ends up wasting the present. Although you might certainly put your best foot forward today to increase the likelihood of a favorable tomorrow, "right now" is the only reality you can fully count on. Own and experience it. Learning to stay in and appreciate the present enables you to get the most out of each precious moment.

What are you missing when you are preoccupied with past and future events? Life. When you forfeit feeling grateful for the beauty of today, you end up wondering how life passed you by so quickly.

Today's PI

Hunt for the good. Be a "flowers at the feet" detective. Set an alarm or a timer to go off every hour. When the alarm buzzes, pause and write down at least three beautiful, positive, gratitude-inducing things you presently see, feel, or are in some way experiencing. Anytime fear or judgment challenges you, choose instead to focus on what is right within yourself and your friends, family, and station. When a negative thought or criticism arises, exchange it for a positive one.

Although things do not always happen for the best, it is always possible to find the best in what's around.

DAY 8

—⁂—

*What you get by achieving your goals is not as important
as what you become by achieving your goals.*

—Henry David Thoreau

It's time to revisit the goals you made on day one. Have you done three things in the last seven days to help fulfill one of your goals? Compare your mission statement to your goals *and* behaviors. Are these consistent with each other? Are you doing what you reasonably can to achieve your goals, develop your character strengths, and forge your destiny?

Today's PI

In addition to reviewing and possibly rewriting your goals, your task today is to help someone else reach one of his or her goals. Simply choose someone, and ask that person if there is anything you can do in five minutes or less to help him or her achieve something today. It could be a goal or even a chore. The giving of your time does not have to be a huge, heroic inconvenience, but try to give someone at least five minutes.

Journal about the assignment. What did you do today for someone else, and how did it feel? Reflect on what you have become by accomplishing past goals. Is what you have become more valuable to you than what you got?

DAY 9

❦

*You must take personal responsibility. You cannot change
the circumstances, the seasons, or the wind,
but you can change yourself.*

—Jim Rohn

The only things you have control over are your intentional thoughts, actions (including speech), and chosen priorities. You are responsible for your life and yourself in this moment. Indeed, you are responsible for no one else.

Resentment (holding on to feelings of hurt, fear, or hate) is among the most common reasons addicts relapse. But resentment hurts the one who is resenting—not the object of the resentment. It can be construed as the poison you drink in an attempt to hurt another person. It casts a negative shadow over your heart and decreases your ability to find pleasure in your days. It creates a hostile internal experience of life that harms you far more than is often realized.

Today's PI
Journal about any resentment you are harboring. This includes any directed inward at yourself—a type that can be uniquely painful and damaging. Ask yourself in the writing assignment what part you played, if any, in the incident that created the resentment, and see what you can do to honestly let it go.

When you journal, simply describe the resentment in a few words or a brief sentence. Use the bulk of your time writing about your part or reflecting on how you can nurture forgiveness. Focus on changing your intentional thoughts, and wish for the other person's well-being.

DAY 10

By far the greatest predictor of happiness in the literature is intimate relationships. Why are social connections so important to well-being? Because good social relationships serve many vital needs.

—Sonja Lyubomirsky

Human beings are social animals. We need others to flourish. People help in hard times and enhance the good times. Positive social ties can improve health, well-being, and longevity.

Relationships and recovery are intertwined. The chances of managing addiction without social support are very low.

<u>Today's PI</u>

Make time today to speak with three people you care about but with whom you do not often interact. Let them know you are grateful for what they bring to your life. If you feel awkward bringing this up, you might choose to tell them you are fulfilling your task for the day. Perhaps the interaction will lead to a visit or a different unforeseen opportunity.

If possible, connect with someone in recovery who is struggling today, and let him or her know you care. Share your experience and your ear. You're living proof that recovery from addiction is possible.

DAY 11

⊷⊶⊷

Fitness—if it came in a bottle, everybody would have a great body.

—Cher

Need a reason to get moving? The extensive health benefits of exercise are numerous. Exercise reduces the risk of cancer, heart disease, high blood pressure, obesity, and depression. It even slows aging. Movement and action increase blood flow to the brain and cause an increase in feel-good neurotransmitters. Exercising for twenty minutes every morning has been shown to boost mood for twelve hours.

Beneficial activities range from the lowest level of exertion to higher-impact cardiovascular exercises. Whatever your current level of fitness, go get active. (Remember, however, to consult your doctor to make sure you aren't engaging in something potentially harmful.)

Today's PI

Exercise your body and mind. First, be mindful of what you put into your body. If you must smoke, have one less cigarette today. Drink one less caffeinated beverage today. Eat fewer processed and more whole foods. Eat a variety of darker (green and blue) fruits and vegetables. Make breakfast your largest meal and dinner your smallest. Tonight, journal about how today's PI made you feel. Perhaps you will want to repeat today's choices tomorrow.

DAY 12

Don't cry because it is over. Smile because it happened.

—Anonymous

It is one thing to overcome hardships and another to survive good fortune with grace. So much has been written about forgiveness and trauma resolution, and people often focus significant energy on learning how to cope with difficult times. They do not, however, apply themselves equally to examining and improving how to navigate good times. Too often people lose their serenity in good times by clutching desperately to those wonderful things they receive. When fortune smiles upon people, it can be easy to forget gratitude and impermanence and begin to expect that these conditions will last forever. Yet the only constant is change—how easily people forget this in moments of bliss.

The mind naturally attaches to the "good," but frequently this is an unexpected source of pain and suffering. When people grasp too tightly to "good" things, they can suffer just as much as when they try to change or push away "bad" things. In attempting to avoid the bad stuff, people sometimes risk striving for artificial and unachievable safe zones. They try to avoid the pain of ever having to lose another thing they love.

Today's PI

What are you holding on to today? Are you living to shield yourself from pain, or are you living courageously? Can you try to let go of fear today? Apply energy today to noticing what you are holding on to and why. At the end of the day, journal about your experience.

DAY 13

The hardest arithmetic to master is that which enables us to count our blessings.

—Eric Hoffer

In the daily grind of the rat race, people easily lose sight of what they are actually working and living for. They become easily preoccupied with temporary and false doorways to happiness, such as money, status, and prestige. Sufficient financial resources are necessary in life, but once basic needs are met, money's contribution is tricky. When precious time and energy are forfeited to pursue fiscal ends, people experience diminishing returns for all the effort.

Instead, be grateful. Practicing gratitude is a healthy and sustainable combatant to the rat race. Gratitude decreases or prevents negativity, helps cope with stress and trauma, increases self-esteem, and builds social bonds.

What do you love most about your best friend, children, family, work, car, home, sobriety, or life that has recently slipped your mind?

Today's PI
Focus on one thing you usually take for granted, and mindfully approach it from an attitude of gratitude. Tonight, journal about any new insights gained from applying the day to appreciating that one thing.

DAY 14

⸺⊰⊱⸺

You can't punish yourself into change. You can't whip yourself into shape.
But you can love yourself into well-being.

—Susan Skye

Love is many things. Love is:

- the most sustaining virtue of humanity and creation's greatest joy;
- the antidote for fear;
- the most effective strategy for silencing your inner critic (the voice that tells you you're not good enough or that you don't belong).

Allowing others to love you and loving others with your whole heart fosters unparalleled positive emotions.

<u>Today's PI</u>
"May all beings and I be free of suffering and the root of suffering.
May all beings and I be happy, safe, and peaceful."

In your mind, say that mantra. Repeat it three times today for five continuous minutes each time. Allow this mantra to increase your "agape" love—love for all humanity. In the hectic pace of life, it's easy to let activities such as today's PI slip through the cracks. Therefore, set specific times when you can find five minutes of solitude to say the mantra with loving intention.

DAY 15

*If one oversteps the bounds of moderation,
the greatest pleasures cease to please.*

—Epictetus

Human beings are hardwired for stimulation, novelty, and fulfillment of desire. Addicts simply take those drives to unhealthy lengths. One cookie is great, so ten is better—right? Too much of a great thing ends up hurting. That is the quagmire. How can people foster more joy and fun, or "healthy positivity"?

Moderation when pleasure is involved is challenging for addicts, but it's not impossible. The trick lies in finding a moderate formula to experience joy without exceeding the golden mean ("the sweet spot"). Discovering that delicate balance is how you enable yourself to lead the best possible life in recovery. Over time this habit will become automatic. The nervous system rewires itself in response to intentional actions. Make your nervous system an ally in your positive recovery by practicing the moderation habit.

Today's PI

Every time you experience stimulation, novelty, and pleasure, pay attention to your contentment. Be mindful of those feelings that counteract it, such as cravings for more. Pause, break from the experience, and savor the pleasant emotions instead of doing more, more, and more. Interrupting something at its peak can also leave the best possible memory for you to return to later.

DAY 16

꘎──◦⊰⊱ ⊰⊱◦──꘎

Most Americans do not know what their strengths are. When you ask them,
they look at you with a blank stare, or they respond in terms of subject knowledge,
which is the wrong answer.

—Peter Drucker

Everyone has strengths—both naturally occurring and those cultivated with intentional practices. "Character strength" describes what's right within you. You already have those strengths inside you, even if you can't yet name them. They constitute your capacity for excellence, which can be nurtured through awareness and effort. Fostering and developing character strengths is one of the most worthwhile investments you can make. Using your strengths can improve your productivity, resilience, and relationships. In addition, leading with your character strengths is the best way to flourish in recovery.

Today's PI

Take the Values In Action (VIA) Classification of Strengths test at AuthenticHappiness.org. (Scroll down the web page until you see the header "Engagement Questionnaires." The VIA test is within this section.) If you have taken the strengths test already, revisit your results. Remind yourself of your top ten strengths. Then, in your journal, write down your top three to five character strengths (your "signature strengths"). These strengths represent you at your best. They feel effortless, and when you use them, you become more energized and alive.

Were you surprised by how your strengths were ranked? If so, how? Your assignment over the next seven days is to use one of your signature strengths in a new way each day. Each night, journal about your experiences, insights, and surprises.

DAY 17

—⚜ ⚜—

Kindness in words creates confidence. Kindness in thinking creates profoundness. Kindness in giving creates love.

—Lao Tzu

What is kindness? Kindness is many things:

- an act of giving
- a virtue in practically every culture
- a pathway to changing relationships, the world, and yourself
- a way to dissolve misunderstanding and judgment
- a way to create unity where there might otherwise be disconnection

Giving ("kindness with legs") is better than receiving. You might think you are giving solely for the benefit of others, but that is quite rarely the case. When you give to another, you engender positive feelings about yourself, greater hope and trust in the world around you, and a valuable sense of durable fulfillment.

Today's PI

Practice five acts of kindness. There are many ways to give: pay for the person directly behind you at the tollbooth or coffee shop, volunteer at a local shelter, put money in random parking meters, greet strangers with warm smiles, use only kind words, or deliver flowers to someone special in your life.

Journal about what you did and how you felt. Did you commit any anonymous acts of kindness? Were the feelings any different, depending on who benefited from your kindness? Were smaller acts of kindness different in any way from larger ones? How has prioritizing kindness affected your outlook on life today?

DAY 18

The real art of conversation isn't only to say the right thing at the right time but to leave unsaid the wrong thing at the tempting time.

—Dorothy Nevill

It's easy to forget that speech is a type of behavior. *Positive recovery* is a verb. It is action. Flourishing in recovery requires being conscious of your thoughts, words, and behaviors. Your best speech includes both things said and not said aloud. Words can be acts of giving and virtue, or acts of harming.

<u>Today's PI</u>

1. *Does it need to be said?*
2. *Does it need to be said now?*
3. *Does it need to be said now by me?*

Filter everything you say through that three-question litmus test. At the end of the day, journal for five minutes about how you felt not saying things you otherwise would have said, and about being more conscious of what you said and how you said it throughout the day. Share your experience and insights at PositiveRecovery.com.

DAY 19

Despite our best efforts to manage our time efficiently, and despite the many time-saving devices designed to make life easier, our lives often seemed filled to the brim. We cram our days with activities, thinking that each one of them is important and absolutely necessary. We schedule virtually every minute of every day. We say we want free time, but few of us can sit still, even for a moment.

—Richard Carlson and Joseph Bailey

One time-saving piece of technology that has essentially become an extension of each person is the cell phone. These little beauties connect us to others, help us get where we need to go, and find us the closest Ethiopian restaurant in less than five seconds, should we fancy some wat atop injera. Cell phones are great, but like most things, they must be used judiciously.

In one study, researchers discovered that the mere presence of a cell phone could decrease the quality of conversations and the trust and closeness experienced between the subjects. While that little bit of information could be shrugged off as self-evident, there are two particularly remarkable findings in this study: the cell phone used in the study did not belong to either person, and the presence of it affected deep conversations but not superficial ones. If you're after relationships as a means to happiness, next time you're with someone, put the cell phone out of sight.

Today's PI

Practice putting the phone away and hiding it from sight. Did it make a difference in you? Was it difficult to do? How were you affected?

DAY 20

What lies behind us, and what lies before us, are tiny matters compared to what lies within us.

—Ralph Waldo Emerson

Looking within yourself is a powerful way to develop emotional sobriety. Indeed, knowing yourself is the first step to growth. Meditation (the practice of calming the mind and developing awareness of the workings of your consciousness) is a foundational technique to enhance meaningful self-knowledge. You will be meditating several times throughout the year in PIs because it is so vital. In fact, consider establishing meditation as a daily practice. Understanding patterns of thought develops emotional sobriety and equanimity. Additionally, meditation aids brain repair and development and reverses the effects of stress on the body and mind.

Today's PI

Sit in silence for five minutes twice today, or otherwise find a comfortable and quiet place on the floor or in a chair, and simply focus on your in breath and out breath for five minutes. Bring your consciousness to the rhythm of your breathing. Pay attention to your thoughts. Observe them as if from a nonjudgmental third-person perspective.

After each meditation session, journal about where your mind took you. Create a special "Where My Mind Wanders" section within your journal, and keep all meditation reflection notes in that section for easy reference and to track your growth.

DAY 21

❧

Let us remember that, as much has been given us, much will be expected from us,
and that true homage comes from the heart as well as from the lips,
and shows itself in deeds.

—Theodore Roosevelt

An addict's loved ones have often heard grand promises about that addict's plans to change, only to be repeatedly let down. Recovery gives addicts the priceless opportunity to make good on those promises and earn back the trust of loved ones. That said, no one should listen to words as much as they see actions. Addicts are measured by what they do more than most, and this is for good reason: actions make us who we are. Once realized, this concept is both freeing and frightening. It means people can be whomever they want based on how they choose to act.

The amends addicts make in recovery are often ritualized. They make lists of what they have done wrong and engage in purposeful actions to try to make each transgression right. However, what about those cases wherein direct action to address the offense is not a viable option? How then are addicts to rectify their wrongs and clean their slates as they begin lives anew in recovery? In these cases (and in a generalized sense), make a living amends—live the best way possible to show you are both sorry for past wrongdoings and grateful for the chance to do better this time.

Gratitude helps you maintain focus while making these living amends. When experiencing gratitude for the second chance recovery offers, you can more easily live according to your highest virtues and ideals, develop character, and forge a legacy.

Today's PI

Make yourself a living amends in what you do, think, and say. See each choice and moment of your day as an opportunity to engage with the world in the best possible way—in alignment with the values and ideals you hold dear in your recovery. Dig deep here. Ask yourself if there is anything you can either do more or less of to be your best self all day.

DAY 22

✦⚬⚬✦

I think we are living in selfish times. I'm the first one to say that I'm the most selfish. We live in the so-called "first world," and we may be first in a lot of things like technology, but we are behind in empathy.

—Javier Bardem

Empathy forms the foundation of relationships and frees you from the bondage of self. Empathy allows you to feel compassion for others, and with practice, it allows you to extend that genuine compassion to yourself.

Everything is connected on a molecular level. Everyone shares atoms with one another and the environment. Quantum physics suggests we are all connected via a web of something that has yet to be fully defined. Since we are all connected, cultivating the concept of empathy is a way to remove the "self" from the whole of "us." Empathy takes practice. It is not an innate skill, but it can be developed and nurtured in everyone.

Today's PI

Apply yourself to increasing your empathy by practicing the skill of empathetic listening. When you interact with others, try to quiet your personal thoughts or judgments and really listen. When they are through, engage in reflective listening. State things such as, "What I heard you say was…" or "It sounds as if that was _____ [hard, fun, exciting, sad, etc.] for you." This helps the person feel heard and allows you to check for the accuracy of your understanding. Try to intentionally get into the head and heart of everyone you interact with today. See if you can step out of your own ways and experience the unity that comes from allowing yourself to feel along with another person.

In your journal, write down any lessons you learned about your thought patterns or how this exercise made you feel. Was it challenging? Did it come naturally? Did others respond to you any differently with this style of listening? Did you feel more connected to others than you do on an average day?

DAY 23

—⚹⚹—

The best way to predict the future is to create it.

—Peter Drucker

Recovery teaches acceptance, which does not strictly refer to powerlessness over addictions. It's a more general Acceptance, with a capital *A*. If you successfully learn this lesson and acknowledge all that is outside your control, you will experience freedom and a deeper level of serenity. That said, you are still responsible for yourself. Where you put your attention and what you do are within your control. While the universe will doubtless place things in your path outside your realm of influence, you do have agency and choice. You are the narrator and creator of your own story. The actions, thoughts, relationships, and attitudes you choose to put energy into today greatly shape your chances, experiences, and potential fulfillment tomorrow.

<u>Today's PI</u>
Visualize and write about your best possible future self for twenty minutes each day for the next three days. First, close your eyes. Imagine you wake up ten years from now, and your life is ideal in every way. Don't worry about how you got there. Just see what your best future self's life looks like in every way. What are you doing, with whom, where, and so forth? The future self embodies your personalized set of cherished goals. Write about your perfect life, your perfect self, and your perfect everything.

If you limit yourself during this activity to preconceived notions of what is possible, when the impossible dream actually shows up at your feet, you won't be able to see it. Change starts with a vision of what is possible—not impossible. So don't limit yourself. Dream big!

DAY 24

Whether you believe you can or you can't, you are right.

—Henry Ford

Self-efficacy (a mixture of self-esteem and self-confidence) is an especially useful trait for recovering addicts. High self-efficacy can prevent relapse and improve happiness, and the good news is that anyone can learn to heighten this valuable characteristic. First, believe your life is in your hands. Second, believe you can either accomplish your goals or learn how to get them done. Third, see problems as challenges; every chance you get, try out new things or learn new skills. Fourth, fall down—and get up. To fail means an attempt made in a particular situation did not work; it does not mean you are a failure. Disappointments provide the opportunity to develop grit—a precious character trait that fuels the development of self-efficacy.

Today's PI

When you are faced with FEAR (Future Events Appearing Real, or Forget Everything And Run), say the serenity prayer: "Grant me the serenity to accept the things I cannot change, the courage to change the things I can, and the wisdom to know the difference." Imagine that your problems are interesting challenges that grant you the opportunity to develop more self-efficacy. The more successful you become at navigating obstacles on the way to achieving goals, the more you will believe in your ability to succeed as future challenges arise.

Don't forget to journal for twenty minutes, doing your best–future-self PI.

DAY 25

Life is 10 percent of what happens to me and 90 percent of how I react to it.

—John Maxwell

Human beings create stories from events that happen in the world. We don't live in one reality but in the strands weaved together in these stories. Judgments, fears, hopes, attitudes, and perceptions impact the gist of every story. Other animals react to stimuli only, and do not make up stories about those stimuli: a dog barks when it hears noises; it doesn't bark when it feels the noise is from someone who shouldn't be making the noise. Human beings are the only animals who react to the *meanings* of stimuli (which we fabricate). Moreover, humans believe their stories are true. What really happens makes up only a small percentage of reality; what we tell ourselves happened, which memories and moods significantly influence, determines a much larger percentage.

The same event can impact you in vastly different ways based solely on your storytelling. Life is ambiguous. Fortunately, you can choose to use that to your advantage. Struggles and hardships will happen. No one leads a pain-free existence.

Today's PI

Strengthen your abilities as the positive narrator of your story. If possible, bring in a trusted accountability partner for this activity, to help you complete today's positive intervention as a "listener."

To start, vividly recall a particularly vexing, negative, or challenging time in your past. As a positive narrator of your own story, retell that experience to your listening accountability partner by being TRUE:

T: telling the best possible story
R: realistically framing the story
U: using a positive storyteller viewpoint
E: ending the story with optimism

Journaling for twenty minutes about the event can help guide you as you positively narrate the event. While journaling, think about the lessons learned from the experience and how you have grown. Focus on how grateful you are that it happened, and identify the strengths you used during and after the event.

Also journal for twenty minutes today about your best future self.

DAY 26

─────※─────

A person with one watch will always know the time.
A person with two watches will always be in doubt.

—Anonymous

As addicts spend more time in recovery, the "road narrows." This means that as they come to their senses and fulfill their potential, they find certain behaviors that were once acceptable to be no longer consistent with their integrity.

Addiction is a very large umbrella. Even when addicts put aside drugs, addiction can manifest in new ways. After an emotional or spiritual struggle, for instance, a recovering addict might seek to escape the pain with sex, food, gambling, or other self-destructive processes.

This tendency mirrors the experience of having two watches. One watch might be set to the true time, representing positive recovery. If addicts are not aware of other destructive patterns that can develop, however, the other watch (a different manifestation of addiction) will display a contradictory time and cause doubt.

Today's PI

Mind your potential "second watch." It might be invisible to you at first, so spend some time introspectively journaling. Try to look at yourself from a third-person perspective. Are there any areas of your life that have fallen out of balance or are trending toward compulsion? How many watches are you wearing?

DAY 27

Everyone is a genius. But if you judge a fish on its ability to climb a tree, it will spend its whole life believing that it is stupid.

—Albert Einstein

There are many types of intelligence. IQ measures only one. Einstein's quote recognizes that every single person has a gift. It might not be readily obvious, but it's in there. Unfortunately, the human brain is magnificently designed to recognize what's lacking: the bad, the negative, and the "out of bounds."

Brains react more strongly to negative than positive stimuli, and people remember negative events more than positive ones. While bad is like Velcro, good is like Teflon. What are people to do? It's simple: counteract the negativity bias by searching for the gold—in yourself and others.

<u>Today's PI</u>
Become a strengths detective. Search for your and others' strengths all day. How many can you spot? Remind yourself of Einstein's wisdom. Many uses of strength (like intelligence) reveal themselves in different ways. Keep a keen eye, like Sherlock Holmes, who was masterful at putting himself in other people's shoes. Use curiosity today as you look for any and all uses of strength. Just for fun, keep track of the number of times you notice yourself using your character strengths and others using theirs.

DAY 28

———◦❈◦———

You're happiest while you're making the greatest contribution.

—Robert F. Kennedy

While increasing one's own pleasure and decreasing one's own pain feels good, contributing to something larger than oneself feels good *and* fulfilling. To those on the self-centered and selfish side of the spectrum, that might seem counterintuitive at first. However, it is a scientifically proven fact that giving is better than receiving.

Nobody knows exactly why human beings enjoy more well-being from giving than from giving, but most thought leaders agree that it stems from a survival need to bond with others and to belong to a group. However, most people aren't consciously choosing to give so that they receive food and protection. Most people give because it simply feels good. At the end of the day, all that matters is this: kindness is a gift that is impossible to give away because it keeps coming back.

Today's PI

Contribute to something outside of yourself. Choose one thing to focus on, and dedicate yourself to leaving it better than you found it today. Contribute your time or resources today to a cause, idea, or ideal you stand for. Try your best to keep this one anonymous, and journal about how you felt.

DAY 29

⬥⸺⸺⬥⬥⸺⸺⬥

*What you focus on expands, and when you focus on the goodness in your life,
you create more of it. Opportunities, relationships, even money flowed
my way when I learned to be grateful no matter what happened in my life.*

—Oprah Winfrey

Many successful people, including Oprah, claim gratitude preceded success. Good things came their way after they changed their perspective from unfilled wanting to satisfied thankfulness. Too often people keep their noses down and lose sight of what they have to be thankful for. In this blindness, they might actually prevent the flow of good things coming toward them. The more we see and cherish, the more we get to cherish. It's just that simple.

<u>Today's PI</u>

Look for verbal ways to express the gratitude you find today. Unexpressed gratitude is ingratitude. There is no journaling tonight—just use words today. Speak the words aloud to whoever is present when you notice something to be grateful for in the course of your day. Notice as many positive actions and contributions of others as you can. You might be pleasantly surprised to feel the improvement within your relationships at home, work, or play when you make an effort to verbally appreciate the efforts of those around you. At first this might seem excessive, but soon it can become a contagious habit. Maintaining your focus on what to be grateful for will also train your mind to look for the good as happiness becomes a habit.

DAY 30

All the world's indeed a stage, and we are merely players, performers and portrayers, each another's audience outside the gilded cage.

—Neil Peart of Rush

Throughout your life you will assume various roles. Sadly, too many people are not aware they are the writers, directors, and actors in their own lives. You are the storyteller in your own life, and the roles you play are not deceptive. Instead, you craft your own identities by what you do and how you do it. The closer your self-indetity is to your behavior, the more authentic you are. Integrity takes courage, but it is worthwhile. If you believe that you are in charge of yourself and that you are a capable agent of change, you're more likely to flourish and prevent relapse.

Today's PI

What role are you playing today? Who are the other key players you are currently inviting into the story of your life? What sense are you making of favorable and unfavorable events? How is your life evolving? What's the purpose in your narrative? Is there anything within your personal realm of influence you would like to change? A change in scenery? New key players? A different storyline? Journal your reflections on these questions and share your insight at PositiveRecovery.com.

DAY 31

—⟡—

Rebellion against your handicaps gets you nowhere. Self-pity gets you nowhere. One must have the adventurous daring to accept oneself as a bundle of possibilities and undertake the most interesting game in the world—making the most of one's best.

—Harry Emerson Fosdick

As my good friend Dave Wright always says, "There's the way things are, and then there's the way things are." What he points out here is that there is reality, and then there is the unreality made of wishful thinking, mental anguish, and suffering. Acceptance is the first step to a life free from addiction. It's also the virtue necessary to transform trauma into growth.

Simply stated, acceptance can help you make the most of any situation. Despite any imperfections, you have strengths, and you are the only one who can choose to embrace and nurture the best of what you have inside. Accept yourself for where you excel, and put in the work necessary to capitalize on your strengths.

Today's PI

Reflect on the concept of yourself as "a bundle of possibilities." Journal about the three to five strengths or innate characteristics you see working in your favor in your current phase of life. Keep those strengths in mind throughout the day, remind yourself to apply them to any challenges or choices, and then journal tonight on the forum.

DAY 32

—————⚜ ⚜—————

Nobody can go back and start a new beginning, but anyone can start today and make a new ending.

—Maria Robinson

The average person has over seventy thousand thoughts every day. Thoughts are not made up of some magical dust. They are physical pathways in the brain. The more you practice thinking of how you can start from here and make a new ending, the more you strengthen that pathway. The more you strengthen that pathway, the easier the message will be to accomplish.

Over time, this thought process can even become an automatic reaction, increasing your resilience. Don't brush this off as something achievable without work. Thoughts can alter your life, so be prepared to dig in and apply yourself. This is worth doing over and over and over again. The rewards will follow your actions. Remember, *positive recovery* is a verb.

Today's PI
Even if you have had a full day of negative thoughts, start over and make a new ending right now. Think it! Thinking about negative situations in more useful, positive ways literally rewires your brain by creating new pathways. This can make you happier and more resilient.

DAY 33

───◦§◦ ◦§◦───

It is easier to fight for one's principles than to live up to them.

—Alfred Adler

Adler's quote exposes the ease of hypocrisy. How many politicians and other policy makers staunchly and publicly fight against promiscuity, fiscal irresponsibility, homosexuality, or drug use, only to become embroiled in scandals involving those exact things they combated?

Perhaps self-loathing or insecurity spurs such energetic oppositions. Maybe it is just plain old ego-driven hypocrisy. Parents often want their children to do what they say and not what they do. After all, knowing what is right and directing others' behavior while doing whatever you please takes very little effort. Words come cheap and easy; actions require much more.

Look searchingly at your conduct for certain principles you espouse in theory but fall short of in action. Many people have easier times championing causes than living up to them. Living by principles is often easier said than done.

Today's PI

In your journal, write down the five principles you value most. These could be virtues (justice, wisdom, etc.), communal creeds (treat others as you wish to be treated), or religious or spiritual beliefs (love thy neighbor. Tonight, reflect on your actions over the past few weeks. Are you living up to your principles, or are you simply fighting for them? What one thing can you do tomorrow to live by these principles?

DAY 34

⌘⌘ ⌘⌘

Fake it until you make it.

—Anonymous

"Fake it until you make it" is a common saying used in recovery fellowships, and it turns out that this cliché is scientifically validated. You can act as if you feel a certain way until you *actually* begin to feel that way. Studies demonstrate that when people's facial muscles are manipulated into a smile (for example, by being asked to hold pencils between their teeth), they feel better. This finding indicates that even when an emotional state is clearly fabricated, a person's brain automatically recognizes that physical state and creates a feedback switch so that he or she experiences a genuine shift in mood. Sure, you generally smile when you feel good, but smiling itself can make you happy. Confidence breeds success, but acting confident produces confidence too. Standing upright produces energy.

If nothing more than a temporary strategy to weather the storm of fear and doubt, acting as if you are already happy is an effective bridge between pain or anxiety and moving into tranquility. Even if faking it seems silly, keep in mind that it's infinitely more helpful than drinking, drugging, engaging in sexual indiscretions, gambling, and other forms of addictive behaviors.

Today's PI

Set an alarm on your watch or cell phone to vibrate every hour. When the alarm buzzes, check your posture to ensure you are standing or sitting upright. Put a smile on your face for a full sixty seconds. If you are in an environment such as a business meeting, where this could be inappropriate, you may wait until you are in a more private setting. However, make sure you get in a full minute of intentional smiling each hour. At the end of the day, reflect on how you feel. Do you notice any improvement in energy or happiness?

DAY 35

━━◦◈◦ ◦◈◦━━

*Just because someone doesn't love you the way you want
doesn't mean that person doesn't love you
the best way he or she knows how.*

—Anonymous

A common mistake is feeling slighted when others don't live up to expectations ("preresentments"). This is especially common in families and romantic relationships. People don't choose their families, and each member comes with his or her own set of challenges. Although people do choose their romantic partners, many mistake passionate love for true love.

Passionate love, the temporary form of insanity brought on by an avalanche of chemicals and lust, is not true love. True love is unconditional, freely given, and accepting of others. It benefits the giver more than the receiver. As Albert Ellis notes, it's also not a sprint: "The art of love…is largely the art of persistence."

Today's PI

Are you accepting others just as they are, or are you living as if they should be who you want them to be? Is your love for them conditional, or is it unconditionally given because you are loving them in the best way you can? Act on your ability to practice love today by doing one thing (above and beyond your normal routine) to show your love for someone else.

DAY 36

✦━━◦❀◦ ◦❀◦━━✦

Boredom is a certain sign that we are
allowing our faculties to rust in idleness.

—William R. Inge

One common trigger for addicts is boredom, and difficulty concentrating usually accompanies the feeling of having nothing to do and lacking interest. Boredom is consistently listed as a major trigger for relapse and can signify a wide state of unwanted, uninvited, and distasteful emotional states of being. Boredom can also refer to being uncomfortable in one's own skin.

The remedy for boredom is to get busy developing positive habits, counteracting the bad stuff, and living the good life. This remedy is also the formula for effectively pursuing happiness. Notice how the formula for flourishing in recovery does not pursue happiness directly. Rather, the path to living the best life possible in recovery is populated with the multitude of actions whose side effects create well-being.

Flourishing in recovery includes developing your character strengths, nurturing deep and long-lasting relationships, and working toward meaningful goals. It involves courageously taking responsibility for your life, practicing realistic optimism, and being part of something larger than the self. Boredom, meanwhile, is a signal you have temporarily forgotten all you can do to get better every day and in every way.

Today's PI

Create a "boredom alleviator" list. Reflect on the paragraph above, and list at least twelve life-enhancing things you can proactively do next time you are bored. These do not all need to be strictly task oriented (journal, go for a walk, etc.). Powerful too is sitting in quiet mindfulness or practicing loving, kindness, and meditation. If you're bored today, pick one activity and practice it. Share your list on the forum and look for other creative ways to stave of the big B of boredom.

DAY 37

❧⸙⸙❧

*Success seems to be largely a matter of hanging on
after others have let go.*

—William Feather

Legendary UCLA coach John Wooten inspired *Positive Recovery*'s definition of success. Wooten said success comes about by striving toward meaningful goals and experiencing the peace of mind that comes from knowing one did one's very best. You won't be examining your goals list again until day ninety, so now is the time to make adjustments.

Sometimes the best you can do is hang on. Other times you have to adjust your sails. Life is complex, and change is the only constant, so adjust or even change your goals when appropriate. Sometimes life is wonderful, often it's challenging, and other times it is downright painful.

No matter the present state of affairs, the road to flourishing in recovery is much like gardening. Dr. Seligman explains that people plant the seeds of achievement (reflect on goals and write them down), nourish the soil with nutrients, water, sunlight, and care (take baby steps to hit milestones), remove decay and disease (remove the negative), and then accept the fruits of the labor (learn to "deal with it").

<u>Today's PI</u>
Review your goals from day one of this book. If you have not yet made goals, refer back to day one and do so. If you have made them, reflect and journal about what you have done so far that you set out to do in the first month. Are you still on task? If not, recommit yourself, or even possibly redo your goals list. Sometimes the wisest and bravest thing you can do, besides hanging on when the going gets tough, is to know when to scrap your current goals and make new ones.

DAY 38

At times our own light goes out and is rekindled by a spark from another person. Each of us has cause to think with deep gratitude of those who have lighted the flame within us.

—Albert Schweitzer

The process of change is usually painful. People often change when the pain of doing the same thing exceeds the pain of doing something different. Perhaps you have been called out for behaviors and have made changes as a result. People can be on the receiving end of loving-kindness and compassion that sparks awareness, a change, or a feeling of inspiration. Other times people can be addressed with force.

If everything felt great all the time, how compelled would you be to improve? When you reflect on your pivotal moments of change, were you completely alone, or was there a helping hand?

Today's PI
This exercise is called the "Gratitude Visit." It has a deadline of twelve days. Write and then hand deliver a letter to someone who has been especially helpful, kind, or supportive in your life, and who you have not yet expressed your gratitude to. Be vague when asking to set up a meeting, and then read aloud the letter with feeling. See what happens.

DAY 39

—❊— ❊—

Good character is more to be praised than outstanding talent. Most talents are, to some extent, a gift. Good character, by contrast, is not given to us. We have to build it, piece by piece—by thought, choice, courage, and determination.

—H. Jackson Brown Jr.

As a general rule, people get boosts of positivity from using one of their top character strengths ("signature strengths"). It's therefore rewarding and easy to use these strengths on a daily basis. However, it's not so easy to use them daily in *new* ways, though the challenge is worthwhile.

When you find new ways to use one of your signature character strengths, you might enjoy greater well-being, fewer symptoms of depression and/or anxiety, or all of the above. Utilizing your strengths also enables you to fulfill your potential.

Today's PI

Focus on the marriage between strength building and character development. Find a new way to use a top strength in order to reinforce a valued aspect of your character. To increase the meaningfulness and efficacy of this exercise, build just one virtue at a time. Lead with your strengths today to practice one of the virtues you want to develop: prudence, courage, justice, temperance, humor, honesty, dignity, discipline, frugality, industry, compassion, service, gratitude, or any other desired virtue.

DAY 40

—⋇—

The test of tolerance comes when we are in a majority.
The test of courage comes when we are in a minority.

—Anonymous

The need to conform to a group is a strong and subconscious survival instinct in human beings. Even though courage is the fiber of growth, physical courage is more prevalent than moral courage. Perhaps that is because it's easier to sacrifice one's body than to overcome the fear of rejection.

Agreeing with the majority by nodding or staying silent is easier than standing alone and taking an unpopular view. Going to war with the masses is easier than standing up alone against them and speaking against violence. The cliques formed in grade school and high school are reflections of "human herds." Later in life, cliques form in families, workplaces, and societies.

Today's PI

Today is only about you: what you do when you are in the majority and what you do when you are in the minority. Do you practice tolerance? Do you act with courage? Keep these questions in mind today, and see where you can increase your bravery and compassion throughout the day. Tonight, journal about your experience and share it with us.

DAY 41

❦

To live content with small means; to seek elegance rather than luxury, and refinement rather than fashion; to be worthy, not respectable, and wealthy, not rich; to listen to stars and birds, babes and sages, with open heart; to study hard; to think quietly, act frankly, talk gently, await occasions, hurry never; in a word, to let the spiritual, unbidden and unconscious, grow up through the common—this is my symphony.

—William Henry Channing

Slow down. Take the time today to breathe and relax. This is not a suggestion; it is a lifesaver. Running in the rat race increases stress and makes it harder to eat well, and chronic stress is the biggest killer in America. Americans work more and take less vacation time than ever before. As a society, Americans also experience greater medical concerns, such as higher rates of depression, anxiety, and heart disease. Too much fat in a diet interferes with the brain's ability to function optimally, and high sugar ultimately makes one sluggish and can even shorten one's life span.

<u>Today's PI</u>
Take at least three ten-minute breaks during the day to sit in silence. Consume less caffeine and fat, and avoid processed sugar all day. Get at least seven hours of sleep tonight by lying down an hour earlier than normal. Don't watch TV. There is nothing to journal. Just slow down and be.

DAY 42

Leave all the afternoon for exercise and recreation, which are as necessary as reading. I will rather say more necessary because health is worth more than learning.

—Thomas Jefferson

While it might not be feasible to take the entire afternoon off, it is possible to find time to get moving before or after work or even during your lunch break. Which is more convenient—exercising for a brief period of time every day, or being dead for every minute of every day?

Exercise is worth the effort. It enhances physical health, makes the mind sharp, and boosts feel-good neurotransmitters. Exercising in the middle of the day can actually make you more productive at work than skipping lunch and working nonstop for hours. Try it. Wellness is one of those blessings money cannot buy, and maximizing your health should not wait for tomorrow.

Today's PI
Get your blood flowing by exercising rigorously for at least twenty minutes (after consulting with your doctor). If you already have a consistent exercise habit, challenge your body and broaden your mind by trying something new today. If you are a "runner," go for a bike ride or a swim; if you're a yogi, try lifting weights (low weight, high repitition); and if you're a gym buff, do your exercise today outside.

DAY 43

He who asks a question is a fool for a minute; he who does not remains a fool forever.

—Chinese Proverb

Asking for help from, falling into, or being pushed into helping hands is how people start the recovery process. Active addiction is generally interrupted involuntarily. Most often the addict is coerced into sobriety, but irrespective of the method, only afterward can the recovery process begin. In rare cases, the recovery process begins without pain, suffering, or leverage. Most addicts, however, require "pushes" into sobriety because active addiction robs its hosts of volition, and because asking for help is often misconstrued as a sign of weakness. The American ideal of rugged individualism, coupled with the illusion that hard work alone can tackle every obstacle, can be self-destructive. Not asking for help can keep people mentally and spiritually small, and it might perpetuate low self-esteem. Asking for help, however, can be a tremendously empowering act of courage. Sir Isaac Newton said, "Greatness is achieved on the shoulders of giants." Don't be afraid to ask for help. More people means more arms, legs, eyes, ears, brains, and hearts. Whether lifting heavy objects with muscles or heavy burdens from hearts, asking for help is a risk for a minute with benefits that can last a lifetime.

Today's PI
What do you need help with today? Reflect on your current life situations, and identify at least one area where you can benefit from the help of someone else. Also identify at least one person you feel safe asking for help from—and then ask. Allow yourself to be vulnerable. Through the practice of allowing yourself to humbly turn to another, recognize that you will in fact increase your strength.

DAY 44

───◦᠅◦───

The most basic and powerful way to connect to another person is to listen. Just listen. Perhaps the most important thing we ever give each other is our attention...A loving silence often has far more power to heal and to connect than the most well-intentioned words.

—Rachel Naomi Remen

It is said that people have two ears and one mouth so they can listen twice as much as they talk. Unfortunately, people often listen one-tenth as much as they speak, as if each person had twenty mouths and two ears. By talking more than listening, people fail to practice mindful awareness, and they risk losing out on the chance to bond with others. Being loved closely parallels being heard. Being heard means you are valued. When you give someone else the gift of value, you give that person the universe.

Listening is one of the most difficult skills to learn, and many people have not fully developed this ability.

Today's PI

Listen in order to give others a gift beyond words. Listen with your mind, heart, and soul all day today. Use the strength of curiosity more today. Pause before speaking, and ask clarifying questions whenever possible to increase the speaker's experience of feeling heard and valued. At the day's end, journal for ten minutes. In doing so, practice listening to yourself.

DAY 45

Kindness trumps greed: it asks for sharing.
Kindness trumps fear: it calls forth gratefulness and love.
Kindness trumps even stupidity, for with sharing and love, one learns.

—Marc Estrin

People can train their brains to be more open, creative, grateful, virtuous, and happy. At any age and in any situation, human beings are amazingly adaptive. It is never too late or too soon to start bringing out the best in you. You have a duty to yourself, those you love, and your greater community to continuously journey toward the best version of yourself.

Practicing gratitude is immeasurably valuable for achieving happiness and fulfillment. Gratitude boosts your mood, helps you bond more with others, helps your brain stay fit, decreases the effects of stress, and helps you live longer. It changes the way you view the world and your part within it. It brings light, levity, and meaning to life. The good news is that the more people practice gratitude, kindness, love, and giving, the more they receive. The more they receive, the better they feel, and the more likely they are to repeat grateful actions. In this way the process always builds and expands in an upward direction.

Today's PI
First thing in the morning and last thing before you go to bed, journal about what you have to be grateful for. Start your day off right by making a ten-item gratitude list of whatever resonates with you as something to appreciate today. At night, write down three great things that happened today and why. Use an optimistic, explanatory style.

DAY 46

Spirituality exists wherever we struggle with the issue of how our lives fit into the greater cosmic scheme of things. This is true even when our questions never give way to specific answers or give rise to specific practices such as prayer or meditation. We encounter spiritual issues every time we wonder where the universe comes from, why we are here, or what happens when we die. We also become spiritual when we are moved by values such as beauty, love, or creativity that seem to reveal a meaning or power beyond our visible world. An idea or practice is "spiritual" when it reveals our personal desire to establish a felt relationship with the deepest meanings or powers governing life.

—Robert C. Fuller

Spirituality can help prevent relapse and be a source of happiness, positivity, health, and vigor. However, spirituality is an emotionally charged concept that either gets confused with religion or dismissed by naysayers. For those who have had a spiritual experience, however, there is no mistaking it. The experience stands true regardless of external opinions or critiques, because spirituality strikes a chord deep within an immeasurable and indefinable soul.

There are no "right" or "wrong" concepts of spirituality. Your concept of spirituality is exactly what it is supposed to be today, and it will continue to be exactly what it is supposed to be as it morphs, shifts, and grows throughout your lifetime. Spirituality can be connection, faith, love, God, or anything that resonates with you. In discussing and exploring personal spirituality, give it a platform where it can expand as necessary and have the most positive effect on lives.

Today's PI
Journal about any spiritual experiences you have had in your lifetime. What did they feel like? What did you learn from them? If you cannot recall any experience you would deem "spiritual," journal about a time when you felt particularly connected to the world or the people around you. Can that connection serve as fertile ground upon which to build a concept of spirituality?

DAY 47

❦

Knowledge of what is possible is the beginning of happiness.

—George Santayana

Happiness, like *recovery*, is a verb, and recovery, like happiness, begins with the knowledge that it is conceivable to live the best life possible. This knowledge alone might not avail people, but it is an important start. Simply knowing you can experience happiness in the upper reaches of what's possible and flourish in recovery is not enough. You must get busy; positive thinking like this is only as powerful as the grit you use to fulfill your potential and forge your legacy. Experiencing the maximum amount of happiness only *begins* with thinking you can maintain stable, long-term recovery.

In active addiction, hope shrinks and withers away. After several unsuccessful attempts to quit, one can feel helpless, dejected, and fearful one will never again live a life free from addiction's bondage. However, after meeting legions of recovering addicts and discovering that people can live in ways exceeding their wishes, people can develop faith in the knowledge that authentic happiness is within their grasps.

<u>Today's PI</u>
Use your past achievements to fuel hope for the future. On a clean sheet in your journal, write down five accomplishments that once seemed distant, remote, or nearly impossible to achieve (e.g., reaching a certain level of sobriety, graduating from school, living in your own apartment or home, working a certain job, experiencing a connection with your spiritual side, and so forth). Next write down realistic and "stretch" (challenging yet doable) goals you hope will be in your future. Afterward reflect on whether you've developed any insights by recognizing your past achievements.

DAY 48

Throw out an alarming alarm clock. If the ring is loud and strident, you're waking up to instant stress. You shouldn't be bullied out of bed, just reminded that it's time to start your day.

—Sharon Gold

Many people unintentionally add stress to their daily lives through lack of mindfulness, conscientious planning for their well-being, or self-care. Alarming alarm clocks are not the only culprit. Unnecessary noise, long commutes, and aggressive people are other examples. Excess stress can prevent the immune system from healing and growing as it should. At some level, unmitigated physiologic stress causes all sickness. Stress relief, then, is not just a good idea—it's necessary for survival.

All these "vexations of the spirit" should be avoided whenever possible. When they cannot be bypassed, create buffers to minimize exposure to their stress. You might not be able to move closer to work or change your home's geographic location, but you can arrange the best possible travel routes at the least stressful times. You can also make conscientious changes, such as listening to a captivating audiobook, to ease the stress of your commute and add serenity to your surroundings. Buying a gentle alarm clock is easy. Start there, and see what other changes come with time.

Today's PI

Take an inventory of external stressors that can be minimized or eliminated in your life today. List five proactive things you can do to destress your life, and share these ideas with an accountability partner. Do your best to implement your actions today to enhance the tranquility in your life.

DAY 49

Collect as precious pearls the words of the wise and virtuous.

—Abd el-Kader

Relationships are invaluable sources of happiness, self-esteem, and resilience. Other people bring joy to your life and can help you cope with the curve balls life throws your way. Since they know you best, your social connections are also filled with wisdom about you and life in general.

People commonly admire traits in others that they themselves possess or are in the process of cultivating. In other words, if you spot it, you got it. Respecting others' traits often reflects overlooked characteristics in *you*. This implies that you value and can enhance traits you might very well be blind to. In addition to asking for help in times of need and multiplying joy by celebrating victories with others, people can learn the virtues they embody from those around them.

Today's PI

Ask five people you respect for their top pearls of virtue and wisdom. Post one of these borrowed quotes somewhere visible in your home or workplace to regularly inspire you. What is your number one pearl?

DAY 50

It doesn't matter how long we may have been stuck in a sense of our limitations. If we go into a darkened room and turn on the light, it doesn't matter if the room has been dark for a day, a week, or ten thousand years—we turn on the light and it is illuminated. Once we control our capacity for love and happiness, the light has been turned on.

—Sharon Salzberg

Many people live their entire lives unaware and unawake—until a significant experience or set of experiences shakes them to their cores and reminds them that what really matters is love, kindness, and happiness. But why wait for unpredictable and illuminating moments of awakening or the end of your life to appreciate that the light already exists within? The time to discover the ability for love and happiness is right now. Fortunately, it doesn't matter how long fear has kept you imprisoned, because love is a more powerful force. It can liberate even the most enslaved, downtrodden, and hopeless person.

Today's PI

"In the light, I can see what's good. May all sentient beings be free of suffering and the root of suffering. May all sentient beings be happy, safe, and peaceful."

In your mind, repeat this mantra three times today for five continuous minutes each time. Set specific times when you can find five minutes of solitude.

DAY 51

——⚜ ⚜——

My God, a moment of bliss. Why, isn't that enough for a whole lifetime?

—Fyodor Dostoyevsky

Addictive substances and processes work in and disrupt the pleasure center of the brain. However, addiction is not a "pleasure-only disease," because long after pleasure is gone, addiction remains.

Savoring pleasurable experiences is one source of human happiness. Many experiences do not remain pleasurable, though, because we quickly adapt to most things. Addicts especially have difficulty maintaining pleasure, because what causes others to feel good and satisfied often causes them to feel angst and longing. They crave more and more.

When in the throes of addictive patterns, addicts are often not satisfied with the pleasure derived from something good. Instead they attach themselves to the never-ending pursuit of "more." Pleasure can be a good thing, but people must be aware of the potential pitfalls of unbridled hedonic pleasure. As the saying goes, "One is too many, and a thousand is never enough."

This does not imply that people are doomed to live without pleasure. Instead the trick is to savor and focus on eudaemonic pleasure—the kind of pleasure associated with meaning, self-awareness, inner peace, love, service, and balance with nature.

Today's PI
Reflect today on the sensory and eudaemonic pleasures you can minimize. What brings you the greatest amount of healthy pleasure?

DAY 52

———⸎⸎ ⸎⸎———

Life's fulfillment finds constant contradictions in its path; but those are necessary for the sake of its advance. The stream is saved from the sluggishness of its current by the perpetual opposition through which it must cut its way.

—Rabindranath Tagore

It is not difficult to find evidence that humans live in a hostile world. Survival mechanisms, refined and strengthened over millennia, cause people to automatically and vigilantly scan their environments for threats. Since crime, wars, violence, and affronts to pride are commonplace, people can sometimes fall into the depressingly pessimistic perspective that "life is tough, and then you die." While it's easy to understand this perspective, it's often challenging to appreciate that life is also full of heroism and virtue.

Tagore's quote illuminates the paradox of growth by using a stream as a metaphor for life's journey. Like the stream, people are always moving. The constancy of change and challenges faced save people from complacency and mediocrity. Recovery will not guarantee a windfall of economic prosperity or fame, but it will give addicts chances to go out and make the most of today. Why were you given an extra chance? What are you going to do with it?

Today's PI
Engage in guided-imagery meditation for ten to fifteen minutes. View yourself and your life as a stream. You are flowing gently over and through the troubles that are natural parts of life. Envision yourself as the water that gradually but ceaselessly flows on. You are able to adapt to your environment without stress or duress.

DAY 53

⚜

There is not a more pleasing exercise of the mind than gratitude.
It is accompanied with such an inward satisfaction that the duty is
sufficiently rewarded by the performance.

—Joseph Addison

One of the best ways to live in the upper reaches of happiness is to cultivate an attitude of gratitude. Over forty studies demonstrate that gratitude boosts happiness and helps people cope with hardships. Practicing gratitude is correlated with improved life, relationship, and work satisfaction, physical health, and sustained recovery. To help these benefits materialize in your life, revisit the "count your blessings" PI below.

Today's PI

This PI appears simple. As you might have found previously, though, it is not easy. For the next four nights, write down three good things that happened to you each day. Explain why these good things happened to you. Finding out why these good things happened is the most important part. Look for qualities in you that played a part. Accept these as permanent and pervasive parts of your life experience. Try not to dismiss them as luck. Be optimistic about the why.

DAY 54

Nearly all men can stand adversity, but if you want to test a man's character, give him power.

—Abraham Lincoln

Ironically, many weather the challenges of harsh circumstances better than the fortunes of windfalls. Everyone has tendencies that are brought to light when they have power over others or more disposable income than they know what to do with. The lure of power and unfettered freedom are challenging foes. To use a *Star Wars* metaphor, this is very much like the dark side seducing someone. Absolute power corrupts absolutely.

Money, fame, power, and ego can render people deaf when they're not mindful of practicing humility. Oftentimes it takes losing nearly everything for people to regain hearing. Only then are they open to hearing suggestions, accepting limitations, and letting go of entitlement.

Even if the dark side does seduce you, all is not lost. You can always choose to nurture your best character. Any fall from grace can have beautiful results if you realize through your hardships that you do deserve happiness, growth, joy, and a full life in recovery.

Today's PI
Give your ego a healthy checkup. Are you acting with exaggerated pride? Are you practicing gratitude? Are there any areas of your life where you are allowing fame, money, or power to take the driver's seat over your deeper principles and values? Remember, things don't make people who they are—actions do.

DAY 55

Of course I'm in shape! Isn't round a shape?

—Anonymous

Why should you bother exercising? Proper exercise improves sleep, helps manage weight, and decreases the risk of cardiovascular illness. In addition, exercise can improve arthritis, high blood pressure, and diabetes. It can also improve your libido and sex life, energy, and mood. Indeed, exercise might manage depressive symptoms as well as, if not better than, many antidepressant medications. Best of all, it can be fun!

<u>Today's PI</u>

Start exercising at your current point of fitness. Take advantage of daily opportunities to exercise more, such as by parking in the most distant parking space, using the stairs, and walking during your lunch break. Choose a fun way to exercise today. Perhaps it can include others. Rotate your exercise regimen to keep it fresh and new, stave off boredom, and engage different muscle groups for maximal benefit. Apply today's strategy most days, and see your mood and shape change.

Please remember to consult your doctor about any questions regarding the most appropriate physical activity regimen for you.

DAY 56

If you've ever wondered Why do we feel emotions?
or What difference does it make if I look on the bright side?
I can tell you. The latest science shows how our day-to-day emotional experiences affect
the very course of our lives.

—Barbara Fredrickson

Emotions are perhaps the most crucial aspect of the human experience. They can literally make or break you. Negative emotions narrow attention and shorten life span, while positive emotions increase creativity and improve health.

Positive emotions have the power to stop negativity in its tracks as well as to enable people to be more resilient during tough times. Positivity allows people to more easily focus on and lead with strengths. This in turn can increase self-esteem, make people more desirable to interact with, and enhance relationships.

Today's PI

Savor moments of positivity. The three main ways are to 1) anticipate future pleasurable events, 2) enjoy present pleasures, and 3) reminisce about past pleasurable events. Bask in, luxuriate in, marvel at, and give thanks for any moments today worth enjoying. Don't shrug this activity off. Don't assume you do this anyway. Savoring requires deliberate mental and physical mindfulness.

DAY 57

There is so much good in the worst of us, and so much bad in the best of us, that it hardly behooves any of us to talk about the rest of us.

—Edward Wallis Hoch

Human beings tend to gossip. Sharing information can be an instrument to discover truth, or it can be a misplaced way to make people feel better when others are put down. Oftentimes people are guilty of the latter, because judgments are frequently automatic and subconscious, while practicing nonjudgmental acceptance is challenging. Whether judgments are directed at the self or another, they can significantly erode peace and serenity.

Putting others down is simply not helpful. No lasting benefits exist for self-esteem or happiness when people judge others. In fact, the intolerances of others are oftentimes helpful clues about areas they have yet to accept in themselves. People are truly their own worst enemies when they criticize or shame others. Many addicts have insecure senses of self and overactive inner critics. These detrimental critics within can significantly block or delay healing and slyly infiltrate cognitive and emotional realities. The disease of addiction festers and feeds on intolerances—of others and the self.

However, you need not remain stuck in a cycle of self-degradation. With mindful effort, you can build new ways of speaking to yourself and viewing your imperfections. Freedom from the bonds of active addiction is the first step. Practicing empathy and self-compassion follow.

<u>Today's PI</u>
Borrow the rubber-band-on-the-wrist strategy to remind yourself to practice nonjudgmental thoughts. From waking until sleep, wear a rubber band around your wrist. Every time you judge yourself or another, snap the band against your wrist once. (This should cause a small stinging sensation, but nothing actually painful.) Replace the judgment with a positive fact.

DAY 58

Then, without realizing it, you try to improve yourself at the start of each new day; of course, you achieve quite a lot in the course of time. Anyone can do this, it costs nothing and is certainly very helpful. Whoever doesn't know it must learn and find by experience that a quiet conscience makes one strong.

—Anne Frank

Incredibly, Anne Frank wrote these words while hiding from certain peril in a desperate circumstance that would have driven most over the brink of sanity. She shared a crowded little space with demanding and noisy relatives, including a crying baby. Threat of discovery by the Nazis overshadowed everything constantly. Still this young woman found the wisdom of sages: peace is found from within. This type of inner peace is more powerful than any army. One major way to foster durable inner peace is through the meaning you place on hardship. Anne Frank is a stunning example of one who looks for the lesson to be learned and applies oneself to fulfilling personal potential despite the intrusion of great hardship in life. Seeking out the valuable implications and hidden benefits of seemingly damaging situations increases resilience, enhances optimism, and allows you to flourish. You will not achieve the upper limits of your potential by accident. Striving for personal excellence takes consistent and mindful effort.

Today's PI
Take a few moments to reflect on your choices, habits, and attitudes as they stand today. Are there any areas where you are not living up to your potential? Pick just one area, identify a positive behavioral change or an approach you can enact today to fix it, and do it. Work on improving yourself at the start of this "new day," as Anne Frank described. For added accountability, share your chosen positive change with a trusted friend.

DAY 59

⬩⸺⧫◈ ◈⧫⸺⬩

I can be changed by what happens to me, but I refuse to be reduced by it.

—Maya Angelou

Life can be hard. At the very least, it is filled with change. Many people's first instinct when they encounter change is to automatically withdraw, which then leads to judgment. That instinct does not define a person, however. Instead, what people do with their resistence to change determines where they lie on the spectrum of responseness versus reactivity.

"Change" merely indicates difference—not necessarily improvement or worsening. Certainly, bad things happen. Even "worse" things do not have to reduce people, though. Change, but don't fall. Many addicts enter recovery with the coping skill set of adolescents, and they find it hard to deal with life on life's terms. Slowly but surely, emotional maturity develops, but it takes time, practice, and patience.

Today's PI

Reflect on a hard aspect of life you are currently dealing with. Realize that all things change and pass, and catastrophizing or finalizing any one event is like putting a period where there should be a comma. As Benjamin Button reminds us, "You never know what's comin'." Look ahead with optimism and hope. Expect the best of all that's possible.

DAY 60

A friendship can weather most things and thrive in thin soil; but it needs a little mulch of letters and phone calls and small, silly presents every so often—just to save it from drying out completely.

—Pam Brown

Of the many key elements to flourishing in recovery, the greatest contributors are relationships and community. Social bonds form the backbone of a healthy, fulfilled life. Friends and social groups (like fellowships) are incredibly powerful sources of health, healing, happiness, resilience, and preventing relapse.

Wonderful as they might be, however, friendships do not just fall from the sky when needed. Meaningful, inspiring, and sustaining relationships take intentionality and work. If you do not reach out during good times to your support system, chances are slim that you will manage to reach out during hard times.

Today's PI

Put energy into shoring up your friendship reserves. Make a list of ten people you can call simply to say hello and ask about their days. If ten people don't come to mind, that's OK. Introduce yourself to a new person on any day you don't have someone lined up to call. Start the calendar countdown. You will be reaching out to one person every day for the next ten days. Foster an enhanced support network through pursuing these small connections. Spreading these calls out makes this exercise doable and provides the added bonus of looking forward to a different person to connect with every day.

DAY 61

In a controversy, the instant we feel anger, we have already ceased striving for the truth and have begun striving for ourselves.

—Buddha

It is entirely human to experience escalated emotions such as anger in the midst of controversy. Anger alone does not denote a failure to search for the truth. However, in arguments with friends and family, anger usually ensues when people make things personal that don't belong to them. In turn, people become more attached to being right than being happy, and in so doing, they lose sight of objectivity or curiosity (honest, humble exploration). Situations then often escalate and degrade.

Fortunately, you can apply communication skills in the heat of the moment to improve a situation. This includes removing the word "you." When interacting in a conflict, use only "I" statements to express your feelings. For example, don't say, "You make me so mad when you are lazy and disrespectful and don't pick up your things around the house." Instead try saying, "I feel _____ [frustrated, angry, or disappointed] when you _____ [factual action, without judgmental adjectives]."

Using that example, highlight the behavior of "not picking up around the house," and leave out the inflammatory portion of the person being "lazy and disrespectful." Using "When you _____, I feel _____" is more likely to engage the other person in looking with you for solutions and genuine common ground. Practice this technique to increase your personal serenity and minimize the need to make future amends.

<u>Today's PI</u>

When you begin to feel anger (today or whenever), pause. Doing so enables you to take stock of the situation and gives you the chance to respond instead of react. Practice using "When you _____, I feel _____" statements today and anytime a situation is escalating, or when you notice yourself feeling intense emotions while communicating.

As a reminder, call a friend or introduce yourself to one new person today to enhance your support network.

DAY 62

Once we recognize what it is we are feeling, once we recognize we can feel deeply, love deeply, can feel joy, then we will demand that all parts of our lives produce that kind of joy.

—Audre Lorde

The disastrous and dreadful deal with addiction is that once the brain discovers how mind-altering substances and behaviors make it feel, it demands that one repeat the experience over and over and over. This removes the person from participating in his or her own life. It ultimately leads to pain and suffering.

In recovery, positive emotions are by no means extinct. Recovery is actually where people experience higher, sustainable pleasures as a result of living virtuously. Giving, loving, appreciating, and nurturing deep, long-lasting relationships creates genuine happiness—the kind the authentic self wants to repeat. While life is not supposed to be one long ecstatic joyride, it's still healthy to enhance love, joy, and pleasure. Feeling more love and happiness takes a little work and lots of habitual reinforcement.

Today's PI

Sit in silent meditation for five minutes in the morning. During that time, recall how you've felt when you've extended love toward another. At night, sit again in silent meditation for five minutes, but this time recall how you've felt when you've been the object of love.

Remember to call a friend or introduce yourself to one new person today to enhance your support network.

DAY 63

If a fellow isn't thankful for what he's got, he isn't likely to be thankful for what he's going to get.

—Frank Clark

The brain is limited in that it can only focus on a small portion of reality at any one moment. Even multitasking is nothing more than shifting attention from one thing to another. Therefore, when you are focusing on gratitude, you are not focusing on fear or want. While there are many false doorways to happiness (money, fame, etc.), there is one that can reliably and directly boost mood—gratitude.

Gratitude shifts your thinking and mood, and it opens up your perspective. Feeling appreciation for what you have expands your visual field literally and figuratively. Gratitude helps you see what you already have and what you already are. It helps you view the people already in your life as valuable beyond measure.

Today's PI

Make three gratitude lists: one for things from your life during your active addiction, one for things from your life in recovery, and one for things since you've been engaging in the work of this book. Place at least ten items in each list. Reflect on what you have gained from each of these chapters in your life.

Again, call a friend or introduce yourself to one new person today to enhance your support network.

DAY 64

It is never too late to be who you might have been.

—George Eliot

In active addiction, people make mistakes. In life in general, people will make more mistakes still. To be human is to be imperfect. It's unwise to think otherwise, and it's within that messy human condition that you can start living this gifted time you have left in recovery. Many addicts are lucky to be alive and capitalize on their second chances with awareness and integrity. In so doing, they write their own stories. They narrate their destinies with every positive, healthy choice they make.

No matter what the wreckage of your past might have been, you can always start over today. You can live according to who you would like to become, and before long, that is exactly who you will be. No other person has the power to dictate who you are. You are the storyteller and dreamer. You are the only one to write your own story.

Today's PI

Make as many choices as possible today to enable you to fulfill your potential. Nothing is too small. Before making any choice (e.g., Should I eat that third cookie? Do I feel like exercising today? Does it matter if I make time for my relationships this evening?), remember that individual choices build habits, and habits build destiny. At the close of the day, journal about your experiences, insights, and any surprises you found throughout the day.

Remember to call a friend or introduce yourself to one new person today to enhance your support network.

DAY 65

———❦ ❦———

For beautiful eyes, look for the good in others; for beautiful lips, speak only words of kindness; and for poise, walk with the knowledge that you are never alone.

—Audrey Hepburn

Perhaps the most important ingredient in developing your character strengths and virtues is loving-kindness. It helps cut through fear, makes space for your imperfections and those of others, and connects you with others.

Today's PI

Every hour on the hour, spend just three minutes extending compassion toward six people of six different types: someone you are grateful for, a loved one, a friend, a difficult relative, a difficult acquaintance, and yourself. Write down the names of these six people, and set an alarm to help yourself remember the assignment. Every hour, take a brief moment to extend loving and beneficial thoughts toward each of these six people. At the end of the day, take a few minutes to reflect on whether you notice any benefit in your mood, productivity, or relationships.

Between these meditative minutes, when you talk, "speak only words of kindness"; when you look, "look for the good in others"; and when you walk, "walk with the knowledge that you are never alone."

Remember to call a friend or introduce yourself to one new person today to enhance your support network.

DAY 66

⟡

Scared and sacred are spelled with the same letters. Awful proceeds from the same root word as awesome. Terrify and terrific. Every negative experience holds the seed of transformation.

—Alan Cohen

Recovery and relapse are opposite sides of the same coin. As bold and dramatic a claim as it might be, every decision you make either bolsters your road to recovery or leads you closer to a relapse. As a recovering individual, you must undertake introspection. Similarly, you must remain curious and vigilant and consistently seek to grow, or else risk collapse.

The hell of addiction can be the springboard for incredible growth. It allows you to engage in the life-changing existence of one in positive recovery. There are no guarantees in life, but pain and suffering are certainly going to fill a life of active addiction.

Today's PI
Train yourself to hunt for the good stuff. As you practice this type of hunting, you might find that most of the bad stuff you used to notice fades smoothly into the background. Make the choice to focus today on what's right instead of what's wrong. Be mindful. Focus on finding the good in every moment, other people, and each situation you encounter today. See if doing so makes a difference in your mood, relationships, and productivity.

Remember to call a friend or introduce yourself to one new person today to enhance your support network.

DAY 67

✦

There are many ways of going forward, but only one way of standing still.

—Franklin D. Roosevelt

It does not matter how slowly you journey. Just keep moving. Reflect on this: dynamite did not create the Grand Canyon. Rather, water tore through rock and slowly crafted one of the most beautiful natural treasures in the world. This occurred over the course of millions of years. Is it different for rock than people?

Do you expect to achieve overnight transformative success for yourself? If so, you might be surprised to learn that overnight success is a myth. Amazing achievements generally result from normal human beings repeatedly doing well many small, boring things for many years. It generally takes a person ten thousand hours of diligent practice before he or she truly becomes an expert in anything. By routinely doing small things with attention to quality, you give yourself the biggest advantage and chance for success. Even 1 percent changes, which are the smallest modifications, such as limiting dessert to once a week, have an enormous impact over time.

Today's PI

Do all the little things the best you can. Brush your teeth as if auditioning for a toothpaste commercial, drive as if tailed by police (without panicking), work as if it were your life's calling, savor every meal, and breathe each breath as if it were your last.

Remember to call a friend or introduce yourself to one new person today to enhance your support network.

DAY 68

True intuitive expertise is learned from prolonged experience with good feedback on mistakes.

—Daniel Kahneman

Everyone has a blind spot. It's the part of you that doesn't know what it doesn't know. Those who think they have small blind spots generally have the largest ones! The good news is that anyone can learn how to shrink his or her blind spot. It's a worthy skill to cultivate, because greatness (in the form of wisdom and intuition) develops from shedding light on and decreasing this blind spot.

Today's PI

Pick three people from various areas of your life (family, friends, work, social groups, fellowships, and so forth). Ask them for honest and open feedback on the following questions.

1) *What are my top strengths? Please give specific examples of when you have observed me use them.*
2) *What would you like to see more of from me?*
3) *Are there times I overuse my strengths? Please give specific examples.*

This PI can be done in person, via e-mail, or over the phone. Let those you contact know you are doing an assignment whose benefit is contingent upon their honesty. Feel free to follow up on their answers if you're confused about any responses or simply curious to learn more. While you read or listen to their answers, be curious. Pretend you are hearing about yourself for the first time, in order to stay open and receptive. This PI can be a bit intimidating, and if it is too frightening, feel free to pass. It's OK to honor your comfort level at this moment. Tonight, journal about any surprises or discoveries.

Remember to call a friend or introduce yourself to one new person today to enhance your support network.

DAY 69

—⊷⊷ ⊶⊷—

Let food be thy medicine and medicine be thy food.

—Hippocrates

Sugar tastes great and causes energy spikes, but is it too good to be true? Is it tasty but deadly? The answer is yes (when referring to the processed type, such as table sugar), because it causes inflammation and can lead to depression, physical ailments, and even an early grave.

Sugar's energy spike also has a downside—the crash. After a brief burst of energy, sugar leads to fatigue and depression. Sugar also causes a spike of do-pamine to release in the brain, which leads to desire and excitement. Buyers beware, though. Similar to all other potentially addictive substances, the body adapts and tolerance develops over time. People's bodies and brains will crave sugar increasingly, but they will also experience diminishing positive returns and increased consequences, such as crashes and even depressive symptoms.

Whole, unprocessed foods, on the other hand, are the healthiest forms of nu-trition. You do not have to live entirely on raw organic foods to feel the benefits of healthy consumption, but you can benefit from increasing your intake of these nutritious forms of fuel while decreasing the junk. A diet full of pro-cessed sugar and other toxic ingredients is one of the leading causes of disease and death in today's world. The closer your foods resemble their natural forms, the healthier. Eating five servings of fresh fruits and vegetables a day can even make you happier.

Today's PI
Have a processed-sugar–free day from dawn to dusk.

Remember to call a friend or introduce yourself to one new person today to enhance your support network.

DAY 70

You can't connect the dots looking forward; you can only connect them looking backward. So you have to trust that the dots will somehow connect in your future. You have to trust in something—your gut, destiny, life, karma, whatever. This approach has never let me down, and it has made all the difference in my life.

—Steve Jobs

Faith and spirituality might be controversial topics, but the truth is that most human beings believe in something greater than themselves. Steve Jobs, for one, was deeply spiritual. Notice how he did not suggest people should commit to a religion. Instead he made the case for trusting in something. Trust is hope and reliance combined into one powerful virtue.

Having faith in a higher power or spiritual connection of your definition could very well be powerful enough to enhance your physical health, mental health, and well-being, as well as to extend your life.

Today's PI

Trust in something. Be mindful of what you trust in throughout the day—friends, colleagues, the sun setting, a higher power, etc. Reflect on or journal about any impact this trust PI had on your day. Were you more peaceful? Helpful? Aware of others? Surprised?

DAY 71

Excellence is an art won by training and habituation.
We do not act rightly because we have virtue or excellence,
but we rather have those because we have acted rightly.
We are what we repeatedly do.
Excellence, then, is not an act but a habit.

—Aristotle

What are you waiting for? What you put off until tomorrow will stay there. After all, current behavior best predicts future behavior. You are what you do. Neurons that fire together wire together. You are essentially patterns of habit.

If you want a sober brain, you must first get sober. If you want a brain full of happiness and excellence that exists at the upper limit of what's possible, you must do as the happy and excellent do. You must do so repeatedly. Good habits are hard to start but easy to break. Bad ones are easy to start and hard to break.

Today's PI
Make a list of good habits that you would like to do. Then make a list of what you are actually doing. Then strike out those items which appear on both lists, and circle any remaining habits that you would like to be doing. Choose one, and start doing it now.

DAY 72

—⁂—

A person however learned and qualified in his life's work in whom gratitude is absent, is devoid of that beauty of character which makes personality fragrant.

—Hazrat Inayat Khan

While knowledge and talent are useful, these alone accomplish almost nothing. When you do not live with appreciation that these and other such blessings are always gifts, then you truly cannot see. Gratitude lifts the veils of fear, comparison, and negativity that prohibit eyes from soaking up the good stuff. Cultivating an attitude of gratitude is an effective path to letting your light shine and opening yourself to a richer, deeper existence.

Even when things are not the best, it's still possible to find the best in what's happening. Things can always be worse. For example, showing a sick person what death is like can make him or her grateful for the sickness. Some religious practices even guide people to intentionally imagine their deaths. This is not a gruesome exercise. It merely awakens people to all they have. Because humans adapt so quickly to what they have, it is simply human nature to take many blessings for granted.

Today's PI

Spend five minutes in silent meditation contemplating the end of your life. Visualize what you are losing in the process. What people, places, and things are most cherished? What will you miss the most? Then spend fifteen minutes journaling about insights and surprises.

DAY 73

We cannot change our memories, but we can change their meanings and the power they have over us.

—David Seamans

When bad things happen to good people, how do you make sense of everything? For those who believe in a benevolent and controlled world, tragedy can smash that belief into a million little pieces. Is that belief really an illusion, though? It's obvious that life can be hard and challenging, and it's undoubtedly short and precious. With these pragmatic truths apparent, how can people keep hope and optimism alive?

The key is Acceptance. It prevents hope and optimism from morphing into cynicism and despair. Acceptance is not one-sided. It includes knowing that life is short, hard, and precious but also full of potential, growth, love, happiness, and change.

Today's PI

Journal about several mildly haunting memories. Focus on how they have been (or will be) springboards for your personal transformation. How will they help you grow? Pen a story wherein you are the hero that overcomes this and any other obstacles that might come your way. Be mindful of the memories you choose for this exercise. If you have significant unaddressed trauma, access professional help whenever possible, and do not attempt to navigate it through this exercise alone.

DAY 74

*When a man dies he clutches in his hands only that which
he has given away during his lifetime.*

—Jean Jacques Rousseau

Every day, you encounter a potentially infinite amount of choices. Some situations are mundane, but others can be pregnant with implications. Addiction turns people inward and leads to self-centeredness. Being focused on others is a challenge. Selfish and self-centered things can consume anyone if a person is not careful. Additionally, acting altruistically and doing the right thing for others might not always feel wonderful while you're doing it. However, giving has many benefits, and it's a worthy way to fill your time. Giving increases social bonding, enhances meaning and purpose in one's life, and is positively correlated with happiness. Giving does not have to be elaborate. Even small gestures matter. It can take the form of a donation, prayer, words, or intentions. Arguably the most precious of all gifts is the gift of time.

Today's PI

Set aside extra time for someone else or a cause. Make the time count. Make it of adequate duration and intensity to be a gift from you. Do not rely on the secondary gains of appreciation or admiration from others by verbalizing that you are giving. Just give with benevolent intent. When journaling tonight, reflect on whether you felt better or more productive today, or whether you noticed any changes in your relationships.

DAY 75

✦✦✦

If you create a character, you create a destiny.

—André Maurois

A common pitfall exists in working diligently to become perfect by trying to remove character defects: you inadvertently make those defects stronger. When you focus intently on what is wrong, you lose sight of what is right—including your strengths. If you want to leave negative aspects behind, focus on your character *strengths*.

Keep in mind that there is nothing wrong with identifying negative patterns of behavior and gaining insight. This form of self-reflection can be quite useful. However, in terms of moving toward the upper reaches of potential, it's even more helpful to look for opportunities to develop your strengths and utilize them in the formation of positive habits.

Today's PI

If you have not taken the strengths test, do so at AuthenticHappiness.org. If you have already done so, pick one of your top three strengths. Start looking for ways to use it in your daily affairs today and for the next seven days. Bring your intention to using the strength in novel ways. Journal each night about the experience.

DAY 76

And the day came when the risk to remain tight in a bud was more painful than the risk it took to blossom.

—Anaïs Nin

Life is hard. Avoiding pain is not possible, and any attempt to flee from it results in fleeing from what is treasured most in life. Perhaps your addiction started because you tried to live life avoiding something unpleasant, such as grief or painful memories. In trying to avoid the "bad," did you escalate suffering instead? Flourishing and happiness are not possible without the courage to lean into life and accept life on life's terms.

When you live life in a way that aims to minimize pain or prevent change, you fail to live. In order to experience anything fully, you can't shut yourself off. Control strategies meant to avoid "bad" experiences also prevent you from being creative, using courage, and taking risks.

<u>Today's PI</u>
Use your journal to answer this question: How are you leaning into both the pain and joys of life? Are you using courage or fear today?

As a reminder, don't forget to keep leading with your three chosen strengths.

DAY 77

Self-esteem isn't everything; it's just that there's nothing without it.

—Gloria Steinem

Not all pride is bad, but there is a very real difference between knowing and owning your strengths and believing you are superior, faultless, or "perfect." Without self-awareness, there can hardly be self-love, and without self-love, you rob yourself of the one true lifelong relationship—the one with yourself. It is not conceited or self-indulgent to be proud of what you have accomplished.

<u>Today's PI</u>
Write about the times in your life when you have felt the most confident and self-assured. Focus your attention on your accomplishments, and write about what you did to achieve them and what character traits you used to make them happen. Try not to let fear of what others might think stifle your writing. Especially explore why you were able to achieve what you did.

As a reminder, call one new person today to enhance your support network, and don't forget to keep leading with your three chosen strengths.

DAY 78

❦

Don't let what you cannot do interfere with what you can do.

—John Wooden

No matter the current state of your health, a little movement is good. It helps your emotional, physical, and spiritual aspects. Moving the body can also help quiet the mind, release muscle tension, and increase levels of feel-good neurotransmitters.

Exercise also keeps stress levels down. Areas of the world where people live the longest (known as Blue Zones) have several things in common. Notably, strenuous, lifelong physical activity is one of them. Sadly, if the bathroom, couch, and refrigerator were not in different places, some might hardly move at all.

Today's PI

Get moving. Do thirty minutes of physical activity. Park your car in the farthest possible parking space, walk to the store, take the stairs, and stand rather than sit. Ride a bike, do yoga, do walking meditation, or move in other ways you are able. Just do it.

Remember to call one new person today to enhance your support network, and don't forget to keep leading with your three chosen strengths.

DAY 79

—⊰⊱⊰⊱—

Gratitude bestows reverence, allowing us to encounter everyday epiphanies, those transcendent moments of awe that change forever how we experience life and the world.

—John Milton

John Milton's quote is a reminder of the potency of gratitude. A simple shift in the focus of thought can realign energy powerfully enough to elevate your spirit and sense of awe. Happiness is not a state of perpetual bliss, nor is it defined by a problem-free existence. Instead, happiness is accepting that life is full of the good stuff, the bad stuff, and everything inbetween.

Happiness isn't cheap — it requires that you don't take the blessings in your life for granted. An easy remedy is at your disposal, though. Simply take the time to pause, notice, and appreciate. Journal to solidify the experience.

Today's PI

Give yourself time for the "easy remedy" of actively practicing gratitude. Take five minutes twice today to journal about what you have to be grateful for. Ideally, do this first thing in the morning and last thing before you go to bed, but any time is good enough.

As a reminder, call one new person today to enhance your support network, and don't forget to keep leading with your three chosen strengths.

DAY 80

❦

*Country people do not behave as if they think life is short;
they live on the principle that it is long, and savor variations of the kind best appreciated
if most days are the same.*

—Edward Hoagland

Many people fall naturally into routines. Some are healthy and stabilizing. Others are destructive or limiting. Either way, people often forget to notice those elements of life that happen repeatedly. You can increase your sense of satisfaction with day-to-day life by learning to savor. Savor the new, routine, invisible, and fulfilling. Savoring can increase positive feelings such as hope, pride, joy, amusement, gratitude, serenity, inspiration, awe, trust, and love. General positivity has the power to change you by expanding your mind and allowing you to see possibilities that negativity can obscure from view. Over time, multiple moments of positivity build resources such as resilience, enhanced relationships, and improved physical health.

Today's PI

Look for opportunities to savor the new or the frequently overlooked in your day-to-day life. Look for elements of your world that your eyes are so used to seeing, they gloss over them without fully appreciating them. Be inspired and amused, and savor these positive emotional states. Seek ways to broaden and build. What can you do to more frequently experience hope, pride, joy, amusement, gratitude, serenity, inspiration, awe, trust, or love?

Remember to call one new person today to enhance your support network, and don't forget to keep leading with your three chosen strengths.

DAY 81

The great majority of us are required to live lives of constant duplicity. Your health is bound to be affected if, day after day, you say the opposite of what you feel, if you grovel before what you dislike, and rejoice at what brings you nothing but misfortune.

—Boris Pasternak

Who you are and what you think might be unpopular or even wrong. However, who you are, what you stand for, and your self-worth are not in other people's hands. If you don't ever take risks and make mistakes, you simply don't grow. It's far better to be taught wisdom than to turn yourself into a carbon copy of who you think others want you to be. Traditional recovery fellowships often borrow a William Shakespeare quote that encompasses today's assignment: "To thine own self be true."

Today's PI

Speak your truth in every situation, unless that truth unnecessarily causes harm. Speak slowly and deliberately. Take your time. Keep in mind that speaking one's truth does not justify saying hurtful things to others. Be mindful that what you say does no harm.

Don't forget to keep leading with your three chosen strengths.

DAY 82

Optimism is the faith that leads to achievement. Nothing can be done without hope and confidence.

—Helen Keller

Helen Keller was not born deaf and blind. Those conditions were consequences of a childhood illness. Before she was born, there was no evidence that any deaf and blind human could have achieved anything close to what she did with her life. Helen Keller was the first deaf and blind person to get a bachelor's degree. She was also a prolific speaker, author, and political activist. She illustrates that adversity does not block the chances for excellence. With the right attitude and actions as heroic as Helen Keller's, adversity can actually affect others in vividly positive ways. For example, Keller was awarded the Presidential Medal of Freedom and elected to the National Women's Hall of Fame. Her likeness was placed on currency, and she had streets named in her honor. She had many other tributes as well, fitting of someone so inspirational.

Today's PI

Write for ten minutes about your best possible self one year from today. Write continuously for only ten minutes about what the best, most heroic version of you is doing one year from now. Be like Helen Keller. Don't limit yourself. Use your imagination and wishful thinking in describing the ideal circumstances and events in your life one year from now.

DAY 83

Early to bed, early to rise makes you healthy, wealthy, and wise.

—Benjamin Franklin

Research reveals morning is the perfect time to be productive. Whether it's exercising, working, problem solving, or any form of accomplishing, self-regulation (willpower) is greatest in the morning. A calm and productive morning is very different from a frantic one. Dr. Samantha Boardman suggests practical ways to maximize your mornings. How you spend your morning sets the tone for the rest of the day.

1) Use a gentle alarm clock rather than one that violently jars you awake.
2) Make your bed. Physical movement is good. Think of it as stretching.
3) Exercise. Just twenty minutes boosts your mood and energy all day long.
4) Be mindful. Pay attention, and be in the moment.
5) Spend time in the fresh air and daylight. Natural light and environments are important for well-being.
6) Eat well. Try some fruit and oatmeal. Skip the sugar.

Today's PI
Follow these healthy guidelines, and plan for tomorrow morning. Wake up earlier than normal, and commit to doing at least one thing that requires self-discipline (going to the gym, doing a school or work assignment, doing those dreaded house chores, or more).

DAY 84

Our most basic instinct is not for survival but for family. Most of us would give our own life for the survival of a family member, yet we lead our daily life too often as if we take our family for granted.

—Paul Pearsall

Today is "family loving-kindness day." People often don't work as hard at home as they do in other relationships. Perhaps it's too easy to take family members for granted. Since family members are less likely to abandon one another, they may have less drive to be on their best behavior. As a result, complacency and carelessness can follow the expectation that you will be loved unconditionally. While unconditional love is a valuable virtue, it's also most precious when continually cultivated and earned.

<u>Today's PI</u>

Practice loving-kindness toward a specific family member all day long. Throughout the course of your day, intentionally think loving thoughts, use loving words, and create loving actions toward that other person, whether he or she is in front of you or not. Feel free to open yourself in loving-kindness to everyone, but focus your intentional energy and behavior on only that specific family member. No matter how small any gesture might be, try to do something loving and kind toward or for that family member once every hour.

DAY 85

There is more to life than increasing its speed.

—Mahatma Gandhi

Slow down. Too often people hurry through their lives at a breakneck speed. However, people just as often find that they are simply running in place. Never before has humankind been able to share so much information so quickly. While humans' success on this planet is largely due to exchanging information, it's nearly impossible to avoid information overload without vigilance. One problem with this deluge is that media overexposure can decrease mood.

However, there's a boundlessness in each person. There is life, love, joy, beauty, and breath. Mindfulness and other meditative techniques allow people to see what Gandhi meant in his quote. In order to find the "more to life", though, people have to slow down long enough to experience it.

Today's PI

Spend one minute every hour in silence. Focus on your breath, and just be. This takes diligence, since it will be easy to forget. Use something to remind you of this positive intervention, such as a recurring alarm, to ensure you stay on task. Tonight, journal about anything you felt, learned, or otherwise became inspired to do from today's PI.

DAY 86

When you get to the end of your rope, tie a knot and hang on. And swing!

—Leo Buscaglia

Humor and laughter are good medicine. Physicians in ancient Greece believed illness actually resulted from an imbalance of internal fluids they called "humors." Naturally, they reasoned that restoring these humors to proper balance created optimal health. Humor frees up some space from (one's reaction to) the bad stuff with a playful perspective and transforming it into less bad stuff. Perhaps a Yiddish proverb words humor's healing's power best, "What soap is to the body, laughter is to the soul."

It is no surprise that laughing helps decrease pain and stress hormones and allows people to make light of (even survive) the darkest times. "Humor" and funniness became synonymous over time. Laughing and amusement were that important to health. Some things are definitely not laughing matters, but humor and laughter are often good medicine.

Today's PI
Plan on seeing a funny movie, going to a funny play, reading a funny book, or watching a funny TV show. Do it today if you have time. Otherwise plan to do it within the next three days. Be mindful of how you feel in anticipation of what you planned, and see if you can savor the reward in looking forward to the experience.

DAY 87

❧ ❧

Gratitude unlocks the fullness of life. It turns what we have into enough, and more. It turns denial into acceptance, chaos to order, confusion to clarity. It can turn a meal into a feast, a house into a home, a stranger into a friend.

—Melody Beattie

People can find gratitude in every corner of their lives if they look. Think about mealtime and how the process of food creation depends on a vast and interconnected network of people and animals. Some toil the land, some transport the food, and some store it. Food ultimately comes from the sun and the earth, but you can choose to be grateful for the short-term work that went into planting, reaping, transferring, cleaning, preparing, or selling the nourishing food. If you're interested in learning more, investigate each step in the food production chain in order to discover and appreciate how intricate and involved the process is.

Today's PI
Determine ways you have benefited from the work, gifts, and beneficence of others. Try to play this game with others. See who can create the longest list by the end of the day.

DAY 88

*It is the mark of an educated mind to be able to entertain
a thought without accepting it.*

—Aristotle

Aristotle's valuable wisdom speaks of courage and acceptance. Allowing the space within oneself to respect foreign beliefs is challenging at times but part of wisdom. Doing so does not require you agree with everything. Instead, by opening up to and acknowledging other views, you practice empathy, nonjudgmental opinions, humility, and acceptance.

It is said that the goal of education is to fill empty minds. How wrong! Truly learned ones are those who replace that emptiness with openness. Although cliché, it's true—the more people learn, the more they realize how much more they have to learn.

Today's PI
Make a list of five things you know beyond a shadow of a doubt. Then write how you know them to be true. Share these with a trusted friend, and try to discover if these are absolute truths or not. See if you can hold space within your mind to acknowledge other possibilities. Perhaps use any insight gained from this PI to look at the world in general with more curiosity.

DAY 89

*What you get by achieving your goals is not as important as
what you become by achieving your goals.*

—Zig Ziglar

It's nice to fit in, and it's an achievement to be powerful, but it's more important
to live authentically. It's important to achieve, but it's most powerful when the
pursuit of achievement results in personal development. Power and achievement
are nice, but they change into weaknesses when they become anchors for
happiness.

If you say, "I'll be happy when _____," you live the lie that happiness
waits. This perspective entraps you in the never-ending search for the next
best thing—something better or different that finally enables you to feel inner
peace. However, happiness is not a destination.

Even if you keep reaching new heights, your happiness is generally short
lived, and this ushers in postclimactic depression and confusion. You are left
wondering, "Where does happiness really exist?" As a result, you usually tell
yourself that happiness awaits in the next achievement. The cycle of illusion
repeats itself, though, as you find happiness elusive because nothing can possibly deliver what you expect.

What you evolve into by pursuing valuable, meaningful goals is far more
important to your overall level of happiness than what you get by actually
achieving them.

Today's PI

*Put aside what you think you are after. Who are you trying to become? Think about this question
throughout the course of your day, and journal about it tonight for twenty minutes.*

DAY 90

People in forty-nine other countries have longer life expectancies (in both years and quality of life measurements) than Americans. We are the richest country, so why are we not living the healthiest and happiest lifestyles? Simple: we want what is easy, not what is best.

—Michael Banz

On average, Americans burn fewer than one hundred calories a day by exercising. Is there a solution? For many people, making a drastic change such as walking to work is unlikely, but most can make small, incremental changes that increase activity over time and enhance well-being and longevity. People can also hide the remote control, eat meals together *slowly*, and take after-meal walks together.

Blue Zones, areas of the world where people live longer and are healthier and happier, are far more active. Moving the body in many Blue Zones is simply a cultural norm. Blue Zone residents also tend to eat a Mediterranean or similar diet, which is rich in fresh fruits, vegetables, healthy fats, whole and unprocessed grains, herbs rather than salt, olive oil rather than butter, and lean protein sources such as poultry and fish. These are associated with a reduced risk of cardiovascular mortality, cancer and cancer mortality, and Parkinson's and Alzheimer's diseases. In addition, Blue Zones stress the importance of eating meals slowly with family and friends, and this naturally enhances bonding.

Today's PI
Live and eat according to the Blue Zone lifestyle. For one day, make informed food choices, create valuable social bonding moments during mealtimes, and make it a goal to incorporate exercise.

DAY 91

What is a face, really? Its own photo? Its makeup? Or is it a face as painted by such or such painter? That which is in front? Inside? Behind? And the rest? Doesn't everyone look at himself in his own particular way? Deformations simply do not exist.

—Pablo Picasso

Which memories and emotions direct people greatly influence what they see. Without awareness, a person often assumes his or her interpretation of events and experiences, which is infused with memory, subjectivity, and emotional influence, is the one true reality. Objectivity is merely an idea. By observing anything, people change what they observe by fixing it with meaning.

Picasso wisely noticed that observation determines what "is." Perhaps John Milton put it best in *Paradise Lost*: "The mind is its own place, and in itself can make a heaven of hell, a hell of heaven."

Today's PI

Relax your inner storyteller. Do not make up a backstory to anything. Take everything as it comes without judgment or attachment. Keep your notebook handy today, and jot down any moments when you notice yourself slipping into assumptions or judgments. Notice when things pan out differently than your internal storyteller would have assumed, and jot those instances down too.

DAY 92

—⁂—

*If we could learn to like ourselves, even a little, maybe our cruelties
and angers might melt away.*

—John Steinbeck

The elusive self-love and self-esteem—oh, where can you be found? Self-esteem and self-confidence are not the same thing. Self-esteem is the core belief in yourself that holds true even when your confidence wavers. *Self-esteem* is a verb as well, and it results from using courage and self-compassion over time. Self-esteem is not a destination but, like life itself, a journey. Many have moments or days when self-confidence wavers, but practicing self-compassion and empathy over time bolsters self-esteem and creates durability where once there might have been fragility. In fact, loving yourself and extending compassion to your imperfections empowers you to love and respect others.

Today's PI

Pamper yourself. Even if you have a busy day, find a little time to spoil yourself. Take an extra long walk at lunch, get a mani-pedi, buy a nice gift, sleep a bit longer, get some sunshine, sneak off to the movies, or exercise. Above all, do not let guilt enter the equation. Do this today because you deserve it. You are not stealing from anyone. It is more than OK to slow down and smell the roses. Why people don't slow down more is baffling. Why are people in such rushes? Where are people really going, anyway?

DAY 93

Beauty doesn't need ornaments.
Softness can't bear the weight of ornaments.

—Munshi Premchand

Ideals of beauty change over time and differ between cultures. Depending on where one is born, beauty might mean obesity, elongated necks, stoic demeanor, or even baldness. Despite potential fringe benefits of physical beauty (higher-paying jobs, better grades, elevated social status, and more), beauty in and of itself adds little to nothing to happiness or recovery. Inner beauty is a soft lightness of being.

A person full of inner beauty is slow to anger, quick to help, and full of compassion. Inner beauty needs nothing else to shine. It is admirable in any packaging.

Today's PI

Enhance your inner beauty. Strive to be slow to anger, quick to help, and full of compassion. Set your alarm at random times throughout the day to remind yourself of today's intention. You and your unique gifts deserve to be here as much as anyone else.

DAY 94

❧

Always be yourself, express yourself, have faith in yourself, do not go out and look for a successful personality and duplicate it.

—Bruce Lee

As Bruce Lee offers, to be yourself, it is important to express yourself. The true self often comes out when you are engaged in creative projects. For that reason, today will be "expression day." Keep today's project to assess the evolution of your spirit over the years.

Today's PI

Express yourself today by making a collage. Find the time to make this project happen. The collage does not have to be elaborate. It can be as simple as gluing a few pictures on a piece of paper, or you might be inspired to make it intricate and more decorative. Choose images that reflect your innermost self and dreams. When you are finished, share it with an ally who is supportive of your creativity and authenticity.

Perhaps you do not consider yourself to be built for today's PI. Even if you do not consider yourself to be creative or artistic, you have the same creative spark that every human being has. Don't dismiss todays PIs as meaningless or "not for me." Do it anyway, and share your experience with us on the forum. Try it once, if it is truly meaningless, you have permission to skip it next year.

DAY 95

In every community, there is work to be done. In every nation, there are wounds to heal. In every heart, there is the power to do it.

—Marianne Williamson

It is easy to throw stones at others. How easily do you see the speck in others' eyes while unaware of the log in your own? Recovery includes taking responsibility for *your* side of the street and leaving the rest where it belongs. Picking easy targets to resent or complain about, such as the government and the justice system, distances you from the one thing you have control over—yourself.

Recovery includes "citizenship," or civic involvement. In turn, your new life also a call for you play an active role the community you wish to live in. Be the change you wish to see in the world. Gandhi and Martin Luther King Jr. knew love and peace resulted from inner love and self-respect. These influential leaders conscientiously chose nonviolence and catalyzed incredible changes through love and peace.

<u>Today's PI</u>

Do one thing that reflects your wish for a better world, such as registering to vote, feeding the homeless, donating to charity, abiding by all the traffic laws, being kind to strangers, creating art, or stopping and giving your loved ones a few minutes of undivided attention. Whatever you choose, recognize that small acts of loving-kindness shared over time by a critical mass of society can truly change the world. Focus today on doing your part. Let others do theirs.

DAY 96

⸺⸻⸺

The true test of character is not how much we know how to do, but how we behave when we don't know what to do.

—John Holt

Responses are the most telling when people don't have a clue what to do. What values, intuitions, or habits carry you through? How does your integrity (what choices you make when no one is looking) hold up under pressure or temptation? Anyone can avoid a charging elephant; it takes very little mindfulness to react to something so large and obvious. Your responses to the small things in life (those easily overlooked or swept under the rug) are compounded over time and make up the bulk of your interactions, activity, and character.

Today's PI

Draw awareness to these tender moments of "not knowing," and draw intentionality to your actions. Wear a rubber band on your wrist today. Every time you are faced with a moment when you don't know what to do, and you find yourself reacting instead of responding, snap it against your wrist. To yourself say the words, "This is a test of your character." When you are alone and are about to or already have engaged in behavior you would not do in front of an audience of other people, snap the rubber band against your wrist. To yourself say the words, "This is a test of your character." Stay away from shame and self-judgment. Simply practice noticing when your impulses or actions go against how you would prefer to respond.

DAY 97

Some people are always grumbling because roses have thorns;
I am thankful that thorns have roses.

—Alphonse Karr

Your initial reactions to people, places, and things can appear valid at first. However, setbacks are often disguised as gifts, and gifts frequently look like setbacks. Perhaps Hugh Downs said it best: "A happy person is not a person in a certain set of circumstances, but rather a person with a certain set of attitudes." This is perhaps what led David Sams (Oprah Winfrey's first TV producer) to say, "My stroke was a lifesaver."

Today's PI
Make a gratitude list of at least twenty good things that are attached to not-so-good things. Use a format similar to Karr's: Which thorns in your life have beautiful petals?

Think about those blessings that you initially viewed as unpleasant. Some examples: I'm grateful traffic teaches patience. I'm glad destitution spurs perspective. I'm grateful not working in Hawaii (my wife wouldn't let me take the job) led me to friends in Houston whom I love and cherish.

DAY 98

※———❀ ❀———※

Never go to a doctor whose office plants have died.

—Erma Bombeck

Caring for plants is a strategy to enhance compassion, health, and happiness. It requires dedication, devotion, and responsibility. Erma Bombeck's quote is humorous but true to an extent. How can a doctor help you if he or she cannot even keep a plant going? Some believe plants can hear what's in people's hearts. Others believe plants literally hear people's voices. All living beings benefit from one another in one way or another, so this proposed emotional symbiosis might not be as farfetched as it seems on the surface. Regardless of your beliefs, plants doubtlessly do better with full attention, and research confirms that people do better when they care for plants.

Today's PI

Buy a plant, plant some flowers or other garden life, or donate money to help plant a tree some-where. Without plant life, humans couldn't survive. Plants provide beauty to the world and, most importantly, life-giving oxygen. Take today to give back to the natural world. For a bonus, spend time practicing gratitude for the plant life you see as you go throughout your day.

DAY 99

We can never obtain peace in the outer world until we make peace with ourselves.

—Dalai Lama

Life provides tests. It is great, but it's filled with trials, tribulations, and hardships. Abuse, major trauma, and abandonment are only a few examples of painful experiences human beings undergo too often. You cannot change the past, but you are empowered in the present. Pain is not optional, but suffering is.

You might have endured great pain in the past, but how much power you allow that past hurt to have over you is up to you in the here and now. This is often easier said than done, as traumas sneak into the psyche in ways that can be extremely difficult to overcome. Fortunately, forgiveness is an especially healing strategy.

When hate, blame, and anger remain, they degrade resilience and erode relationships. If you harbor those emotions (no matter how justified), they erode your ability to love and be loved. If you're tired of the past robbing you of living the best life possible, practice forgiveness. It is the one peacemaking activity you primarily do for yourself.

Today's PI

Pray for forgiveness or for the willingness to forgive. See the people who hurt you as human beings—not perfect beings. Try to envision their thought processes to help shed light on their behavior. This is for you and only you. Today, you are letting go of the past bit by bit and leaving it where it belongs.

DAY 100

✦━━⊰⊱━━✦

Love is more than a noun—it is a verb; it is more than a feeling—it is caring, sharing, helping, sacrificing.

—William Arthur Ward

Positive recovery, *recovery*, and *gratitude* are all verbs, and as Ward says, *love* is a verb too. If living the best life were possible in dreams and thoughts alone, people could all be hooked up to respirators and other life-sustaining machinery so they could merely coast in comatose, blissful, illusional states. That life is no life at all, though. Despite the promise of bliss, people need to behave like people—not like a bunch of cells. In all of its messiness, life's payoff is love. Love means caring when it's hard, helping when you don't want to, and sacrificing when it's inconvenient. Love requires us to *act*. As the antidote to fear, love really does conquer all.

<u>Today's PI</u>
Put your love into action. Write and send a letter (e-mail or handwritten) to someone you love. Tell that person what he or she means to you, what you love about him or her, and what you're grateful for. Externalize and act on your love. Journaling this evening about your experience in sending the letter is optional but suggested.

DAY 101

It's not the load that breaks you down; it's the way you carry it.

—Lena Horne

Most find that asking for help is challenging because people are taught that good old-fashioned self-reliance should be able to tackle anything. Unfortunately, adhering solemnly to this self-reliance principle leads to unnecessary agony. People are actually empowered in so many ways when they open themselves to receiving help, and they can also realize how much strength there is in working with others.

Today's PI

Everyone struggles sometimes. Instead of being afraid or too proud to ask for help, invite others in. Share your burden with others today by expressing what, if anything, you have been silently carrying around.

If you are struggle free, call one friend at a time until you can be of service to someone who shares that he or she is currently carrying a burden. Either way, today's PI is about sharing a challenge—yours or someone else's.

DAY 102

Love yourself—accept yourself—forgive yourself—and be good to yourself, because without you the rest of us are without a source of many wonderful things.

—Leo F. Buscaglia

Instead of focusing on what you lack that everyone seems to have, think about what you offer that everyone else doesn't have. Leo Buscaglia was right: you are unique and special because you are the one and only you! Fear gets in the way of loving, accepting, and forgiving yourself. Fear conditions you against self-love or pride. If you feel proud, you risk the potential fall from grace that fear tells you will hurt more the higher up you are. However, loving and accepting yourself does not have to be so extreme as to cause arrogance, and self-love and pride do not set you up for pain. You can find balance between humility and taking joy in your successes, which can empower you to achieve sustainable self-love that is maintained despite those inevitable human setbacks that fear tells us must be painstakingly avoided.

<u>Today's PI</u>
You are the object of the assignment today. Practice a transcendental-meditation technique for twenty minutes twice today. Find a quiet place and either sit comfortably or lie down. With your eyes closed, focus on your breathing. You can use the given mantra or choose your own:

"I am loving and lovable. I am good and getting better every day, in every way. I forgive myself."

DAY 103

Half of the troubles of this life can be traced to saying yes too quickly and not saying no soon enough.

—Josh Billings

Boundaries are borders that define where a person ends and another begins. Setting strong emotional boundaries is key to maintaining self-esteem, balance, and healthy relationships. Without adequate boundaries, damaging or unhealthy people and thoughts can take up rent-free space in your head and heart. Consequently, you allow yourself to "own" what's not yours to begin with. This includes others' feelings or behaviors, and you experience avoidable shame and hurt.

While this is common sense to many, people still find themselves taking responsibility for others' feelings or saying yes when they should say no. This is out of a sense of guilt, a desire to gain favor and please people, or both. When you do this, you forgo your own needs for the perceived needs of others, and most importantly, you risk the safety and health of the one person who truly needs your care—you.

Today's PI

Choose a relationship of yours you think might need boundary bolstering. Identify one boundary you can put into action today, and do it. Some boundary-strengthening activities include sharing a previously silent need with someone, asking someone in your life to stop doing something that has been making you uncomfortable, or asking for that favorite book or article of clothing back from the friend who borrowed it ages ago but whom you've felt anxious about requesting it from. Also identify a neglected area of your life: Are you saying yes enough to your physical, emotional, and spiritual needs?

DAY 104

No one is as capable of gratitude as one who has emerged from the kingdom of night.

—Elie Wiesel

By definition, traumatic events are deeply disturbing and confusing. It's normal to feel anxious, angry, or depressed after traumatic events. It's also normal for these events to lead to posttraumatic growth. Wiesel's quote sheds light on how traumatic events can usher in major personal transformations. In those cases, people don't bounce back to where they were before the event. They "bounce up" to even higher, more fulfilling states of being, with more gratitude and equanimity. Living a sheltered life might be safer or nicer on some levels, but without challenges and pain, you would miss some of the blessings your personal trials and tribulations could afford you.

Today's PI

Write a poem of thanks for all you have been given through the challenges you have faced in life. If you wish, write about those gifts you will receive in the future. Today's PI has no rules, so don't worry about rhyme schemes or any other constraints. Write creatively and from the heart. Practice courage and boldness by sharing your work with someone else.

DAY 105

It takes seventeen muscles to smile and forty-three to frown.

—Anonymous

Did you know that merely smiling can trick your brain into thinking you are happy? Science reveals that if you try smiling, you often feel better, expand your creative thinking, and start to see possibilities you never knew existed. When you are down in the dumps, smiling can help lift you out. You can literally fake it until you make it.

With so many different languages in the world, this is still one message clearly understood all over the place. Smiling is the universal welcome sign. The world might be vast, but it's also a mirror. When you smile, the world smiles back. When you scowl, the world will give that back too. In any language, smiles can counteract the effects of frowns and confuse grumpiness.

Today's PI
Every hour on the hour, smile with your entire face. Smile for fifteen seconds straight every hour. Make sure it's not a smile with only your mouth. Crinkle your eyes—one sign of a genuine smile. When you feel ready, try laughter on top of your smile. Chuckle quietly or laugh boisterously. Either way welcomes joy.

DAY 106

There is nothing noble about being superior to some other person.
The true nobility is in being superior to your previous self.

—Hindu Proverb

It has been said that once a person strays off the path of righteousness, his or her character is forever tarnished. This program disagrees wholeheartedly. Nobility and good character are not birthrights. They are earned. Living a life full of good character and nobility starts when a person acts venerably, provided that vanity is not allowed to seduce him or her into darkness.

People do not improve when they are the only ones leading themselves. They become better versions of themselves by learning from and even emulating others. Yet when you view as inferior those whose teachings enabled your growth, it is akin to eating your own limbs for nourishment. You might temporarily survive, but soon enough you will have less than what you started with.

Today's PI
Journal for fifteen minutes today on a person or group you feel greater than, while looking within that person or group for caches of hidden wisdom. What can you learn from that person or group? What strengths does the person or group possess that you could emulate to help improve yourself? What gratitude can you find for having that person or group in your life?

DAY 107

Feelings of oneness come and go, not at random, but in step with your feelings of joy, gratitude, love, and the like.

—Barbara Fredrickson

Positive relationships transform you in amazing ways. Moments of connection occur within what Fredrickson calls "micromoments." These fortify the connections between the brain and heart, and they even improve physical health. They can also expand awareness of your surroundings and dissolve the barriers that are erected to keep you safe from harm but that actually prevent you from making authentic, positive connections. Micromoments empower you to see through self-imposed boundaries and appreciate how few divisions between you and others actually exist. Over time, Fredrickson notes, these moments relax "distinctions between you and others. Indeed, your ability to see others—really see them, wholeheartedly—springs open. Love can even give you a palpable sense of oneness and connection, a transcendence that makes you feel part of something far larger than yourself."

Today's PI

Focus on forming a new connection. Reach out to someone who you know but would like to know better. Perhaps challenge yourself by reaching out to someone completely new. Invite that person to lunch, coffee, a movie, or a meeting. Put yourself out there, and trust the process. Connections are not built overnight, but each relationship starts somewhere. Open yourself up to the possibility of something new.

DAY 108

If you want others to be happy, practice compassion.
If you want to be happy, practice compassion.

—Dalai Lama

One key to emotional sobriety is compassion, but what exactly is that? Compassion involves feeling what another is experiencing *and* being moved to help that person. This skill uses empathy and expands the circle of connection with both you and the world at large. It widens the circle of who you are and what is included when you use the term "us."

Compassion is necessary to counteract the "bad stuff" in life, because your automatically negativity-biased brain separates you from others and tells you the world's resources are finite and limited. If you're not careful, you can view others' gains as your losses. This allows jealousy to fester within and subconsciously robs you of meaningful connections. Humans are, after all, social and herd animals. It is compassion that allows people to see others as they see themselves and themselves as others see them. The power of compassion and kindness sweeps away judgment, sarcasm, and other fear-driven actions. In their wake, compassion ushers in higher amounts of well-being and attracts positive relationships.

Today's PI
Offer to help a friend in need or write a congratulatory letter to someone in your life who has done something admirable lately. While helping, imagine what it's like to walk in that person's shoes. While writing, allow yourself to feel truly happy for that friend. Savor the joy of using generosity of spirit.

DAY 109

The temptress fear has many guises, and she weaves the illusion of pride, loss, abandonment, power, helplessness, and craving to lure us off the mount of self and higher purpose the way the Sirens did to the great Ulysses. We are to ride on and true if we are to rise above and new.

—Toots O'Donnell

Taking things personally is a form of selfishness disguised as pain. When you perceive someone else as acting out toward you or when you are rubbed the wrong way, it is a clue that you are holding on to something you shouldn't. Do people really act out *at* others, or are they navigating through the world as best they can? Are you reacting with intolerance toward someone else? Maybe the negative trait you see in that person is one you would rather pretend does not exist within yourself.

Fear would have you believe you are the center of the universe. Do all things happen to you, for you, or because of you? Can you concede for a lifetime, year, month, day, or moment that all people are equal spiritual visitors here to have physical experiences?

<u>Today's PI</u>
Develop awareness of your judgments as they arise. Keep a journal with you throughout the day, and when you find your mind wandering to judgment of someone else, write down the thoughts. At the close of the day, look over your list, and ask yourself if any of the topics are areas where you could enhance compassion for yourself. Do as Toots does: Allow fear her song, but ride on, and ride true. Allow fear to sing or shout, but stay steady on your trusted mount.

DAY 110

Humility is to make a right estimate of oneself.

—Charles H. Spurgeon

Humility is not a lack of healthy self-esteem. It's also not the opposite of pride. Humility is one of those mysterious virtues. Once you realize you have it, it's lost just as quickly. There is no award for the most humility.

Humility is actually a balance between acknowledging your strengths and simultaneously appreciating that everything you offer is part of a vast world that is greater than the sum of its parts. People's joys, hopes, fears, cravings, and other emotions are ultimately fleeting moments in the grand totality of it all. People are spirits here for physical experiences, all part of the same oneness.

<u>Today's PI</u>
"No less than space, no more than my place.
No less than space, no more than my place.
No less than space, no more than my place."

Twice today, sit in quiet meditation for five minutes and repeat this mantra. It reinforces that you have a right to take up space while allowing others to have theirs as well.

DAY 111

⚜

It is better to take many small steps in the right direction than to make a great leap forward only to stumble backward.

—Proverb

Happiness does not come from achieving goals as much as it comes from pursuing goals. A goal does not need to be as lofty as winning the Super Bowl. Any goal that challenges your strengths and is consistent with your values can result in happiness if you take time to savor the journey.

Today's PI

Look at your goals from day one again. Ask yourself if you are on the right road or if there are steps to make, sails to adjust, or even new goals to design. In any case, reevaluate the goals to make sure they are in line with your values and meaningful to you. Remember that success comes from repeatedly taking baby steps—not from making one enormous leap.

It is said that addicts want what they want when they want it—and they want you to pay for it. That trite cliché reflects how poor people can be at practicing delayed gratification. The same applies to goal achievement. Have you given up because you haven't crossed the finish line fast enough? Has the lack of quick success discouraged you? If so, don't fret. Keep going. Look at what you can do by breaking up the task into small, manageable tasks.

DAY 112

A true friend never gets in your way unless you happen to be going down.

—Arnold H. Glasow

People come and go in and out of your life over time. Having one or two close confidants is more valuable than having millions of "followers." Even when nine out of ten or ninety-nine out of a hundred let you down, the one who stands by you is worth more than the grand total of everyone else.

When everything else is gone, a friend can mean everything in the world. A true friend is worth more than gold. Friends are the ones standing beside you when you are falling down. They are there for you in the good times and when it's inconvenient, and they remind you of your goodness. Friendship has no survival value but gives value to survival.

<u>Today's PI</u>
Listen to the song "Stand by Me." Allow the lyrics and message space in your heart and mind. Reflect on who you have in your life that is a true friend, and on the ways in which that person has earned that friendship. Practice gratitude for the people who have stood by you in your life. Once you're in the gratitude space, write one friend a brief letter expressing what you feel.

DAY 113

You cannot do a kindness too soon, for you never know how soon it will be too late.

—Ralph Waldo Emerson

Kindness is a skill anyone can enrich, and it has an interesting implication. Immanuel Kant, considered by many to be the father of modern rational philosophy, argued that kindness is not only a good idea but a duty. If he is correct, kindness is both a moral imperative and a strategy to improve happiness.

Are you freely giving kindness? If not, is it because others do not deserve it from you? Are you perhaps unable to find it from within to give kindness to others or yourself? Are you protecting yourself against harm? No matter the reason, it is never too late to start practicing kindness (like many behaviors that enhance well-being). Once you start, you'll find that giving kindness is a gift that keeps giving back. Over time, the practice of kindness morphs into instincts of kindness. When that happens, you'll also discover your capacity for kindness has grown like a muscle.

Today's PI

Practice kindness today in a new, intentional way. Do something kind for someone else, and reflect on the feelings that arise during and after the experience. If you like the way it feels, feel free to repeat this activity as many times as you like.

DAY 114

Our fears are more numerous than our dangers,
and we suffer more in our imagination than in reality.

—Seneca

Nothing keeps you from living the best life possible more than what fear fabricates. Creating and then fretting over future events can actually stress your mind and body as much as—if not more than—actual life-threatening scenarios. Living as if future events are real is potentially detrimental enough to kill. Stress is stress to the body, and chronic exposure to the stuff can lead to heart disease, anxiety, and depression. It can even shorten longevity. Stress is stress to the mind, and in an attempt to mitigate the discomfort, people often resort to old measures like avoidance, numbing, and suppression. These are not useful approaches, and they increase the chances of relapse.

Fortunately, you can counteract the magnetic power of fear with mindfulness. When you do so, you get out of your own way. When you quiet the chatter in your mind, you become free to make choices, take responsibility, and ultimately flourish.

Today's PI

Dedicate twenty minutes twice to sitting in quiet meditation. Either follow a guided meditation or repeat a mantra during a quiet and uninterrupted practice of mindfulness. Focus on your breath while you repeat the mantra of your choice twice today. (Detailed instructions are located in the appendix.)

DAY 115

—⋇⋇⋇—

Earth and sky, woods and fields, lakes and rivers, the mountain and the sea are excellent schoolmasters, and teach some of us more than we can ever learn from books.

—John Lubbock

Nature is a source of learning as well as positivity and health. Your connection with nature does not have to be elaborate. If you simply get enough sunshine on your skin to boost absorption of vitamin D, you might experience fewer depressive symptoms. Sadly, most people spend most time indoors and commuting to and from indoor places—work, school, movie theaters, stores, and so forth.

In the modern world, people can spend several consecutive days (perhaps even weeks) engaging more often with computer screens than with other people, let alone the great outdoors. We are animals on a beautiful and abundant planet. We breathe in the products of the plants, and the earth, sun, and water sustain us. Even the most convincing virtual reality cannot compensate for all that is sacrificed through prolonged periods of disconnection from nature.

Today's PI

Locate at least five nature-connect points in your community, such as nearby parks, trails, gardens, and other natural spots where you can get away briefly. If you are able, visit at least one of them today. If you cannot, intend to spend at least thirty minutes enjoying the outdoors within the next five days.

DAY 116

❦

*The significance of a person is not in what he or she attain
but in what they long to attain.*

—Kahlil Gibran

Achieving goals is clearly linked to well-being. As it turns out, the purpose and meaning that fuel the pursuit of goals are even more significant than the success that follows from achieving goals. A person *is* what he or she repeatedly does. What drives a person reflects his or her core values, and if that person can prioritize and enjoy the journey itself, the destination becomes less vital to sustained happiness than setting and striving toward a goal.

Making money for the sake of making money is not as valuable as making money for the sake of providing for our families, developing self-respect through self-sufficiency, or helping others. Giving in order to receive is not as fulfilling as savoring the process of giving for the happiness it brings and the basic value of giving.

Today's PI
Take the time to reflect back on whatever journey you've chosen for yourself. Can you clearly identify your goals? Reflect on where you were when you started, what you have learned along the way, and what next steps you can make. Then spend fifteen minutes journaling your thoughts.

DAY 117

Hatred is the rabid dog that turns on its owner. Revenge is the raging fire that consumes the arsonist. Bitterness is the trap that snares the hunter.

—Max Lucado

There is no single reason why people should forgive, but this much is clear—harboring anger and resentment is physically, mentally, relationally, and spiritually unhealthy. Even justified anger can be every bit as self-destructive as addiction itself. Both can feel good yet be toxic. This is a good example of why you should use the past as a guidepost and not a hitching post. People who are unable to forgive themselves or others have more depression and are less kind toward other people.

Ask yourself if you are holding on to anger, a desire for revenge, or resentment. If you are, is it helpful? Is your life better as a result of allowing these anchors to the past to mire you down in unwanted emotions? If the answer is no, then remember that your life is your own creation. Where you apply your attention will make your experience. So attend to helpful thoughts. Let go of resentments. Forgiveness is really more about your relationship with yourself than about whom or what you are forgiving.

Today's PI

Decide to reclaim your power. Evict anyone who is living rent free in your head. Journal for fifteen minutes about what your life will look like when you have released the resentment beast. How will you feel and act when you are free?

DAY 118

———⦿⦿———

Courage is doing what you're afraid to do.
There can be no courage unless you're scared.

—Anonymous

The mind is a craving mind. Cravings are part of the human experience. Even monks crave. It's simply hardwired in the brain. Everyone craves safety, security, pleasure, money, power, love, and so forth. While these cravings can be overwhelming at times, they should not be feared. Instead they should be embraced and used to your advantage.

It might be easy to forget how often you have been brave. Every time you face and let pass a craving to use, act out, or engage in old behaviors such as hiding, stealing, lying, or cheating, you have grown stronger. Every time you successfully navigate a road bump, you emerge freer than you were before, having accessed your courage.

Today's PI
Journal about a few times when you have looked fear squarely in the face and stayed true to your integrity. Examples could include times when your resolve for recovery was tested, your morals were challenged, or your mood was a challenge. This practice will help remind you that you can act heroically and overcome obstacles. Share these experiences with a trusted confidant or on the website. You might find all people are heroes.

DAY 119

✦━━◦❦ ❦◦━━✦

The biggest human temptation is to settle for too little.

—Thomas Merton

At any age, the human body (including the brain) responds to its environment by adapting or changing itself. The only constant in the universe is change. However, people can become so accustomed to a habitual way of living that they arrest potential personal growth and development by failing to challenge themselves. Following routines is helpful because autopilot saves energy, but you can only take advantage of your body (including your brain) by challenging your strengths and welcoming opportunities to master new processes and information.

Impulse control is key in developing resilience and maintaining long-lasting recovery. Despite the self-deprecating humor often used among addicts, impulse control is a skill anyone can learn. That's right—even addicts can strengthen self-control. But doing so requires they get out of their routines from time to time. Leading behavior-control researcher Roy Baumeister found that practicing self-control activities for just a few weeks improves willpower. These can be small activities, such as using your nondominant hand when brushing your teeth or eating, or they can be meaningful, such as improving money management. Baumeister's studies show that overriding habitual ways of doing things by exerting deliberate control over actions improves self-control over time.

Today's PI
This might seem strange and difficult, but do it anyway. Do everything differently—brush your teeth with the other hand, hold your coffee or tea with the other hand, use less cream and sweetener, drive to work via a different route, eat different foods, call different people, and sleep on the other side of the bed.

DAY 120

⠶⠶⠶⠶

*I wanted to change the world. But I have found that the only thing one can
be sure of changing is oneself.*

—Aldous Huxley

Reflect back on the sum total of your behaviors over the past four months, and
see who or what has been fundamentally changed by your behaviors.

Next, think about missionaries or Peace Corps volunteers who work overseas
and give tirelessly to others. What is happening, above all else, is that missionaries and volunteers are acting like givers. No matter their intention, they are in
the process of making themselves useful to others. At the end of the day, they
are becoming the helping sort.

In contrast, think about those who sling criticisms from the "cheap seats"
(to borrow from Brené Brown). What are they in the process of becoming?
Ultimately, you become tomorrow what you do today. Ask yourself if you
believe your tomorrow self is going to live differently than your present self.

Today's PI
*Choose one thing about yourself you would like to improve, eliminate, or change. Then identify one
specific action you can take today to move toward that change. Write it down in the morning, and
act accordingly for the entire day. In the evening, reflect on how well your actions matched your
intentions and whether you experienced any surprises or gained new insight.*

DAY 121

⚜ ⚜

Don't dig your grave with your own knife and fork.

—English Proverb

The raw-food diet is a diet of uncooked food. It stems from the belief that uncooked food is healthiest for the mind and body. Cooking food at high temperatures can neutralize the effects of natural enzymes present in raw foods, and enzymes help the body digest and absorb nutrients.

The typical American diet consists of mainly processed foods or cooked natural foods. American bodies, therefore, have to work extra hard in order to digest and absorb the diminished nutrients still remaining in most food. As a result, people suffer from anxiety and depressive symptoms, accelerate the aging process, gain weight, have less energy, and develop digestive problems. A pure raw diet might be healthy, but it is probably entirely unfeasible for most people in today's culture. You do not, however, have to be all or none in this endeavor. Every little bit helps.

Today's PI

Eat a diet that is at least 50 percent raw. If possible, pick fruits and vegetables that are less than three days off the vine (picked within three days of consuming). Be mindful of any changes in energy or mood. Who knows? You might continue this trend indefinitely.

DAY 122

In daily life we must see that it is not happiness that makes us grateful, but gratefulness that makes us happy.

—Brother David Steindl-Rast

The natural instinct to survive has hardwired a negativity bias in people that causes them to focus on past failings and negatives in the present and threats in the future. If you allow the brain to assume its energy-saving autopilot mode, it's far too easy to fail to appreciate all the positive events in your life. That's why you must actively counteract negativity by choosing to direct time and attention to the good stuff.

Gratitude transforms negativity into positivity, expands awareness to new and different blessings in your life, and reinforces the recovery-enhancing attribute of humility. Humanities professor Javy W. Galindo put it best when he said, "Happiness is not the result of *what we bring* into our life, but the consequence of *how we choose to experience* our life."

Today's PI

Infuse your internal "meaning maker" with gratitude. You are the storyteller of your own life. You fabricate and respond or react to the meanings you perceive behind events. Utilize the positive associations gained from an attitude of gratitude to mindfully enhance your own life narrative. Write down five core things you are grateful for and write a short explanation of why each good thing happened. Dedicate five minutes tonight to reflecting on what went well for you today, and another five minutes to uncovering possible experiences you might have taken for granted.

DAY 123

As an alcoholic, you have no appreciation for your wife or your children's feelings, but I'm making up for that now. I'm winning my children's trust back.

—Maurice Gibb

Over the course of one' active addiction, many lose the ability to say with true conviction, "I am sorry." Those words, perhaps muttered often, are just words. With recovery, however, you are given the golden opportunity to put some meaning back in those words with your behavior. With adequate intentionality and mindfulness, your life symbolizes how you feel when you make a "living amends."

A living amends is a way of life—a decision to demonstrate (through actions) that you regret past indiscretions and have actually amended behavior as a result. There is no refuting the integrity of someone who gradually puts trust and faith back into his or her relationships through right actions.

Today's PI

Ask yourself, "Am I still making a living amends?" Even with years of recovery, are you mindful of a possible debt to those who supported you? Identify one or more actions you can take to increase your confidence in the fact that you are practicing "living amends." Commit to engaging in this action tomorrow.

DAY 124

All experience is an arch wherethrough gleams that untravelled world, whose margin fades for ever and for ever when I move.

—Alfred Lord Tennyson

Media and marketing send signals that you will be made whole, powerful, and more popular if you will only purchase certain wares. From money and assets to beauty and prestige, Americans live in a culture that persistently urges people to focus on getting more. When people make these extrinsic goals the priority, however, their well-being erodes, and unfriendly, competitive behavior increases. You can only enhance and solidify your positivity through experience, not material objects.

Experience is something that illuminates the horizon and makes the future clear. Experience's unforgiving hand (either gently or firmly) reveals how learning is applied. In that way, experience is the gateway to wisdom. When sought strategically, experience can enhance well-being.

Today's PI

Foster a life-enriching experience. Spend time planning a vacation or another way to spend money on an experience that involves you and other people. The benefits of this exercise start the minute you begin the planning process. Savor every step of the way. Do some research, write your vacation plan down, commit to it, and share your plans with others.

DAY 125

Before enlightenment—chopping wood, carrying water.
After enlightenment—chopping wood, carrying water.

—Proverb

Are you still looking for the one colossal experience that can make you profoundly happy forever? Many movies and novels perpetuate the myth that everlasting happiness is possible when the right partner is found or the definitive *aha* moment is realized. Fantasies such as that only happen in make-believe, however. Here in the real world, real people create the lives they truly desire through the sum total of repetitively doing the minor and mundane.

Happiness does not come through rare, momentous windfalls, but rather through small acts and conveniences that happen many thousands of times a day. Similarly, stable, long-term recovery happens one day at a time by doing the right thing and then the next right thing. Recovery empowers you to make mindful choices free from the exhausting bonds of compulsive living. You make thousands of small choices each day—what to wear, how to interact with other people, how late to sleep in, whether or not to make time for exercise, and more. Each day is precious if you can appreciate it for the simple joys, lessons, and experiences it brings. Make choices that bring you ever closer to being the person you want to be.

Today's PI

Bring mindful awareness to experiencing the path you are on in each moment. Be mindful of the little decisions you make throughout the day. Prior to each choice, take the time to ask yourself, "Is this choice in line with the type of person I want to be?"

DAY 126

⚜

Buddha was speaking in a village square one day, when one of the inhabitants started to abuse him. Buddha paused and said to the man, "If you offer me a piece of paper and I refuse to accept it, what happens to the paper?" "Why, it stays with me, of course," the villager replied. Buddha smiled gently. "And that is exactly what I am doing with your abuse," he said. "I am not accepting it; therefore, it stays with you."

—Buddha

Brain scans reveal evidence that humans are naturally more reactive to hostility than to kindness. A brain lights up with more activity when viewing angry faces than happy ones. This poses a natural challenge for those focused on fostering positivity. Buddha's ability to not react to abuse comes from the "ordinary magic" everyone can and should learn. Keep in mind that this does not mean you should allow evildoing in the world without a response. Instead it is a higher calling. Choose not to assume ownership of negativity placed in your life. Choose empathy for yourself and others. You can find the ordinary magic Buddha realized in his life when you come to appreciate this: nobody has power over your mind but you.

Today's PI

Ask yourself, "Do I want to be right or happy?" Whenever approached today in button-pushing fashion, pause and do not absorb any negativity. Allow bad drivers to pass on and disgruntled people to have and keep their turbulence. Don't get the last word, and practice doing whatever it takes to maintain your ordinary magic. Choose to practice being happy, and remember to use lots of empathy on yourself for being imperfect. (This is a tough PI.)

DAY 127

Character is like a tree and reputation like its shadow.
The shadow is what we think of it; the tree is the real thing.

—Abraham Lincoln

There is the idea you have of yourself, and then there is an image you portray to the world. People are often preoccupied with the shape and quality of their shadows and can lose themselves temporarily in trying to act in ways they think will get others to like them. Like the tree with its shadow, however, you don't have control over how others perceive you. In the short term, perhaps others see only a distorted shadow, but over the long term, your true character shines through.

Actions shape character and enhance overall well-being. The happiest people are those who embrace themselves for who they are and don't allow judgments about their shadows to distract them.

Today's PI

This might feel a bit intimidating, but if you are up to the challenge, ask three people whom you feel safe with to describe the person they perceive you to be. Be mindful of things they say that resonate as true and anything that seems surprising. Do these people see the character you see? At the close of the day, journal about your experience.

DAY 128

⊱⊰

Modern science is still unable to produce a better tranquilizer than a few kind words.

—Anonymous

When you think about past harms that still linger today, how many were physical and how many were verbal? Some people have experienced painful physical traumas, and these are not to be minimized or ignored. That said, virtually everyone can recall past verbally inflicted hurts.

Words are actions that can inflict more pain than a knife. Similarly, however, using healing speech in most day-to-day situations is more powerful than a scalpel or a pill. If a picture is worth a thousand words, kind words are worth a thousand good feelings. Kind words paint the world, feed others, and enhance personal well-being.

Today's PI

Use right speech. If you have a sharp tongue, hold it. If you have a clever but sarcastic wit, keep it in your head. Most importantly for today, say as many sincere kind words as you can. Say what you mean, and mean what you say.

DAY 129

The world when seen through a little child's eyes, greatly resembles paradise.

—Anonymous

The innocent goodness people are born with does not have to be diminished throughout adolescence and adulthood. Children play and learn without having to be taught to do either of these things. People all share the same nature, but at some point, many stop having unbridled and unstructured fun—that is, people learn the "cool," "proper," and "accepted" forms of fun. Many stop breaking into the spontaneous dances and songs that children often explode with, because they worry about how they will look or be perceived. They don't want to be rejected. A purely honest, fear-free exercise is to give yourself permission to be spontaneous and fun.

Today's PI

Give yourself permission to be spontaneous and fun by doing something you have never done before. Do this as long as the moment is appropriate. Give total strangers high fives, break into a dance in public, or sing your favorite song aloud. The point is not to attract attention or make a fool of yourself; no one has to be around when you get spontaneous and fun. This might be challenging, but do it anyway. Who knows? You might like it. Allow the experience to help you get in touch with honest mindfulness in the present moment.

DAY 130

Until I feared I would lose it, I never loved to read.
One does not love breathing.

—Harper Lee

When you have a toothache, you long to be free of that burden. Immediately after it's fixed, you are usually grateful to have no more toothache. Soon thereafter, though, you lose that gratitude and take the "no toothache" state of being for granted. This is a normal aspect of the human experience. It's known as hedonic adaptation—the process through which people grow accustomed to pleasures.

Some spiritual advisors in rehabilitation have addicts practice gratitude for simple, mundane, and even base activities. They encourage people to be grateful for the ability to wake, breathe, chew, urinate, and all the rest. At first it might seem absurd, but with time, the deeper implications of what Harper Lee meant will become clear.

Today's PI

Practice gratitude for all the physical acts you do today. As you wake, realize what a gift that is. With the ability to eat, drink, breathe, urinate, and all the rest, appreciate what blessings all these things are. As you do these things, imagine what your life would be like without each one of them.

DAY 131

———❦ ❦———

The best thing one can do when it's raining is...to let it rain.

—Anonymous

Many people struggle with acceptance and subsequently suffer. Suffering is only as intense as the depth and width of the chasm separating desire and reality. Since addiction uses denial as a self-perpetuating tool, nonacceptance becomes habitual. That denial is largely unintentional, but avoiding reality leads to nuclear-grade suffering. Many people have very little emotional sobriety (resilience) when they first get sober. Avoiding acceptance is often a rote behavior, but this largely unintentional practice further challenges already-stretched coping abilities.

Acceptance does not mean resigning yourself to fate, lying down, and letting it rain all over you. Acceptance is not a struggle or fight. It is simply knowing and living in reality and accepting that you have certain powers to change how you feel and what you do for the next step. When it rains, make a shelter. If you can't, seek refuge temporarily in someone else's.

Today's PI
Practice acceptance. Say the serenity prayer every hour: "Grant me the serenity to accept the things I cannot change, the courage to change the things I can, and the wisdom to know the difference." It might help to set an alarm on a watch or a cell phone to remind yourself of this practice.

DAY 132

❧⸺☙

Freedom is not worth having if it does not include the freedom to make mistakes.

—Mahatma Gandhi

Many people judge and shame themselves when they are not perfect. This is especially true for anyone with a predisposition toward perfectionism. Trying to be perfect is a fear-based attempt to prove to the world and yourself that you are enough. "Perfection" is a subjective ideal people mentally create. It does not exist in the real world. The best people will ever be is human. Addiction is a prison; recovery is freedom. Expect the freedom recovery brings to be full of mistakes. Hopefully you have few to no relapsing mistakes, but even then, you must avoid the shame trap. Addiction is a chronic, relapsing disease. The goal is 100 percent sobriety, but as with every chronic disease, 100 percent perfect remission is the exception rather than the rule.

Today's PI

Write down five mistakes you have made this year so far. Look at your part in these mistakes, examine patterns with the help of a trusted partner, and make a living amends by changing your behavior if you haven't already done so. Recovery bestows on you the additional gift of learning to make (and hold true to) meaningful amends. You are going to make mistakes again and again and again. That is part of the beauty and pain of being human. Living a program of recovery allows you to appreciate the intrapersonal and interpersonal joys of circling back with a spoken (and living) amends as a means of establishing true freedom from the weighted ties of perfectionism.

DAY 133

Either we're growing in goodness, becoming more creative and resilient, or we're solidifying our bad habits, becoming more stagnant and rigid.

—Barbara Fredrickson

Positive psychologists such as Fredrickson have discovered that, in terms of positivity and negativity, people expand and grow upward by what they actively think and do. Conversely, they wither and slip downward when they entertain pessimism and allow fear to rule.

In terms of recovery, every action you take either leads toward a life of positive recovery, resilience, and emotional sobriety, or it inches closer to relapse. The luxury some nonaddicts have of being cavalier with every little decision cannot be safely applied to the life of a recovering addict. Those two groups are not the same. Addicts have a disease that lies temporarily dormant. It patiently waits for the addict to slip up so it can pounce like a hungry beast.

<u>Today's PI</u>
Share with your group, people online, and/or your partner about how your life was narrow and negative before entering recovery. Share at least a dozen ways positivity and freedom have increased in your life since then.

DAY 134

—⟡ ⟡—

The cure for boredom is curiosity. There is no cure for curiosity.

—Ellen Parr

Love of learning is one of twenty-four universal human character strengths. Whether it's among your "signature" strengths or lower strengths, learning is important. Human beings' evolutionary advantage stems from the accumulation and sharing of information. However, information alone guarantees neither knowledge nor wisdom. While information is factual, knowledge is an appreciation of how to apply that information, while wisdom understands the relevance of context, values, and the whole; wisdom recognizes the role people play in the universe and the limits of knowledge. Even vast amounts of knowledge cannot predict the future.

Wisdom provides the most compelling guide to action, and it arrives in various packages. Others' faults that push your buttons teach you about yourself. Mistakes teach you how to improve. Learning from your enemies teaches you tolerance. Change is the only constant. Those who choose not to learn remain in the past and stagnate. Whether you learn new factoids or practice curiosity, learning something today will keep you open, alive, and moving forward.

Today's PI
Learn five new facts. You choose them—fun facts, random facts, industry or professional facts, facts you didn't already know about your friends, family lineage facts, and so forth. Practice love of learning, and see what space it opens up internally for you.

DAY 135

⟶───◦❦◦─❦◦───⟵

The family you come from isn't as important as the family you're going to have.

—Ring Lardner

Friends are the family you get to choose. You exist within multiple families or communities (the biological, the social, the fellowship of recovery, and more). Other people matter. The Ring Lardner quote today basically points out that friends cut sorrows in half and double joys. Strength, healing, and happiness largely come from relationships. What defined past relationships can be left in the past in exchange for focusing on a better today and more hopeful tomorrow.

Today's PI

Call at least three people from each of your "families." Say hello and make plans. If you are extremely busy, tell them you are just calling to say hello because of this dang workbook. If it feels right, turn them on to it. What is a better gift to yourself (and to others) than to expand your positive recovery support circle?

DAY 136

Your task is not to seek for love, but merely to seek and find all the barriers within yourself that you have built against it.

—Rumi

The path toward developing the best life includes repeatedly getting out of your own way. Your fear can be a mountain. It isolates you and hinders connections where you need them most. Some people behave badly, and you might subsequently be the victim of wrongdoing. However, being wronged only matters when you hold on to it. Loving yourself is not wholly possible while you wish pain on another.

You can enhance compassion, defeat fear, and dismiss resentment by praying for or wishing well the objects of your anger or scorn. Loving and forgiving yourself is necessary before you can love and forgive others. Consequently, forgiving others increases your ability to love yourself.

Today's PI
Pray for yourself and another whom you resent or are mad at. Do this every day for the next ninety days. Use the following prayer, or pray for the other to have all you wish for yourself:

May [_____] be filled with love and peace.
May [_____] be free from pain and suffering.
May [_____] receive happiness and fulfillment.

DAY 137

Although men are accused of not knowing their own weakness, yet perhaps few know their own strength. It is in men as in soils, where sometimes there is a vein of gold, which the owner knows not of.

—Jonathan Swift

Those who are fortunate enough to have "callings" that feed careers enjoy the privilege of using strengths daily. Many people have not realized their callings, however, and work in jobs that pay the bills but do not necessarily provide deeper fulfillment. If this describes you, don't fret.

With a little effort, you can redefine your work in alignment with your strengths and values. Leading researcher Amy Wrzesniewski coined this process "job crafting," and research reveals it can lead to more well-being, greater job satisfaction, and higher engagement.

Today's PI
Find new ways to use your strengths at work (if applicable) or at play. Look at your VIA results from day sixteen. Ask yourself, "Which three strengths can I use more often at work or play that can maximize what I do best?"

DAY 138

―――◦◦◦◦◦―――

Gratitude...goes beyond the "mine" and "thine" and claims the truth that all of life is a pure gift. In the past I always thought of gratitude as a spontaneous response to the awareness of gifts received, but now I realize that gratitude can also be lived as a discipline. The discipline of gratitude is the explicit effort to acknowledge that all I am and have is given to me as a gift of love, a gift to be celebrated with joy.

—Henri J. M. Nouwen

Nouwen is dead-on. Gratitude leads to love, joy, generosity, and kindness. These positive emotions rewire the brain and activate specific genes that mitigate stress effects. It is no surprise, then, that gratitude is an important part of most (if not all) spiritual practices. Gratitude also leads to wisdom. Positive emotions alleviate the distress caused by self-centeredness and broaden perspectives. Gratitude nurtures a larger and more unreserved view of the world. Gratitude connects. It even reminds you that you are part of something bigger than yourself that is shared with all sentient beings.

Today's PI

Write a small note of appreciation to each of the five people in your life whom you were reminded of when you read today's quote and passage. Then mail the notes, and talk about the experience on the forum.

DAY 139

—❈❈❈—

There is no passion to be found playing small—in settling for a life that is less than the one you are capable of living.

—Nelson Mandela

Nelson Mandela is easy to admire. He realized his potential (a feat in and of itself), but he also embodied passion. Passion's role in flourishing is crucial. It ignites curiosity and creativity and snuffs out fear. When you find your true passion, you will be luminous, and people will flock to see your glow. Passion also catalyzes the transformation you make as you more swiftly realize your potential. The importance of discovering the passion to do what you were made to do and using the courage to make that happen cannot be overstated.

Today's PI

Are there any areas of your life where you are settling? What are you accepting as "good enough" when you could reach up and make something better a reality? Are you stuck in a loveless relationship? Are you procrastinating on your physical health or mindfulness practice? Are you waiting for your boss to give you a raise? Are you stuck in a job that does not make use of your strengths? If any of these topics resonate with you, journal about it and then take some action. Brainstorm proactive steps you can take to get out of a given rut. As you explore, share with someone close to you to establish accountability for making positive changes where you are stagnant.

DAY 140

❀—❦ ❦—❀

Remain a witness to your emotions
as if from a great distance
an eagle's eye view
slowly this simple knack
of remaining a detached witness to your subtle emotions will grow stronger.

—Osho Rajneesh

Few things help people develop emotional sobriety quite as effectively as meditation. Masters such as Rajneesh have been informing people for thousands of years that meditation leads to equanimity. What a gift! To rise above the noise of the emotional center and respond to life, rather than react to it like a puppet on a string, is a noble pursuit. Conquering the negativity within your mind is the greatest way to personal power in existence.

Today's PI

Practice witnessing your thoughts and recognizing your emotions in a meditative practice. Find twenty minutes to sit and practice. With closed eyes, observe your thoughts as they come and go. Do not follow these thoughts or any stories your mind creates about them. To detach from your thoughts, view them as air bubbles rising and disappearing above the surface in a huge body of water. Practice doing this "thought-witnessing" practice with detachment. Don't judge yourself for having a racing mind or for where it races to.

DAY 141

If I have seen farther than others, it is because I was standing on the shoulders of giants.

—Isaac Newton

Recognizing that your parents, caregivers, mentors, and role models assisted you in your growth allows you to have a humble perspective and sheds light on a deep truth. Realize that you might see as far as you are able in part because they blazed some of the trail in front of you. Some people with children can appreciate this kernel from both perspectives—the student and teacher. The best teacher humbly recognizes that when the learner absorbs all that he or she could give, the student can see things even farther than the original mentor.

When all is said and done, you have been able to achieve because you have had mentors along the way. Within families, communities, and the species, you have achieved due to the combined efforts and sacrifices of the whole.

Today's PI

Reflect on the "giants" in your life whose shoulders you have stood upon to gain perspective and knowledge. Think about your achievements and the people (current or past) who have made them possible. Write a list of at least a dozen people who have helped you (in small ways or large) get to where you are today. Reflect with gratitude on the effect these people have had on your life.

DAY 142

I refuse to let other people and circumstances impose on my joy, because I know, as we all should, that I have a limited time to live.

—Bernie Siegel

Everyone experiences self-doubt. To use a personal example, I was deathly afraid of writing any book—much less one with sophomoric leanings. My inner dialogue sounded roughly like, "Who am I to make a daily guide?" The self-critic answered, "You're a meshugga poser. That's who you are! No one will like it, anyway, and it's only a matter of time before you're exposed as a fraud. So don't bother. Stay safe and out of sight. Say nothing, make no waves, and remain as invisible as possible."

Each journey has led you to this exact point, and your voice and actions are, if nothing else, at least authentically you. Everyone has to take the frightening hero's journey in order to fulfill their potential. Instead of allowing fear, shame, other people, and circumstances to dictate your mood and choices, decide to venture forth into the wilderness wholeheartedly.

Today's PI
Keep your journal handy throughout the day. Every time you feel your mood slip due to other people and events, write down the event, the fear, what you stand to lose, and how you feel. Then consider what your feelings would be if you knew you were going to die tomorrow. Bring the insight online or to an ally in your personal life.

DAY 143

—⊱♦⊰—

Those who think they have not time for bodily exercise will sooner or later have to find time for illness.

—Edward Stanley

In *Eat, Move, Sleep,* author Tom Rath points out that people don't have to prove exercise is good; research has already clearly established its benefits. While exercise can improve mood and extend life, however, Americans are more obese and use more pain medications than any other country.

Walking at least ten thousand steps a day has proven benefits, while walking less than two thousand might be costly to your health. More strenuous exercise is beneficial as well, but not always necessary. Do what you can after clearing it with your physician. Weight-resistance training increases bone mass and enhances metabolism. Swimming and biking are excellent activities if you have knee or back pain, because they lessen the load of your weight.

Today's PI

Buy and start using a pedometer. Wear it daily to record your average daily steps in the normal course of your daily routines. Set a goal, and find creative ways to increase your steps to over ten thousand each day.

DAY 144

When I first got sober, I completely lost my identity. I could no more keep up the illusion that I was what you wanted me to be than I could've been the Queen of England. From then on, I saved my energy and have been who I am. No more, no less, just me.

—Landry Rack

When people stop using and acting out, they often have no idea what to do or who they really are. The process of living a new life in recovery means you get to be authentic, but in order to do that, you must discover who you truly are. However, in the recovery journey, you are constantly changing and growing. The only constant is change, and if you are applying yourself, you will be fulfilling your potential more and more every day. What you were yesterday does not define you as much as what you are today.

Today's PI

Today is show-and-tell. If you are doing this work with a partner, next time you meet, bring a sacred object and share its significance with that person. If not, share about the item on the forum, with a sponsor, or with anyone else you can meaningfully confide in. Allow yourself to show a part of the authentic you by describing the importance of something deeply relevant to you. Ask your partner or group to do the same. Express what the object signifies and why you cherish it. Tell the story out loud.

DAY 145

—◦◦—

One generation plants the trees, and another gets the shade.

—Chinese Proverb

Resting in the shade is nice. If you enjoy ample shade, why should you bother planting more trees? It is said that people inherited the world from their parents and are borrowing it from their children. If you only soak up the shade from others' labors, you leave nothing for those who follow. Will you only take and let others worry about themselves? If so, you risk losing sight of what has been done for you. More importantly, you ignore your (twelfth step) responsibility to help others. People are responsible for one another. Anything you do or don't do will have an effect. It's like the ripples on a lake that come back to you as well as spread out to others.

Today's PI
Giving and giving back are mood boosters, but they also reinforce a sense of community—in and of itself a tool for flourishing. Today, get out there and do something to help others. Feed the hungry, clothe the needy, and find other ways to metaphorically plant trees that provide shade for someone else.

DAY 146

Today's PI

Today's reading and PI are one. This positive intervention is quite unique. Use the reading in three ways. First, read the following poem aloud three times. Next, write it down in your journal. Finally, use it as a gratitude lighthouse when you need a mood boost, wish to expand awareness, or want to counteract negativity bias.

Be Thankful

Be thankful that you don't already have everything you desire.
If you did, what would there be to look forward to?
Be thankful when you don't know something,
for it gives you the opportunity to learn.
Be thankful for the difficult times.
During those times you grow.
Be thankful for your limitations
because they give you opportunities for improvement.
Be thankful for each new challenge
because it will build your strength and character.
Be thankful for your mistakes.
They will teach you valuable lessons.
Be thankful when you're tired and weary
because it means you've made a difference.
It is easy to be thankful for the good things.
A life of rich fulfillment comes to those who are
also thankful for the setbacks.
Gratitude can turn a negative into a positive.
Find a way to be thankful for your troubles,
and they can become your blessings.

—*Anonymous*

DAY 147

Feelings like disappointment, embarrassment, irritation, resentment, anger, jealousy, and fear, instead of being bad news, are actually very clear moments that teach us where it is that we're holding back. They teach us to perk up and lean in when we feel we'd rather collapse and back away. They're like messengers that show us, with terrifying clarity, exactly where we're stuck. This very moment is the perfect teacher, and, lucky for us, it's with us wherever we are.

—Pema Chodron

Emotions and thoughts come from somewhere and nowhere. You cannot just stop fear from occasionally entering your mind any more than you can stop water from being wet. You can, however, learn from even your harshest thoughts and most painful emotions. Perhaps your instinct is to fight against negative emotions, push them away, escape from them with drugs and acting out, or deny they are even there. But reality cannot be fabricated. Persistent emotions are teachers.

Today's PI

Journal about ways you are holding back. Journal about uncomfortable feelings and any events or people you are avoiding. Once you have identified your "stuck points," use courage to write down ways you can face the fears and take some action to process and move past them.

DAY 148

If I ever have this thing figured out, shoot me!

—Eggar Eissen

There is never a point in time when you will have "recovery" for good and forever. Relapse rates level off after five years of sobriety, but they never hit zero. Addicts live with a chronic disease that mandates persistent effort in order to stay in remission. Many relapses start with a person's delusional thought that he or she is "cured." The process of relapse begins with a deterioration of the recovery lifestyle, especially when stress is applied to the system. When you think you have it made, when you get complacent, or when you stop directing your attention to pursuing the good life, you head backward.

The world moves quickly. You don't stagnate when you fail to add to your and others' growth and well-being; you reverse. How can you ever have it made? Who know what tomorrow will bring? Instead of knowing everything, get curious. Curiosity is a hallmark of many successful recovery programs. Maintain your ability to be a student throughout your lifetime, and stay open to suggestions from people you trust and respect.

<u>Today's PI</u>
This PI can be challenging for many people, but remember what Chris Peterson said: "Other people matter. Period." Reach out to at least three people in your life who know you are in recovery and whose opinions you value and trust. Ask them for their perspectives on how you can apply your top signature strengths to improve an aspect of your life or perhaps to reach a goal that might have stagnated recently.

DAY 149

⟞⟨⟩⟢

*A pessimist sees the difficulty in every opportunity;
an optimist sees the opportunity in every difficulty.*

—Winston Churchill

Each person has an "affective style" that describes his or her overall outlook on the world. In simple terms, are you a glass–half-full or glass–half-empty kind of person? While people generally inherit their affective styles and typically favor one perspective over the other, even low set pointers with pessimistic tendencies can develop habits that nurture high amounts of overall well-being. If you are a born pessimist, you are not forever doomed to see the half-empty portion. With intentional effort and practice, you can train yourself to appreciate life's fullness. Natural-born optimists might start ahead in the "attitude shapes experience" phenomenon, but they too occasionally need help enhancing their resilience. The usefulness of the following happiness pearl cannot be overemphasized: you choose your own reality. Thus, you chose how you experience life.

Today's PI

Reflect on one particularly challenging time in your life that has been resolved. Write about how you felt before it was resolved and how your life has improved as a result. Then journal about one challenge you are facing in this moment. Specifically, think about the opportunities this challenge presents and what you can learn from the experience. What unacknowledged benefits might result from the challenge? Map out a plan of action you can realistically apply yourself to. See if you can change your perspective from one of difficulty to one of opportunity. This can empower you with motivation, energy, and hope.

DAY 150

✦✦✦

One minute of patience, ten years of peace.

—Greek Proverb

Patience is no simple matter. It's tough. Rather than simply waiting passively, patience is active. It's a mindful acceptance of the fact that only time can do time's job. Yet delaying gratification is not an addict's signature strength. Addicts want what they want when they want it because they want it! Unfortunately, impatience often creates trouble. In failing to accept that you are not in charge of the universe, you lose out on the wisdom to know when you should flex the patience muscle by distracting yourself.

Today's PI

Make a list of ten healthy distractions you can fall back on when you need help practicing patience. Many find it helpful to first turn "it" (the fear, worry, anxiety, etc.) over to your higher power. Follow this with the serenity prayer. Together, these activities help to engage with humility and remind you of the benefits of living life on life's terms. In any case, make a list of ten things you enjoy that can help provide distraction until you gather your senses and can act mindfully. The only rule is to fill the list up with healthy distractions and not escape plans in disguise. Follow this rule, and before long you might develop the positive habit of not catastrophizing each challenge you face. Healthy distractions empower you to pause and allow the dust to settle so you can approach the situation with a calmer and more detached mind. Keep this list accessible, and circle back to it as needed.

DAY 151

⚜⚜⚜

There are shortcuts to happiness, and dancing is one of them.

—Vicki Baum

Dance—to some it is a pastime, a chore, an expression of the soul, or an art. To others, dance is a painful experience of vulnerability, and this becomes especially true when others are around. Public dancing is not the only way to practice this "shortcut" to happiness, though. You can also dance as if no one is watching when no one is watching. Dancing is good medicine: dancing releases endorphins, quiets the mind, and enables the expression of feelings. Quite simply, engaging with music helps fill your life with positive emotions. Research reveals that those who engage more frequently and wholeheartedly in dance, laughter, and song experience more happiness. Allow your body to be free. Dancing is optimistic body posturing.

<u>Today's PI</u>
Dance! Whether with loved ones, strangers, or alone in your kitchen, make time today to let your body move to music you love. There is no wrong way to do this. Let go of the preoccupation with how you look or what others might be thinking. Let yourself have fun with this!

DAY 152

Look at me. I am "shoulding" all over myself.

—Stuart Smalley

Do you "should" all over yourself too? Maybe your inner voice says things such as:

- I should be richer.
- I should be better.
- I should be in a more powerful position.
- I should be smarter.
- I should be smaller.
- I should be perfect.
- I should be more beautiful.
- I should be different.

Today's PI

Be just right. Be exactly what you are in this moment. Every time you hear a "should" today (for yourself or others), stop and pause long enough to allow a feeling of permission and acceptance to rise to the surface. Allow yourself and everyone else to be where they are today. Keep your journal handy so you can look at just how much or little you "should" on yourself and others too. Short directions do not signify a less important PI. You should do this one all day. (Pun intended.)

DAY 153

Even the Lone Ranger had a sidekick, and that made him unlonesome.

—Anonymous

The myth of the Lone Ranger capitalizes on the ideal of self-sufficiency, but even he had a companion named Tonto. The Lone Ranger and his sidekick, Tonto, lived by a code that reflected the value they placed on community and commitment to serving others. Some of their code included the following:

- All people are created equal, and everyone has within himself or herself the power to make this a better world.
- Be prepared physically, mentally, and morally to fight for the right cause.
- "This government of the people, by the people, and for the people" shall live always.
- People should live by the rule of what is best for the greatest number.

Today's PI
Reinforce or develop your deep, long-lasting friendships by performing acts of service together. Invite your friends to a "service party," and ask them to block off four hours either after work or on a weekend. Make arrangements to purchase sundries or food, and then deliver them together to a local shelter. Or, if your group enjoys the outdoors, arrange to work together to clean up a local park or trail. If you know an elderly or handicapped person, offer to spend time on his or her property doing yard work or house maintenance. You are never too young to benefit from service work, so consider inviting along any children!

DAY 154

I can think of no more stirring symbol of man's humanity to man than a fire engine.

—Kurt Vonnegut

It's not hard to find "bad stuff." Life can be difficult. Humanity is full of stirring symbols. In a way, firefighters and other prosocial, procommunity professionals (armed services, police, and so forth) are capable of loving humanity in a wholehearted, almost supernatural way. Think about it: What could motivate a human being to run into a burning building to rescue a complete stranger? These are not jobs everybody is willing to do for a few bucks.

Firefighters, police officers, armed servicepeople, and so forth are just people, but they risk their lives to save others. Everyone has a place and contribution, and most people contribute to others' well-being; we are all indispensable. One person is not better than another. The point is that some professionals don't talk about community; they live it. In their courage and willingness to make the ultimate sacrifice, they deserve gratitude in action.

Today's PI

Locate and visit your local fire, police, or other positive civil department. If you cannot afford to bring them gift cards, snacks, or flowers, bring them your gratitude in the form of you. Let them know in one way or another today that you recognize and truly appreciate their service and sacrifice. If you cannot access your local fire department, or if you feel called in another direction, show your appreciation for another civil servant.

DAY 155

—※—⊹※ ⊹※—※—

How far you go in life depends on you being tender with the young, compassionate with the aged, sympathetic with the striving, and tolerant of the weak and the strong. Because someday in life you will have been all of these.

—George Washington

George Washington led a successful revolution against the world's dominant empire and then became our fledgling country's first president. The wisdom of his words reveals that leading others or having ultimate authority, land, or other belt notches will not measure a life's worth. Individual success depends on tenderness, compassion, sympathy, and tolerance. Numerous surveys reveal that the single most important quality a person wants in a partner, friend, or even a boss is love. It's easy to take others for granted, but even easier to ignore personal character development.

Today's PI

Reflect on your recent behaviors and attitudes over the past week, and fill in the chart with examples of each character strength. Use this experience to draw awareness to areas where you are living up to your potential and areas where you would like to apply more effort and make improvements.

Tenderness	Harshness
Compassion	Judgment
Sympathy	Apathy
Tolerance	Intolerance

DAY 156

Physical strength can never permanently withstand the impact of spiritual force.

—Franklin D. Roosevelt

Making room for a higher power can make some people uncomfortable. Perhaps merely seeing the words "spirituality" and "higher power" made you want to skip today's exercise. A person with faith can also shut down when he or she thinks, "I'm good with God, thank you very much." The million-dollar question is this: Are you open to whatever comes? This openness in and of itself can be a form of spirituality, because it allows the space within to be part of something greater than the self. Many need this dimension in order to thrive. Addiction puts itself above all else in life and closes off light and openness. Addiction is a false idol that shrouds lives in darkness.

Today's PI

Practice openness. At ten minutes past every hour, take a moment to open your heart and mind to accept and be guided by whatever force larger than yourself you have accepted or could imagine accepting. Pray for (or meditate on) guidance in being an empty vessel open to direction, rather than being full of self in all actions today. At night, spend a few minutes journaling about your experiences today as compared to other days. Ask yourself if today's PI is a happiness-boosting strategy you can repeat more frequently?

DAY 157

Vision is the art of seeing the invisible.

—Jonathan Swift

We live in what many are now calling the age of distraction. Images and information travel at the speed of light and expose themselves to us via every imaginable avenue. Television, printed media, radio, Internet, smartphones, telephones, billboards, and the like are constant sources of diversion. Combine all this with the fact that Americans work more and take less vacation time than every other major wealthy nation in the world, and it's no wonder that many struggle with savoring life moment by moment.

Learning to quiet the noise in life can be the perfect remedy against the onslaught of sensations and data. Regular meditation enhances your ability to focus in the face of distractions, decreases stress and protects you against its physically damaging effects, and increases resilience. Best of all, it is widely available and convenient. Many PIs in this book involve meditative practice. Today, however, you will take a slightly different path to help bring awareness to and savor more richly a life with minimal distractions.

Today's PI

Limit the amount of "noise" and distraction in your life. Choose to abstain from TV, radio, Internet surfing, shopping, or thumbing through magazines. Lean into the challenge this will pose. Be curious about what comes up for you as you remove or limit these standard daily distractions. Use the quiet space to meditate and reflect on what it is like to be a "human being" rather than a "human doing."

DAY 158

For somehow this is tyranny's disease, to trust no friends.

—Aeschylus

The world is full of those who would deceive and take advantage of others, but the remedy is not to universally dismiss everyone as untrustworthy. Prudence is a character strength that involves caution but not avoidance. Prudence involves taking calculated risks. Trusting no one is a type of insidious "tyrannical disease" that leads to a painful imprisonment of isolation and doubt.

Even though positive relationships increase happiness, health, and chances of staying in recovery, trusting others can be very difficult. Perhaps you have good reasons to struggle with trust. Maybe friends or family have let you down, or perhaps you have let yourself down. You can only truly trust others when you are trustworthy. Trust is the most vital currency in the world.

<u>Today's PI</u>
Extend trust as a gift to others and the world. In social and business affairs, extend the unbridled intention of trust. This is not to suggest that you should hand the keys to your kingdom over to anyone. Instead, catch yourself when you entertain thoughts of paranoia or persecution. Change them around to gifts of trust. View those you interact with today with positive associations and assumptions. You might be surprised by what peace you can find through approaching the world in this way. It will bring you closer to others and closer to happiness.

DAY 159

We learn wisdom from failure much more than from success.
We often discover what will do, by finding out what will not do;
and probably he who never made a mistake never made a discovery.

—Samuel Smiles

Many people try to avoid mistakes and discomfort and the ensuing emotional turmoil by making sure they at least appear infallible. Perfectionism (the fear of never being good enough) is a commonly used but impotent countermeasure to these painful emotional tugs. Perfectionism is not benign. It robs its host of living a life full of learning, growth, and joy.

No one can be perfect. Fortunately, though, everyone is already good enough. Everyone is perfectly imperfect. Fear doesn't drive those who know this to be true, and those people know that sometimes "good enough" can be fabulous. A simple change in perspective can move you from self-punishment to self-discovery. Looking at challenges as opportunities instead of times to feel downtrodden can open doorways to self-efficacy, meaningful personal development, and happiness.

Today's PI

Embrace your imperfection. Throughout the day, remind yourself that mistakes are chances and not absolute reflections of character. Write small notes reminding yourself that you have permission to be "imperfect" and that "mistakes" are positive opportunities for growth. Use whatever language resonates with you on these notes. Place them where you will see them throughout the day—on a bathroom mirror, a desk, or a smartphone with frequent alarms set to remind you to glance at the note. Make room for yourself and others to learn, and see how much more peace you experience when you embrace life's imperfections.

DAY 160

You can make more friends in two months by becoming interested in other people than you can in two years by trying to get other people interested in you.

—Dale Carnegie

When you think about your favorite friends, which specific qualities do you admire most? Chances are you value that person's support, kindness, and how he or she makes you feel better about yourself. Yet being a true friend also requires authenticity. It's nearly impossible to feign affection forever.

However, there is one technique you can cultivate in order to become a better authentic friend—active constructive responding (ACR). ACR is a positive way of responding when someone else shares good news with you. It enables you and your friend to relive the moment and savor the joy.

Today's PI

Practice ACR. You can find examples and an explanation on PositiveRecovery.com. Look for opportunities to listen with focused attention, and then ask questions that intentionally engage the sharer of good news. When responding, use curiosity. Seek to learn more details and ask about the person's feelings. This supportive listening style is a powerful strengthener of social skills and bonds. Do this all day whenever possible. Avoid the temptation to talk more than necessary about yourself. At the day's end, journal about how today's exercise made you feel.

DAY 161

The trouble with the rat race is even if you win, you're still a rat.

—Lily Tomlin

We are "human beings," not "human doings," but most act as if they've never heard of the latter. That is why many *Positive Recovery* assignments include variants of today's theme—*stop racing*. In working more, vacationing less, pausing less, and trying to accumulate stuff ad infinitum, people lose touch with the magic of silence and stillness.

Strategic pauses and the use of blank space make music and art more powerful. Empty space is needed in order to accentuate what is present. Learn from this method. Rest and quiet refuel your tank and help you savor the space between the pauses.

<u>Today's PI</u>
Practice slowing down. Throughout the day, pause before making hasty decisions to fill your empty and silent space with doing. Allow yourself to sit in stillness long enough for the monkey mind to stop chattering. At first, even a few extra seconds might seem like an eternity. Don't worry. As challenging as stillness is at first, the rewards of practice are proportionally great.

DAY 162

As irrigators lead water where they want, as archers make their arrows straight, as carpenters carve wood, the wise shape their minds.

—Buddha

One cannot build the "good stuff" simply by removing the "bad stuff." Enhancing happiness is not the same as decreasing sadness. For example, "dry drunks" have managed to remove one of the key negative factors from their lives, but they have not found the inner serenity and wellness that typify flourishing in recovery. People find strength, durability, and happiness in recovery when they not only acknowledge character defects and past failures and wreckage, but also embrace and build strengths and successes.

For many, the task of identifying and becoming comfortable with owning strengths is a process. Throughout this book, you have been engaging in this process, and you might be experiencing growth. Continue to follow Buddha's advice, and get to know your own mind. This includes knowing your strengths. Today you will reflect and build upon the work you have already started.

Today's PI
Look back at your VIA results from day eighteen. Choose one of your "signature strengths" to focus on throughout the day. Look for any and all opportunities to use that character strength today. Journal about how you see that strength positively affecting your life and how it has grown since you started this work.

DAY 163

Be thankful for what you have; you'll end up having more. If you concentrate on what you don't have, you will never, ever have enough.

—Oprah Winfrey

Gratitude begins with appreciation of life itself. People too easily slip into subconscious patterns of fear and craving. They look for things to find fault with and criticize themselves into Shamesville. Some people gossip and judge others in order to feel better about themselves. Some convince themselves they can achieve meaningful happiness with material possessions or temporary successes. All of these reasons and more render gratitude elusive for many.

Gratitude is a doorway to true, lasting happiness. As such, focus intention on it every day. Practice it in a formal way in order to maximize its effectiveness. Remember that discovering what is possible is to be found in the doing and not in the wishing.

Today's PI

Help realize your potential by practicing gratitude through searching for the good stuff. Make a list of twenty-five blessings in your life. Look in some less obvious corners, such as appreciation for lungs that breathe or eyes that see. Post your list where you can reference it daily.

DAY 164

Good humor is a tonic for mind and body. It is the best antidote for anxiety and depression. It is a business asset. It attracts and keeps friends. It lightens human burdens. It is the direct route to serenity and contentment.

—Greenville Kleisser

Life is short, but it can seem awfully long without a sense of humor. A humorless human is like a car without shocks. Every bump, turn, and imperfection on the road will jolt both mercilessly. Fostering your ability to laugh at yourself is like installing a super shock-absorbing defense system.

Humor can help you cope because it softens the sharp edges of what can sometimes be a very harsh reality. Laughter is medicine. It releases feel-good, pain-relieving neurotransmitters in the brain and literally helps to alleviate pain.

Today's PI

Laugh. Set aside one minute every hour of today for laughing. This can be done alone or with others. If life has not provided material to naturally incur laughter, laugh independently in front of a mirror, watch a few minutes of a show you find particularly funny, or read text you know you find humorous. Make sure not a single hour passes by today that you do not engage in laughter and allow yourself to embrace the spark of joyful medicine this brings.

DAY 165

Aging and death are treated very differently in different cultures throughout the world. Some view the aged with deep respect and reverence. Others turn away from the elderly without regard for the valuable lessons they could teach. All humans are in the same ultimate dilemma, though. No one gets out alive.

—Anonymous

Rather than dying with addiction, choose to live with it in recovery. Look for similarities rather than focusing on differences. Ask for help when you need it, and acknowledge that you do not have all the answers. If you do not seek out the wisdom of elders, you leave yourself vulnerable to repeating the mistakes they made as young, shortsighted, and self-centered individuals. At the least, you miss the opportunity to be enriched by what those who have gone before you have to share.

Asking for help can teach you humility, and it can also give your life richness and meaning. Many come to recovery lost, but through opening themselves up to the teachings and support of others, they are found.

Today's PI

Find an elder in your life. Visit or call that person merely to listen. Ask that person how he or she feels and how his or her day is. Encourage the conversation to evolve through active constructive responding. If you know of no one to call, visit a local retirement home, and do the same exercise.

DAY 166

What is more inconvenient: one hour of exercise or a lifetime of no life?

—Anonymous

Exercise is a great tool for stress reduction, mood improvement, cardiovascular fitness, weight management, and personal development. Exercise requires both physical and mental strength. After all, it is human nature to want to rest or quit when something gets hard. The benefits of exercise (longevity, physical fitness, emotional stability, and mental clarity) have been well researched and validated.

Exercise, however, is not an effective stand-alone tool for weight loss. Exercising more in compensation for eating more will not work. In fact, this strategy might actually increase weight and decrease life span. Don't make "table muscles"— the muscles needed to lift food to your mouth—the only ones you develop. Jump up and down—not to conclusions. Run with your legs—not away from problems. Step to the beat instead of sidestepping responsibility. Do push-ups; don't push your friends away.

Today's PI

Get moving! Challenge yourself by trying to exercise with someone else today. Companionship increases the likelihood that the activity will become regular and provides the added bonus of strengthening relationships.

DAY 167

People are often unreasonable, irrational, and self-centered;
Forgive them anyway.
If you are kind, people may accuse you of selfish, ulterior motives;
Be kind anyway.
If you are successful, you will win some false friends and some true enemies;
Succeed anyway.
If you are honest and frank, people may cheat you;
Be honest and frank anyway.
What you spend years building, someone could destroy overnight;
Build anyway.
If you find serenity and happiness, some may be jealous;
Be happy anyway.
The good you do today, people will often forget tomorrow;
Do good anyway.
Give the best you have, and it will never be enough;
Give your best anyway.
In the final analysis, it is between you and your God;
It was never between you and them anyway.

—Kent Keith

Today's PI

Repeat this poem (sometimes attributed to Mother Teresa) three times today: upon rising, after lunch, and with at least one other person at dinner or bedtime. Do you want to be right or happy? Choose happiness, and let "right" be in your right action, right heart, right speech, and rights for all.

DAY 168

━━━╼◦ ◦╾━━━

Each of us should frame life so that at some future hour fact and our dreaming meet.

—Victor Hugo

When you dream about your future, your mind and heart open. This type of hopeful prospecting improves overall well-being, and it cultivates those emotions and strategies that actually help you achieve your goals. Athletes are taught to "visualize the win" because the same areas of the brain activate during visualization and participation. Hopeful prospecting can guide you onward, facilitate valuable insight about your motivations, and enable you to prioritize your goals and passions. Dreaming and doing are certainly different, but start with the dream, and then make it happen.

Today's PI

Use a "vision board." This is a creative project that enables you to focus on your hopes and dreams by crafting a representation of a desired future. Before you begin, spend a few moments centering yourself and meditating on what you would like your life to look like in five to ten years. Let yourself feel the emotions from this positive future projection of yourself.

Create your vision board using any artistic medium—pens, pencils, charcoal, paint, magazine cutouts, words, images, or photos. There is no wrong way to do this assignment. Your vision board can be made on something as small as a single sheet of paper or as large as a poster board. When you feel complete, set your vision board somewhere you can easily see it. Allow it to inspire you in the weeks and months to come, and share it on PositiveRecovery.com.

DAY 169

─❧ ❧─

If there was a simple formula for success and it was easy to follow, everyone would be doing it.

—Edward C. Johnson III

The same is true for addiction. If recovery were easy, everyone would be free from the hell of the disease. Undoubtedly, certain behaviors help prevent relapse and increase chances for success. However, life is full of twists and turns. Relapse prevention is a personal, lifelong process that is much more complex than plugging someone or something into an assembly line.

Before inventing the light bulb, which is now a staple in homes and businesses around the world, Thomas Edison suffered through many "failures." The effort toward this discovery seemed futile, and no one would have faulted him for throwing away the pursuit altogether. Yet through striving and grit, Edison learned what he needed to know to bring the invention to life.

"Failure" can be the best teacher. When you persevere, you discover that your current path should be altered. Persevering does not mean sticking to the original path. Steadfastness is valuable in some pursuits but can break you apart in others. Adapting to and then accepting obstacles is the key in life to emotional sobriety, recovery, happiness, and success. However, the ego inhibits new perspectives and keeps you from appreciating that your current view is limited. Worse still, the ego keeps you from asking for help.

Today's PI
Do you reframe failures as opportunities, or do you see failures as dead ends? Can you adapt and reevaluate your treasured goals? Can you do this with help from others? If not, why?

DAY 170

—⊰⊱—

The thing about love handles is...the more you have the less you get.

—Anonymous

I was on a diet, but there wasn't enough to eat, so I went on three diets.

—Anonymous

Whenever I feel like exercising, I lie down until the urge passes.

—Anonymous

Exercise is easy fodder for parody. Humans once had to physically work at strenuous jobs in order to survive. Now you can earn a living by hardly moving at all. Since this is far from a healthy form of existence, and because many consume copious amounts of readily available food, people must get moving in some form or fashion. Otherwise people's bodies and minds will suffer unnecessary agony.

Make exercise inspiring! A piece of exercise equipment in the corner, without much flair, is about as inspirational as a melted snowman. Splurge by purchasing exercise clothing you actually want to don. Also get a great pair of shoes that beg to be worn. These are not frivolous purchases or attempts to buy happiness. They are investments in your life, spirituality, health, happiness, brain fitness, and self-love.

Today's PI

Purchase or make a commitment to purchase at least one inspiring piece of exercise gear. An optional second assignment is to do yoga or walking meditation for forty-five minutes, or find another meditative exercise to do. In any case, move your body!

DAY 171

The seventy-five years and twenty million dollars expended on the Grant Study points to a straightforward five-word conclusion: Happiness is love. Full stop.

—George Vaillant

Love recognizes no barriers. It jumps hurdles, leaps fences, and penetrates walls to arrive at its destination full of hope.

—Maya Angelou

The antidote to fear, love, can truly conquer all. Love is freedom from the bondage of fear and self. Service is an act of love. Acceptance is an act of love. Kindness is an act of love. Integrity, honor, courage, faith, friendship, respect, character, and beauty are all actions or features of love. Where there is love, there is pure goodness and the best of humanity.

Love removes your masks and allows others to bond with you rather than your fears. Anyone can pretend. Only the fearless stand boldly as themselves. You should not look for love but instead look within. Your own barriers to loving yourself and others prevent love's flow and power from working.

Today's PI

Love as if your life depended on it. What does it mean to love? Accept, be kind, hope, give, honor, respect, look for beauty, and be brave. Intentionally practice love, and be cognizant of when you are choosing to act in love today. At the close of the day, reflect on how you felt throughout the experience, and share your reflections on the website if desired.

DAY 172

The hardest arithmetic to master is that which enables us to count our blessings.

—Eric Hoffer

Time is a relative concept. In recovery programs you are taught to live one day at a time but to pause at significant milestones to celebrate continuous days sober. Some people in recovery wield their times like boastful trophies. Others ignore the convention and stop keeping score. Losing appreciation for time in recovery, however, increases the chances you might relapse. It takes work to maintain gratitude for time in recovery, free from the chains of active addiction.

Today's PI

Count your time in recovery. Cherish and share it. There are several computer programs and apps that count your time for you. Use these, or make it an annual event to throw a (big or small) celebration for yourself and those who helped make your journey possible and meaningful. Share your experience on the website. Other people might discover your ceremony enriches their own senses of recovery gratitude!

DAY 173

—⊸⊱ ⊰⊱—

I long to accomplish a great and noble task; but my chief duty is to accomplish small tasks as if they were great and noble.

—Helen Keller

Helen Keller became one of the world's most famous people and stands today as a household name in many countries throughout the world. Like other giants who have contributed in so many ways, she reminds people of how to live. Not only do people need to do all the little things as if they were great and noble deeds, but they must see doing so as their duty. Great athletes who win many competitions can all agree that they play like they practice. When given the opportunity to excel, great and noble deeds are possible because several thousand hours were spent in preparation.

You can't practice recovery alone. You need others to maintain good, long-lasting recovery. This disease cannot be managed alone, but at times the telephone seems as if it weighs a ton; in especially challenging situations, it can seem as if it weighs five tons. If you fail to practice recovery within mutually supportive relationships, you can't expect others will be there for you when you need them most.

Today's PI
Reach out to six people who are in your recovery support circle. E-mail, call, text, or tweet them, or post something on their social media sites. Use a carrier pigeon. It doesn't matter. Just practice staying connected to keep that habit strong for times when you'll be glad it's there.

DAY 174

Simplicity is the nature of great souls.

—Swami Ramdas

Living simply is an acceptance that you are already enough. Letting go is a way to rest the mind and soul. A reflection of greatness is letting go of the complications in life (many of which are self-created).

It is said that you can never be too dumb for recovery, but you can be too smart. "Keep it simple, stupid"—this saying speaks to the busy mind's knack for complicating things.

Today's PI
Simplify your life. Look at this exercise as spring cleaning. Clear out nonessential items in your home. In this cleansing process, separate any items suitable for donation, recycling, and trash. Make it a group effort to donate items together. Use this activity as a metaphor for getting rid of the junk in the mind. Think of situations, resentments, or challenges you are holding on to, and "turn them over" like you turned over and threw away your stuff. Remember to keep it simple. Turning it over is an act of both simplicity and greatness.

DAY 175

Humility is not thinking less of yourself but thinking of yourself less.

—C. S. Lewis

Egocentrism is not limited to grandiose thoughts. It is easy to confuse humiliation with humility. Thinking less of oneself in an exaggerated, self-critical fashion is a close parallel to thinking more of oneself in an exaggerated, arrogant fashion. Both are forms of self-centeredness. Each of these self-absorbed thought habits sets you apart from those around you and prevents you from authentically connecting with others. Both create a false sense of self-importance that limits your capacity to thrive.

Today's PI
"No more than my place, no less than my space."

Repeat this mantra for five minutes three times today as you sit quietly and focus on your breath. This means you take no more than your lot and allow others theirs. You also don't forfeit your lot to others in the name of "martyrdom" or meekness. You deserve a lot, but not too much. This practice will allow you to see others as having equal status, and this opens the door to connection. Share on the website or with a trusted person how you might have felt or acted differently today by engaging in this practice.

DAY 176

Affirmations program the mind in the same way commands and scripts program a computer.

—Remez Sasson

Who and what you are begin with your thoughts and intentions. Self-doubt and fear are part of the human experience. Although these will never completely disappear, you can counteract them with positive thoughts and affirmations.

Even though most of these positive recovery intervention strategies consist of one activity per day, this exercise lasts for a bit. Stick with today's assignment. It can help you realize your potential.

Today's PI

Make a list of five things you want in life. Then write positive affirmations about each one, and post them on your bathroom mirror so you can say them every day for the next ninety days. For example, if you want to be healthy, write, "I exercise and eat healthy foods." If you want to be more trusting, write, "I am trustworthy and trust others." If you want to be more optimistic, write, "Everything is going to work out for the best." Make the affirmations in the present tense. This will help you embody them as you move forward. Set an intention to say your five positive affirmations every morning for the next three months.

DAY 177

Treat others as you would be treated.

—Anonymous

Today's quote is essentially the heart of interpersonal spiritual and religious instruction across the ages and throughout different cultures. Sometimes referred to as the Golden Rule, it is very often incredibly difficult to put in practice—especially when emotions block the way. Furthermore, many could benefit from twisting the Golden Rule back on themselves and learning to treat themselves quite a bit better.

Sadly, many fall into treating those who love them worse than complete strangers. People are often on their best behavior at work or social gatherings but are less sweet, kind, loving, and respectful to their partners, roommates, children, parents, and siblings.

Today's PI

If you must let loose, do so everywhere, but with those closest to you. This includes you, your family, and your close friends. Practice being "on" with that group in ways you would normally reserve for work, strangers, or acquaintances. Treat yourself and the ones who love you as you would truly like to be treated.

DAY 178

We are what we eat.

—Anonymous

It is not a secret that medical doctors do not receive a lot of training in nutrition. Doctors are taught about major deficiencies, but those who want to learn about how to use food for optimal health have to seek that education independently. This lack of prioritization of nutrition seems incongruent. Doctors are exposed to the latest cutting-edge treatments and taught about the incredibly detailed mechanisms of the human body and all its processes. Some even receive further training in very specialized, esoteric fields. However, experience is the best teacher. Most doctors learn how true "you are what you eat" is. That saying is so valid as to be considered a natural law.

Today's PI

Do five minutes of journaling. First, close your eyes and take a few breaths. Imagine you have to leave your body for thirty days. The catch is that you must leave your body to someone you know who can be trusted to take care of it for the thirty days. Journal about why you have chosen that person, what traits that person has that are worthy of your temple (body), why you trust that person, and how that person will treat your body. Imagine next that you are the one entrusted to safeguard your body for the next thirty days. What will you do differently?

DAY 179

How many desolate creatures on the earth have learnt the simple dues of fellowship and social comfort, in a hospital?

—Elizabeth Barrett Browning

Don't wait until your last breath to appreciate the power of fellowshipping. One of the ways fellowships work in recovery is through mutual support. Another way is through forming deep connections with other people. A third way is through the open, honest expression of experiences, hopes, fears, challenges, and strengths. Fellowships of all kinds provide these benefits to their members. Addicts do not have a monopoly on groups or benefits, but they are lucky to have so many places to go to develop strong bonds.

Whether it's a higher power that speaks through other people, a mysterious energy present in the rooms of fellowships, or a "higher power with skin on" (the people in the rooms) infusing you with a sense of peace, you can't get the benefit of fellowships without participating.

<u>Today's PI</u>
Find a recovery-related meeting to attend. Arrive thirty minutes early, and help set up chairs, make coffee, clean, and help newcomers. Stay thirty minutes after the meeting. Allow yourself to connect with those who have been through similar things, and appreciate the strength found in fellowship.

DAY 180

Given the amount of unjust suffering and unhappiness in the world,
I am deeply grateful for, sometimes even perplexed by,
how much misery I have been spared.

—Dennis Prager

Imagine you are waiting in line at a crowded grocery store one day. Suddenly, masked and armed robbers enter. "This is a stickup!" they shout. "Everyone down!" Then you hear a shot and feel warmness running down your arm. Intense pain follows as you realize you are the one shot.

What is your immediate reaction? Are you mad? Do you feel unjustly targeted? Do you wish someone else had been hit instead? Are you resentful at the inconvenience of it all?

Are you instead grateful that someone else wasn't hurt, such as the children present in the grocery store that day? Are you feeling lucky it was only your arm instead of your heart or your brain?

Today's PI
Meditate on the scenario, but feel the second group of grateful emotions. Do it three times today for just a few minutes each time. Practice going there in your mind. Go to a place of gratitude for being shot only in your arm, and for others being spared. Try to use this attitude all day, and then share your experience online.

Jason ZW Powers, MD, MAPP | 183

DAY 181

Nothing will ever be attempted, if all possible objections must be first overcome.

—Samuel Johnson

Daring ideas are like chessmen moved forward; they may be beaten, but they may start a winning game.

—Johann Wolfgang von Goethe

Today's PI

Today's PI is yours. Make up your own intentional strategy for boosting overall well-being. Trust your instincts. You have it in you to come up with something inspiring and moving. Even if you don't perceive creativity to be a strong character strength, you will be surprised by how your perspective can indeed help countless others.

If you are so moved, share your intervention online. Who knows? It might go viral or make it into a later edition of this guidebook. In any case, people learn from one another. There will surely be those in this community who will benefit from your experience and perspective.

DAY 182

⚜

The making of friends, who are real friends, is the best token we have of a man's success in life.

—Edward Everett Hale

When you are down, does your car offer solace? How about fear and a killer sound system? Does one cancel out the other? Will working extra hours or a recent award alleviate your poor health?

When you have great news, can your 150-inch plasma-screen monitor join in your joy? When you get that impossible task done, get a raise, or otherwise succeed in fulfilling your dreams, is the shag carpet able to lift your mood even more?

Friendships and other deep, long-lasting relationships are one of the secrets to health, happiness, recovery, and overall flourishing. You cannot nurture your friendships too much. It is impossible to give your friends too much friendship. You can stalk them or suck them dry with codependence, but that is not giving friendship. Friendship is reciprocal, balanced, and patient. Friendship is loving, genuine, and empathetic. Friendship is built on many things, such as joy and laughter.

Today's PI
Make plans with one or more friends to do something that involves laughter. See a comedy together, reminisce about good times, or otherwise find a laughing medium you can all share.

DAY 183

When the power of love overcomes the love of power,
the world will know peace.

—Jimi Hendrix

Power is a false doorway to happiness. Fear makes you mistakenly believe that if you can amass enough power, you can overcome the precariousness of existence. Fear tries to make you use power as a way to acquire inner peace. Accumulating power is not the road to peace—inner or outer. If power equaled immunity, then the laws of physics and biology would not apply to influential individuals. Even the president puts his or her pants on one leg at a time, eats, breathes, maintains physical and mental health, and engages in other nourishing, predictable, and reproducible behaviors.

Power does not insulate one from harm. Power also does not fill the happiness tank for any sustained amount of time. A new position, more money, and novel spheres of influence might boost levels of happiness at first, but they do nothing for long-term happiness or peace. When your love of power becomes separated from responsibility, you can become convinced that the means justify the ends, and subsequently end up with anything but peace.

Today's PI

Use your "power" to forward love and goodness in the world. Pick a charitable cause that resonates with you, and give a bit of your time, treasure, or talents.

DAY 184

If you want to build a ship, don't drum up people to collect wood and don't assign them tasks and work, but rather teach them to long for the endless immensity of the sea.

—Antoine de Saint-Exupéry

What are you passionate about? People can feign many things, but passion is something that has a built-in lie detector. People naturally love to see passion in others. It's inspiring and reminds people of their own passions. In terms of leading others, your passion is the best tool at your disposal. It's the music of the soul. If nothing else, let it lead you to brighter shores, happier moods, more prosperous living, stronger recovery, and more fulfilling relationships.

Today's PI

Either find your passion or rekindle it. Start journaling. Make a list of fifty things to pursue in life. Allow them to flow without concern for formatting them in an outline, list, or any other form. They don't have to be connected in any way. Just write them down. Then look for some recurring themes among them, and write those down. Keep repeating this until you have a handful of ideas and things to try. Ask for help from other passionate people who know you well. Then get moving on one or more of them. This might lead to visiting a museum, buying a karaoke machine, or starting a new project or career. Who knows? Share the fruits of this labor on the website.

DAY 185

*No pleasure is a bad thing in itself,
but the things which produce certain pleasures entail disturbances many
times greater than the pleasures themselves.*

—Epicurus

Positive psychology reveals that happiness, which can include pleasure and other positive emotions, isn't defined by experiencing positive emotions. Instead, happiness includes the entire range of human emotions, including sorrow, fear, pain, and anger. Hedonic pleasure is one of the false doorways to happiness. Attempting to live life without negative emotions while the pleasure bell is rung repeatedly is a hallmark of the addicted individual. Addicts learn that this futile exercise does indeed cause disturbances many times greater than the pleasures themselves.

Today's PI

Think of your addiction and how much pleasure was gained toward the end. Perhaps you were living mainly to avoid pain. Reflect on the wreckage of the past. Look for ways you might be seeking happiness by excessively opening the pleasure door in your life today. Are you acting out with food, sex, or shopping? Journal for a few minutes, and share any insight with someone you trust.

DAY 186

Security is mostly a superstition. It does not exist in nature,
nor do the children of men as a whole experience it.
Avoiding danger is no safer in the long run than outright exposure.
Life is either a daring adventure, or nothing.

—Helen Keller

Addicts do not do well with change. Change requires living in the gray zone of life where people let go of outcomes. Change is the only constant, yet all humans yearn for safety. A person might think, "If I could only control everything, the power to avoid pain would be mine." However, trying to control people, places, and things is like steering a toy wheel attached to a log floating down a river.

Many have wrestled with this dilemma, and some have gone so far as to conclude that since people have no control beyond themselves, life is too scary. Some construct lives dominated by ritual, repetition, and resistance. Others choose fear and joy and embrace life as an exciting adventure. These people agree with Keller. To dare is to live. To hide is to die.

Today's PI

Reflect on your current life and seek any areas where you have been hiding from pain. Have you been trying to control a relationship or an outcome? Have you been masking yourself with perfectionism? Identify one area and dare yourself to embrace the vulnerability and uncertainty of life. Stop hiding. Set a boundary with a friend, family member, or coworker whom you have been too afraid to confront. Spend a day not wearing makeup or not talking about any of your accomplishments or connections. Choose not to watch the television show that helps you numb the stress of your day. At the end of the day, journal about your experience.

DAY 187

⊱━⊰⊱⊰

The secret of life...is to fall seven times and to get up eight times.

—Paulo Coelho

Everyone has the unbridled ability to tap into the same resilient human spirit. The question is to what degree you have accessed your grit. Deep within each person lies the ability to overcome insurmountable odds. Tenacity mixed with patience and courage is within your grasp—no matter your lineage, education, environment, or other differentiators.

Falling down is not a failure or loss when you learn something from it. In fact, success is often made possible through rebounding from failure. One surefire way to beat a defeat is to practice patience. Like the recovery journey, you must make peace with starting over. When you get up from falling from your disease, you are woken up, reborn, and restarted.

Today's PI

Use your experience, strength, and hope to help someone who has fallen. Do not limit yourself to helping only addicts. Expand your view, and look for any human who could use a hand to see that the power to get up lies within. You might choose to engage in twelfth-step work—call a friend who you know is struggling, volunteer some time with those less fortunate, or engage in anything that focuses on fostering the resilience in others you have found in yourself through recovery.

DAY 188

Be not afraid of growing slowly; be afraid only of standing still.

—Chinese Proverb

Newly recovering addicts often need to slow down their expectations. They cannot experience the fruits of recovery without planting the seeds, tending the soil, and allowing time and nature to work their magic.

Seasoned recovering addicts also need to be reminded that there is no destination or finish line. Learning to live in recovery is an exercise in being in the here and the now. No one can live more than the present moment at a time.

Today's PI

Be grateful for the journey you are now on. Don't fret about your progress. No matter the distance, if you are facing the right direction, you have much to be grateful for. Set an alarm to go off five times today. Each time it sounds or vibrates, allow yourself one full minute to reflect on being grateful that, if nothing else, you are not living in active addiction today.

DAY 189

We only become what we are by the radical and deep-seated refusal of that which others have made of us.

—Jean-Paul Sartre

Addiction is still poorly understood. It's a biopsychosocialspiritual disease. The illness affects bodies, emotions, spirituality, and relationships. Addiction leads people to engage in unsavory behaviors, and it's easy for others to judge addicts as "rejects" with low moral character. These judgments are typically held by those who have not yet sought out knowledge of the true nature of the disease. Perhaps this is due to resentment, apathy, or simple ignorance. (They don't know what they don't know!)

Ignorant judgments, though painful, are not true. Addicts don't need to accept external or internal shaming stories. After all, who has the right to write your story? Does someone else get to tell you who you are, what you stand for, and how you choose your perspective? Do you have to listen to a negative story, even if it comes from within your own head? The answer to both these questions is a loud, resounding no!

Today's PI

Write your story in less than three paragraphs. Who are you, and what are your core values? What have you overcome, and how has your past created the person you are today? Include how the past was required to produce this version of yourself today, armed with what little experience you had when you were in your disease. Include where you are headed in this moment.

DAY 190

❦

We need old friends to help us grow old and we need new friends to help us stay young.

—Letty Cottin Pogrebin

Friends are precious. They can be hard to find, but they give people's lives Meaning (with a capital *M*). One or two good ones make a person lucky indeed. It is easy, however, to take old friends for granted. New friends are "the unknown" and are, therefore, risky. Old friends know you. Even with large distances and spans of time, old friends can pick up with you where you left off. The work in a time-tested relationship still exists, so it is easier to engage, as there is already trust and companionship.

New friends require vulnerability and energy. You must build trust through courage and seek space outside your comfort zone that might lead to strange, new places. New friends, in this way, help you stay young and freshly inspired. They force you to learn, risk, and change.

<u>Today's PI</u>
Invite one new friend into your life every day for the next week. Ask that person who captivates you at the meeting if he or she would like to join you for coffee, invite that coworker to a weekend picnic, and see if the person you enjoy talking to at the gym is interested in jogging together. Challenge yourself to make the first move, and welcome new friendships into your orbit. Is this a tall order? Yes. Do it anyway. It's not a scavenger hunt. Be discerning and make the effort, even if you are not thoroughly successful.

DAY 191

※———❦❧———※

Outside show is a poor substitute for inner worth.

—Aesop

Beauty can imprison you. If you hope to maintain your outer beauty forever, you will eventually be suffocated by self-criticism and fear. Beauty in and of itself is not "bad." In fact, appreciating beauty is one way you can savor life's blessings. The grave mistake is to equate beauty with happiness. People will age, their skin will wrinkle and sag, their bodies will function less effectively, their hair will fall out, their muscles will atrophy, and their vision and hearing will fade.

Those who do not experience aging are not experiencing anything. Invest your time and energy where you can find happiness and self-efficacy—engaging in relationships with others, contributing to others or a meaningful cause, growing daily toward reaching your potential, or enhancing your recovery. These are anchors of happiness that travel with you and keep you fulfilled at every stage of the way.

Today's PI

1) *Take your beauty-happiness inventory, and ask yourself if you want to keep your happiness anchored in your looks.*
2) *Look for the inner beauty in people, places, and things. Every flower is beautiful insofar as it represents a "flower." Every honeybee is beautiful as a "bee." Every person is a beautiful representation of a "human." Buildings, rocks, and water are beautiful when you appreciate their unique natures.*

Remember also to make one new friend today.

DAY 192

Although gold dust is precious, when it gets in your eyes, it obstructs your vision.

—Hsi-Tang

If you are like most people, you probably think you need more money to be happy. After your basic needs are met, however, money contributes a decreasing amount to your overall well-being. Like beauty, money will enslave you if you equate it to happiness. There can never be enough to satisfy the needs of materialism. Money is not bad de facto. Using it for other people's sake is beneficial for the giver's happiness. The question is how you approach it. Is your vision clear, or is gold dust obstructing it?

When you look at where you spend your treasure, you can see whether or not your vision is askew. Are you purchasing excessive material goods, or are you spending money on travel to see friends and family? Does the bulk of your money go to providing for your household or for quality education? Are you using money to engage in life-enriching experiences? To support family? Pets? Gifts? Charity? Your spending habits reveal the values you choose to pursue and can provide valuable direction.

Today's PI
Go online and look at your bank statements. Explore where your money is going, and ask yourself what that says about your values. Is there anything you would like to change? If so, draft a rough budget for the following month's spending that is more congruent with your principles. Write yourself a reminder to check back on your bank statement a month from now to see what progress you've made.

Remember also to make one new friend today.

DAY 193

I hope I shall possess firmness and virtue enough to maintain what I consider the most enviable of all titles, an honest man's character.

—George Washington

Addicts are generally only as sick as their secrets. One lie can wreck a life otherwise well lived. Honor, integrity, and character are but a few virtues that cannot stand in the house of a lie.

Why did the late great George Washington consider the most enviable of all titles the character of an honest person? Perhaps it's because honesty is pure acceptance of everything. It's taking things as they are and not how you wish them to be. In that way, honesty is also a form of "letting go" of consequences. Honesty doesn't try to manipulate or control other people or circumstances. It's pure, simple, and durable.

Today's PI

Be that most enviable of characters—the honest person. Don't forget to spare people's feelings. Remain compassionate as well as honest. Without causing direct harm, be honest in all your affairs. Be honest with yourself. Be curious about any little alcoves of safety you have created for yourself by bending the truth or outright lying. Practice bravery and perseverance, and maintain honesty throughout your day.

Remember also to make one new friend today.

DAY 194

⊷⊷⊷⊷⊷⊷⊷⊷⊷⊷

Abundance is not something we acquire. It is something we tune into.
There's no scarcity of opportunity to make a living at what you love.
There is only a scarcity of resolve to make it happen.

—Wayne W. Dyer

People might read quotes such as this and retort, "Easy for you to say. You are rich. How could someone make a lot of money if what they loved was being a teacher?" If you have an active inner grump or cynic, Wayne's quote might nauseate you. However, before you dismiss the concept of abundance as a delusional pipe dream, pause and ask yourself, "Do I live in a world of finite or infinite resources?" In a world of infinite resources, hope and gratitude are the strengths that prevail. According to this worldview, you neither despise someone else's gain nor view it as a loss. There is ample opportunity for everyone to succeed. That "success" is not limited to the financial. It might take the form of financial prosperity, abundant loving relationships, flourishing satisfaction or fulfillment, excellent health, a dynamic and emotionally healthy family, and so forth. When you enjoy abundance, celebrate others for their successes, and remain open to the vast opportunities the universe has in store for everyone, you can thwart envy and enhance your overall level of happiness.

Today's PI

Utilize the word "abundance" as your inspiration. Get creative and think broadly as you journal about where you see abundance in your life. Look for where you perceive it in the lives of others. Then offer a meditation or prayer of gratitude for what they have. Practice this openhearted way of perceiving life's abundances throughout your day, and share this experience online.

Remember also to make one new friend today.

DAY 195

⚬⚬⚬

No man is free who is not master of himself...Is freedom anything else than the power of living as we choose?

—Epictetus

Addictive drugs and behaviors were at one time effective tools for recovering addicts. They helped them feel better and enabled them to escape discomfort. Once those addictive substances and behaviors stopped working, it was too late to make any adjustments. Once activated, addiction is not a disease that spontaneously goes away.

Addiction is a process whereby unsuspecting people's hijacked brains enslave them. Unknowingly, they invite the terrorists right into their bodies. From the moment their free will is overthrown, they are not their own masters. They lose their freedom.

Today's PI

Make a list of how your freedom was stolen from you during your active addiction. Next to it, make a list of the freedoms you enjoy today. What are you doing now that you only dreamed of doing before? What positive, healthy habits are you able to do today? What are your sources of joy? When complete, compare these lists, and take the time to savor the gifts of freedom.

Remember also to make one new friend today.

DAY 196

Death is what makes life an event.

—Francis Ford Coppola

In Western cultures, many either ignore mortality or else pretend death does not exist. It's not uncommon to attempt to avoid death at all costs. Some even attempt medical "miracles" to hold desperately on to life despite the consequences.

All the money, beauty, and power in the world cannot stop death when it inevitably comes. The stronger the ego, the more powerfully attached one is to the delusion one won't die, and the more resistance there is to accepting death. However, death defines humans. It's a great instructor. It makes life an amazing event. Death does not have to be degrading or depressing. When people stop pretending it won't come, they report feeling incredibly liberated. Releasing themselves to fate can be a source of expansive living and joy. Indeed, many start living the best chapters of their lives only after having a near-death experience.

Today's PI

Imagine you have been given notice that you will die within the next five years. Meditate on how you would wish to live out that final precious time. What about your current choices would you change if you knew your time was limited? What if you were given notice that your life would end within the next five months? What then would change? Avoid the temptation to fall into morbid reflection. Rather, practice courage and curiosity. Look inward to find who you want to be in this life and what actions you can take in order to fulfill that ideal version of yourself. Resolve to put at least one life-enhancing change, no matter how small, into practice this week.

DAY 197

Nothing is more desirable than to be released from an affliction,
but nothing is more frightening than to be divested of a crutch.

—James Baldwin

Chemicals and behaviors that turned into addictions were once highly prized tools for addicts. At one time these assistants ameliorated the problems of their day-to-day lives. Whether coping with painful issues and emotions or enriching positive ones, chemicals and behaviors served a purpose. As when any coping skill is abruptly discontinued, however, the addicts were left naked and afraid. How were they to face angst and fear without escaping? How were they supposed to enhance pleasurable experiences? They didn't automatically discover a new set of effective coping skills simply by breaking free from the bondage of addiction. Remember that every addict in good, long-lasting recovery started at exactly the same place. The trick is to be patient.

Today's PI

Reflect on your current coping skills, and search for anything you continue to use as a crutch in the absence of drugs and/or addictive behaviors. Do you turn to mindless marathon television watching? Food? Shopping? Isolating yourself? Meaningless sex? Self-criticism? Judgment of others? Obsessive thoughts? Take stock of what you can stop, but also make a list of those healthy coping skills you have fostered over your recovery time, and commit to utilizing those rather than any of your existing crutches.

DAY 198

———⁂ ⁂———

In any moment of decision the best thing you can do is the right thing, the next best thing is the wrong thing, and the worst thing you can do is nothing.

—Theodore Roosevelt

Every day people are faced with thousands of decisions, have thousands of thoughts, and are exposed to thousands of other stimuli. It is no wonder that there is so much confusion. Keeping life simple can be very challenging. If you only had the luxury of living at a mountainside retreat without the stress of traffic, rent, taxes, and other hot pokers, couldn't you live in peace?

Not necessarily. In traditional recovery fellowships, it is often said that you should "do the next right thing." You cannot afford to do nothing. Passive existence is not a full life. Addicts have lost the luxury of being on decision vacations. Every decision matters immensely. True, the noisiness of modern life requires you continuously choose what to ignore, what to attend to, and what to assess as threats. However, you would do these things even if alone in a cave.

Today's PI
Be mindful all day about "doing the next right thing." Take a moment to evaluate your decisions as you make them, and act with integrity. Be present at each moment of decision making. Then journal tonight about any insights gained.

DAY 199

━━◦◦◦ ◦◦◦━━

When you surrender to the air, you can ride it.

—Toni Morrison

You are not in control of events, people, places, or things outside of yourself. You are also not in control of the emotions and thoughts that come your way. The human mind is wandering, and fear is a powerful subconscious force. Both of these operate independently from your will. As an addict, fear, cravings, or old patterns of reacting often guide your first thoughts. You are not responsible for your first thoughts, but you are absolutely responsible for what you do with them. You are not a helpless bystander. You don't have to act on every thought or emotion that flashes within you.

Today's PI

Set an alarm to go off five times throughout the day. Take sixty seconds each time to repeat the following: "All life is in your hands." When you say this, you are saying all life, events, and other uncontrollable elements are in the hands of your higher power, the universe, or whatever you believe in higher than yourself. If you do not connect with the Western concept of a higher power, consider turning yourself over to "principled living" or the Eastern philosophies of living in accordance with right intention, action, speech, etc.

DAY 200

—⊰⊱—

It is one of the most beautiful compensations in life that no man can sincerely try to help another without helping himself.

—Ralph Waldo Emerson

There is a causal relationship in the world that goes by several names— the Golden Rule, karma, the law of attraction. "What comes around goes around"—human beings have been teaching this maxim across cultures and times. Some people engage in prosocial behaviors out of self-sacrifice for another's sake, while others engage in altruistic actions for personal benefit. Research proves that when people reach out and help one another, the happiness-enhancing benefits boomerang back to the givers. How people treat others also reflects how they view themselves, and practicing outward-focused love and compassion enhances self-esteem and self-love too.

<u>Today's PI</u>
Find three people to help. They can be coworkers, strangers, people in need of charity, or family members. If you cannot afford to help with time or money, help with prayer and good thoughts. Sending anything helpful their way will benefit them and you, and it will increase your karma bank account.

DAY 201

A man would do nothing if he waited until he could do it so well that no one could find fault.

—John Henry Newman

At one time or another, everyone is afraid he or she isn't worthy or good enough. Many think the antidote involves trying to be perfect. Perfection, though, does not pave the road to happiness. It's impossible to please everyone, and attempting to do so leads to exhaustion and loss of true identity. Worse still, when your inner critic runs the show, you consistently feel anxious, deflated, or pained. You cannot thrive when perfectionistic ideals bind you. Often you cannot even act. If you wait until all possible objections are overcome, you risk never making a move.

Today's PI
Answer these questions:

1) *How do I try to be perfect?*
2) *Which group of people do I try to please?*
3) *If I could believe that I'm already "perfect" just by virtue of being me, what space would be freed up in my life? What could I do with that extra energy?*

The object is to use self-awareness to do what you can and what you love regardless of external acceptance. Happiness and self-esteem will be forever elusive if you live in order to please others.

DAY 202

Joy, temperance, and repose, slam the door on the doctor's nose.

—Henry Wadsworth Longfellow

"An apple a day keeps the doctor away" is synonymous with "an ounce of prevention is better than a pound of cure." Science or medicine cannot undo what you do with your mind and body. You have the power to be healthier, live longer, and lead a richer, fuller life.

Happiness protects against getting sick. Consequently, happy people live longer. The effect on longevity is comparable to whether or not a person smokes. Longfellow's quote reflects this wisdom that happiness, moderation, and emotional sobriety are good for health and longevity. They're so good that they can literally prevent doctor visits.

Today's PI

Do something new for your health. Even if it's just for today, try not to eat processed foods, stay away from tobacco, exercise (more), drink more water, eat more fiber, meditate a bit longer, or schedule that appointment to take care of a lingering health issue. Also practice prevention by exercising joy, moderation, and emotional sobriety. These three are the apple a day that keeps the doctor away.

DAY 203

*Worry never robs tomorrow of its sorrow,
it only saps today of its joy.*

—Leo Buscaglia

Worrying about events that have not happened (and most likely never will) is not an effective way to shield yourself from sudden misfortune. When and if bad events ever happen, the "sting" is very rarely as bad as the imagination says it will be. No matter how much you worry, the future is going to unfold as it is going to unfold. The future will unfold without consulting your fears and desires. Spending energy and giving away serenity by creating catastrophes in your mind robs you of joy and serenity today, and it also does nothing to prevent the unknown from happening. You can, therefore, make the choice to create extra problems, or you can let go of the future and focus on what joy there is in today.

Today's PI

Be mindful throughout the day of times when your mind departs the present for the future. When that happens, make a note of what you are worried about, and at day's end, see if you notice any patterns in your worries. This exercise is aimed at giving you insight into those areas of your life where you have the most trouble letting go.

DAY 204

Caught up in a whirlwind, can't catch my breath.
Knee-deep in hot water, broke out in a cold sweat.
Can't catch a turtle in this rat race.
Feels like I'm losin' time at a breakneck pace.
Afraid of my own shadow in the face of grace.
Heart full of darkness, spotlight on my face.
There was love all around me, but I was lookin' for revenge.
Thank God it never found me, would have been the end.

—"Tightrope" by Stevie Ray Vaughn

Vaughn's lyrics tell the story of a recovery journey. In active addiction, people definitely lose time at a breakneck pace. The song later talks about the light at the end of the tunnel and the love, compassion, and kindness that come from experiencing the gifts of recovery:

Lookin' back in front of me, in the mirror's a grin.
Through eyes of love I see, I'm really lookin' at a friend.
We've all had our problems, that's the way life is.
My heart goes out to others who are there to make amends.

Today's PI
Journal about what your "tightrope" was like. Journal also about what you're doing differently now. Here is the catch: try to write it in poem form, using no more than one page. Creativity is an exercise that stretches and enables you to come from an authentic place.

DAY 205

*Those who have one foot in the canoe and one foot in the boat
are going to fall into the river.*

—Native American Proverb

People are not, as French philosopher René Descartes thought, mechanical clocks. There is no longer any doubt about the mind-body connection. What affects one part affects the other. Still, the mind, spirit, or essence of a person has yet to be sceintifically isolated and measured, and it probably never will be. In just one cubic millimeter of a brain, there are more connections than there are stars in the solar system.

When you enter recovery, you make a journey of spiritual *and* bodily renewal. While it is good to develop your emotional, interpersonal, and spiritual potential, and it's equally good to become a grateful and giving soul, if you smoke or eat a toxin-laden diet, you are stealing from your mind and body's growth. On the other hand, if you are running marathons but avoiding recovery actions, you are also living one-dimensionally.

Today's PI
Rate your physical, emotional, spiritual, relational, and overall happiness dimensions on a scale of one to ten. Where are you now in each category? Be curious. Are there ways you could redistribute your time and energy to create more balance and growth in your life?

DAY 206

✦✦✦

*I have found the paradox, that if you love until it hurts,
there can be no more hurt, only more love.*

—Mother Teresa

Answer everything with love. Fear clouds selfish and self-centered inclinations, and love cannot work its magic. It is only when love is felt in every cell of the body that fear and selfishness become subdued. A very challenging prospect arises when you have justified anger. Resentment, after all, warps reality and poisons opportunities for happiness. Even justified anger does nothing to meaningfully rectify a situation. It also doesn't hurt the culprit. You are the one harmed by harboring resentment.

Resentments typically come from fear and other deeper insecurities. You increase your protection against a relapse when you use love to counteract fear. Love also heals hurt, enhances happiness and relationships, and nourishes. Love is very much like an oil lamp. Filled once and lit, the source of light will run out, and the candle will dim. Your job is to keep pouring oil into the lamp so it stays lit and casts its glow over fear.

Today's PI

Give love unconditionally. Either follow a loving-kindness meditation (found on PositiveRecovery. com), or search your life for a lingering hurt. Love the person, place, or thing that still holds that hurtful energy. Love yourself, whether or not you are the source of hurt, for doing the best you could at the time. Love is its own reward. Savor the experience it brings today.

DAY 207

The irony of willpower shall forever cripple humankind. The force of will accomplishes great deeds just as often as it causes devastation and despair. The illusion that we can alter reality by sheer force of will is perhaps the greatest lie perpetrated by fear.

—Spiro Phernophocles

Wouldn't life be easier if willpower alone could save people from the grips of addiction? Too much willpower actually enables addiction to keep going as the illness progresses. Discipline and diligence are required to keep using and acting out in the face of mounting negative consequences. That's right: addicts actually have too much willpower.

Willpower is not bad. It's necessary in living the best life possible. Self-control allows people to persist, overcome challenges, and accomplish meaning-ful goals. Too much self-reliance, however, is not the wise use of willpower. Immense strength awaits when you are courageous enough to let go of your *self*-will and ask for help.

Today's PI

Ask for help. Spend a few moments in quiet reflection about something challenging in your life. You might journal about it if that helps. Once you have identified a problem area, look for someone from whom you can ask assistance. Embrace the strength of humility, and enable yourself to be empowered.

DAY 208

Chase after money and security and your heart will never unclench.
Care about people's approval and you will be their prisoner.
Do your work, then step back.
The only path to serenity.

—Lao Tzu

Happiness comes from within—not from temporary pleasures, money, power, or approval. Chances are, however, that you are still holding on to some false hope that you are different. These false hopes lead you to chase after artificial means of happiness that generally lead to suffering. Perhaps sexual conquests still occupy your mind, or maybe you seek a nurturing embrace in a bowl of ice cream. Maybe gambling, shopping, or work is the escape you are not aware of that keeps you from taking a step back and focusing on the things that could actually bring you sustainable happiness.

Happiness can only come from getting off the hamster wheel of immediate or superficial gratification—not from running faster. Resting refuels your tank and allows new and fresh perspectives to enter your thoughts. Resting heals the body and mind. Resting is part of living the best life possible and can be that step back Tzu speaks of.

Today's PI

Engage in purposeful rest. Spend at least twenty minutes today intentionally resting. This could be in the form of napping, meditating, or spending quiet time alone in nature. Savor the restful nature of this twenty minutes. Do your best to allow your mind and body to be at rest.

DAY 209

We should not pretend to understand the world only by the intellect.
The judgment of the intellect is only part of the truth.

—Carl Jung

Carl Jung was an intellectual and scientist. He knew better than most what objective scientific data could yield, and he was dedicated to using science in order to find the truth. He was highly respected for his technique as well as his wisdom. Jung knew that the truth does not exclude the spiritual dimension. Carl Jung was actually one of Bill Wilson's influencers in formulating Alcoholics Anonymous.

Jung was mostly quiet about his beliefs, because he couldn't measure divinity, spirituality, or soulfulness. Today people still cannot measure these things, yet most people have always believed in something larger than themselves. Scientific proof is apparently not necessary for human beings to claim a spiritual dimension in their lives. Intellect of the mind is only one medium to discover the world. The heart, soul, and intuition also teach people volumes that cannot be ignored.

Today's PI

Focus on appreciating the wisdom of your mind (intellect), heart (emotions), and soul (spirituality). All three are useful tools in making wholehearted and life-enhancing decisions. Turn to your journal, and write a brief gratitude letter to each of these three components. The letters need not be long, but they should encompass what you appreciate about your heart, mind, and soul, how each have helped you in the past, and any commitments you would like to make to each of these aspects of your inner self. Share these on the website too.

DAY 210

❦

Sometimes it's hard to find what you're looking for when it's right in front of your nose. Fortunately, a smile is happiness you'll find right under your nose.

—Tom Wilson

Many are prone to reacting strongly to situations—especially negative ones. This is self-sabotaging, since those situations inhibit joy and steal harmony. It's easier to be on autopilot than to be mindful of thoughts and pause before acting. The former takes little energy but is more likely to lead to road rage, self-criticism, self-pity, and more. The key to balancing your reactivity and preserving serenity in life is to remember that many positive things are right under your nose. Take this line of thinking one step further to turn misfortune into fortune, especially with a sense of humor. If you cannot laugh at yourself, life can be very long and painful. On the other hand, when you can laugh your foibles away, you make room for imperfection and accepting yourself just as you are.

Today's PI
Keep things in perspective by looking for hidden sources of gratitude and humor. Keep your journal close, and every time you find yourself stressing over minor imperfections, write down a description of the event at hand and your feelings about it. Take the time to explore new ways of looking at the situation so you might recall the smile right under your nose.

DAY 211

—⊰⊹⊱—

Friendship needs no words.
It is solitude delivered from the anguish of loneliness.

—Dag Hammarskjöld

Other people matter. Happiness flourishes when you meaningfully connect with others and choose to be giving of yourself in friendship. People make us happy, and we can make them happy. When you call a friend on his or her birthday, the friend gets the message that he or she matters to you—the ultimate compliment. A friendship really does not need words, and it does more than deliver you from the anguish of loneliness (although that is quite an amazing by-product)—it can also double your joy.

Today's PI

Choose three friendships you would like to put energy into enhancing, strengthening, or rekindling. Write these chosen friends letters (e-mails are permissible) expressing what you are grateful for in your relationships with them. Be brave. Let them know how much they mean to you. This will most likely brighten their days as well as increase your happiness. Share your and their experiences on the website.

DAY 212

Any idiot can face a crisis—it's day-to-day living that wears you out.

—Anton Chekhov

It is said that addicts' biggest problem is not dying but living. Addicts struggle more with all the daily hassles of life than with dying. Think about it. A person only dies once. In terms of managing life's problems, it's far easier to notice and evade a large elephant stampeding toward you by running to safety than to see the smallest of events that can wreak true havoc, like the microbes and insects too tiny to avoid that make you sick. Translated into real life, these microbes and insects are supermarket lines, the neighbor's car or manicured yard, your partner's snoring, your children's grades, your age, your body fat, your bank accounts, anxiety about what others think, worries about the future, and so forth. Individuals in recovery have lost the luxury of allowing themselves to get wrapped up in excessive worry about the small stuff. In recovery you learn to live life on life's terms and experience the beauty of letting things roll off your back. Letting go is a gift that allows you to release the small stuff and disempower it from ruining your sense of serenity.

Today's PI

Focus on letting go when life's minor irritants disrupt your peace and equanimity. Choose at least one frustrating "small stuff" thing that causes you repeated discomfort. Write down on a piece of paper, "Today I choose to let _____ go." Carry that piece of paper with you. Set an alarm to go off six times today, and each time pull out your written reminder to let go and reflect on how you're doing.

DAY 213

We measure success by accumulation. The measure is false. The true measure is appreciation. He who loves most has most.

—Henry van Dyke

Even in relationships, no two people can love each other the exact same amount or in exactly the same ways. While another's generous love adds to your happiness, a larger boost happens when you are the one who loves *others* most. When you utilize the strength of love, you open yourself to a positive, warm, and inspiring world full of potential and hope. You enable yourself to develop deep, meaningful, and trusting relationships with those who have earned it—the ones who can see you through the good and bad times. To love without fear is to live in gratitude. Imagine if the love race replaced the rat race.

Today's PI

Put a copy of today's quote on your bathroom mirror, and leave it there for the next thirty days. Take the time to read it mindfully every morning and night. Allow it to remind you to look for opportunities to love with an open, generous heart. Today, start writing an inventory of all things that bring you delight, enjoyment, joy, happiness, and a sense of fulfillment. Then, over the next thirty days, see how many items you can add to that list, and share it on the website.

DAY 214

Don't put a period where there is a comma.

—Anonymous

Outside of death, there is no "period" when setbacks occur. There are only commas. Often things do not go your way or turn out as you planned. Other times you get exactly what you want but find out later it's not what you wanted. Other times what you dread most comes to pass, and it turns out to be a blessing in disguise.

Looking for opportunities instead of looking for the wall of doom requires you to look for chances to grow rather than reasons to cry. For most, this does not come naturally. It is, after all, easier to cling to preconceived convictions about wants and needs. The fallback position, dictated by fear, is to see the sky falling at the slightest hint of rain. Fortunately, you can learn to instead respond to challenges by looking for opportunities, but you must be diligent and disciplined with your attention.

Today's PI

Reflect on at least three setbacks in your life that turned out to be blessings in disguise. Write about the events (setbacks) and what you gained and/or learned from them in the end. Over time, this simple exercise can strengthen your ability to choose an optimistic perspective. Use your character strengths of perspective, gratitude, curiosity, and hope.

DAY 215

The foolish man seeks happiness in the distance,
the wise man grows it under his feet.

—James Oppenheim

Happiness is not achieved at some final state of being. It's found in how you travel along the way. When meaning and purpose lead your journey, lined with supportive relationships and positivity, you are more likely to experience authentic happiness than if you open false doorways to happiness (sexual conquests, money, hedonic pleasure, and more). False doorways open to emptiness—a constant state of yearning to fill up a hole with more and newer distractions.

According to Joseph Campbell, "The way to find out about happiness is to keep your mind on those moments when you feel most happy, when you are really happy—not excited, not just thrilled, but deeply happy. This requires a little bit of self-analysis. What is it that makes you happy? Stay with it, no matter what people tell you. This is called 'following your bliss.'"

Today's PI

Journal about a day or time when you found bliss. First close your eyes, and center yourself on your in breath and out breath. Do this for five minutes. As you breathe, transport yourself to that blissful experience. Recall as much as you can about it. When you practice this "positive recall," you can boost your mood and discover values and ways to achieve your goals.

DAY 216

Trust in God, but row away from the rocks.

—Greek Proverb

Isn't it curious how mysterious the nebulous line is that separates free will from coincidence and destiny? Where do you end, and where does something larger than yourself take over? Humans are equally capable of trying to control too much and not enough. At times we find ourselves paddling madly against the current using invisible oars. Other times we wonder why we are sitting in the boat so passively as opportunities come and go. We simultaneously experience and discover the mystery by dancing harmoniously or, as the Greek proverb notes, rowing away from the rocks.

Today's PI

Experience and discover your ability to manifest change as well as your powerlessness. You are a valued but tiny part of an awesome species within a massive ecosystem. Throughout the day, be mindful of your power to create, but do not forget that with every action, there is a part outside your control. If you have a verbal relationship with whatever you conceive as your higher power, try asking for guidance as you make decisions. See if there is any change in what you would have done without asking for that help. If you do not have a verbal relationship with a higher power, observe throughout the day what actions you took that were within your control and what aspects of the day were outside your influence. At the day's end, journal about your experience.

DAY 217

―――❧ ❦―――

When you help someone up a hill, you find yourself closer to the top.

—Brownie Wise

You cocreate a healthier, happier reality for all when you give. Study after study proves that giving to others is the gift one gives oneself. People need one another for sustenance, and we are connected in more than just immediate ways. We affect others and they affect us. Helping others engenders positive emotions within the giver precisely because we are profoundly connected to one another. We literally *need* to help one another. It is how we help ourselves (as a group) the most. How successful a city, state, country, or planet is depends on how it treats its individuals.

Today's PI

Find someone and help that person reach his or her goals. In any way possible (nothing is too small), help another in his or her journey toward success. Whether you are aware of someone who needs words of encouragement or whether you can facilitate an introduction to someone in the field, write a good review online, or help with a project, make today about someone else's success. Through kindness, generosity, and focusing on being a positive member of a shared humanity, you might find you not only feel better but also move closer to your goals.

DAY 218

———❦❦———

The way to a man's heart is through his stomach.

—Anonymous

Vast differences exist from person to person in preferences, opinions, and habits around food. Some see food as an opportunity to access sensory joy, and they savor every morsel. Others think food is nothing more than fuel to get them through their days. Others engage in battles with their food choices and strive to maintain dietary protocols.

What people know for sure is that food choices matter. What a person eats impacts physical health, energy level, mood, emotional balance, and the ability to live life to its fullest. In that way food is a way to one's heart. The influence diet has on different aspects of overall well-being has been scientifically proven. Eating too much, too little, or too out of balance can have significant consequences on the ability to flourish.

Today's PI

Be mindful of every food choice you make. Before eating or drinking anything today, ask yourself, "Is this a healthy choice?" Practice mindfulness, and take your time to avoid overeating. Practice gratitude and savoring to enhance the joy of mealtimes.

DAY 219

In Hebrew, the word for "hello" and "good-bye" is the same: shalom. Like two sides of the same coin, shalom's energy is equal at both acknowledgment and valediction. More incredible is the fact that the same word for hello and good-bye also means "peace." Shalom is actually more like a three-sided coin that imbues each greeting and departure with harmony and goodwill. Now that's a community-oriented culture!

—Anonymous

Togetherness fosters health, happiness, and recovery. Cultures across the globe that have ceremonial rituals involving togetherness frequently have higher scores across every measurable indicator for healthy minds and bodies. It is no wonder that the highest life spans occur among groups with extremely strong social bonds and family units.

Today's PI

Create a family or friend ritual. Make an annual or monthly event when you can get together in order to celebrate one another and your bond. Have a monthly block party and call it happy hour (without the booze). Have your friends over for the "third Saturday in March party," or plan a trip with some of your core friends and/or family. Commit to making the trip a yearly affair. Be realistic, but get creative, and make this a reality starting today.

DAY 220

✦━✤✦ ✦✤━✦

Between the optimist and the pessimist, the difference is droll.
The optimist sees the doughnut; the pessimist the hole!

—Oscar Wilde

Gratitude (like optimism) is a matter of perspective. Optimism is not merely seeing the glass half-full. It is seeing both the liquid and air, and choosing to look at and appreciate the half-full portion. Gratitude is also grounded in reality. It's an appreciation for the best of what's around with complete awareness of life's stark and often harsh reality. Gratitude is an attitude, choice, and decision. Even the most pessimistic-by-birth person can learn to look for the good. All people can train themselves to move mountains with gratitude, but for many the change is tough, and many give up prematurely.

Positive recovery describes the act of fulfilling your potential to flourish while staying sober. It cannot be done without gratitude. Gratitude is awareness of the present moment without fear of the future or boggy regret of the past. Gratitude is an expression of the deepest heartfelt humility. When you realize you are owed nothing and that all you have in life is a gift, you are more likely to adopt the most useful perspective to lead to flourishing.

Today's PI

Journal for ten minutes nonstop about what you are most grateful for in this moment. Before you begin, make this gratitude entry fresh by thinking about what you most cherish. Do not try to live up to anyone else's expectations or ideals of you. Stay true to what you cherish. Write, read, and discover. Share it on the website as well.

DAY 221

*The road leading to a goal does not separate you from the destination;
it is essentially a part of it.*

—Charles DeLint

Enjoy the path. That is all there is. Achieving a goal is awesome, but it is a fleeting feeling. The longer and potentially more gratifying experience is the road you take to get there. The journey lasts far longer than the split second it takes to complete it. Unfortunately, too many put blinders on and keep their heads down while waiting to be happy at those points of completion. The inherent flaw in this way of thinking is that you lose out on the present by anticipating a golden future that never comes. There really are no finish lines—only paths.

Today's PI

Examine your goals for the year. What can you do to succeed? Reinforce your path by summoning help and making more specific short-term goals. Then stop and look around at the path under your feet. Take at least ten minutes to reflect on what you have gained solely from your journey. Journal if you like. Don't ignore the now for tomorrow. You might be waiting for a world that is not yours.

DAY 222

Pour me! Pour me! Pour me...a drink.

—Anonymous

Victimization can take several forms. When many addicts first come to the realization that they are powerless over chemicals or behaviors, it's as if shackles of blindness and imprisonment are lifted. Often this one momentous insight is enough to catalyze acceptance of the disease and generate the choice to take the recovery path.

Many other addicts, however, feel betrayed by themselves, God, their parents, or more. Instead of taking responsibility for their lives and empowering themselves with positive choices, some choose to throw themselves pity parties. Perhaps addiction was simply one of many reasons for feeling sorry for themselves. Do you feel as if fate is against you? Does life owe you anything? Do you blame your parents, boss, or spouse? If so, try to take responsibility for your life and your actions now. You have enormous control over what you are doing. This includes what you say and what you intend to do right now.

Today's PI
Be mindful of whether you've assumed the victim role in your addiction or in any other area of your life. Choose to take full responsibility for everything you do, say, and set your mind to. Choose a song you feel represents empowerment and gets you pumped up to take healthy control. Listen to your empowerment song at least three times today, and focus on being responsible.

DAY 223

When people believe in themselves they have the secret of success.

—Norman Vincent Peale

More than a self-fulfilling prophecy, success begins in a belief and an intention. If you think you can or can't, you are right. Unfortunately, too many suffer from low self-efficacy. You are neither the greatest of the great nor the least of the least. Everyone contains the entire dynamic range of human potential. If you accept that this is true about yourself, you could harness positive intention's unbridled energy. Who you think you are is how the world treats you because you set the standard. No one else is inside you—you have the best seat in the house. If you can't see your light, the world will see only darkness.

Today's PI

Think about whom you cherish and admire in your life (besides your romantic partner). What mentors and role models have really made an impact on your life and an impression on your soul? Once you have one or more heroes in mind, write for five minutes without pausing about the honorable characteristics they embody. Then pick out a few of the most poignant virtues, and see how you are (or can be) more like them. People admire in others what they are or can be. If you spot it, you got it.

DAY 224

It's only when we truly know and understand that we have a limited time on earth and that we have no way of knowing when our own time is up that we will begin to live each day to the fullest, as if it was the only one we had.

—Elisabeth Kubler-Ross

Today's PI

Today, we go straight to the PI. Close your eyes, focus on your breath for a couple minutes, and then imagine. See your life as a long voyage on a sailboat. When you are born, you board the ship. You do not choose the winds that blow across the sea, so envision yourself as the captain. You are able to steer the ship but not control the winds. You can adjust only your sails.

There will be many other people-boats on the journey. See some come and go and some stick alongside you for different periods of time and at different distances. There will be some who tie up and share the course, some who drift away, and some who follow behind. See that once you boarded and set sail (however long ago), the ship was immediately but slowly sinking.

Every ship is on a one-way journey that will inevitably end at the bottom of the sea. Everyone is on his or her own ship, and every ship is sinking at a different rate. Some command their ships as if their ships do not obey this law. They live in the what-if rather than the what-is. You, however, are awakened to the what-is and enjoy the journey. You no longer attempt to control the winds or change the nature of the ship. Appreciate that, and live your life to the fullest.

In your guided-imagery meditation, focus on feeling the ocean water lapping at your sides and the fresh breeze across your face. Give yourself to the joy and beauty of the present moment. Ignoring the here and now and living in the what-if is to stay asleep at the wheel.

DAY 225

———⬦ ⬦———

Two thoughts cannot coexist at the same time: if the clear light of mindfulness is present, there is no room for mental twilight.

—Nyanaponika Thera

Self-awareness shapes and enhances resilience and spirituality. You aren't any worse off than all other human beings when it comes to practicing self-awareness. The "self" is the same fundamental barrier in everyone, and when you discover how to get out of your own way, the results are truly remarkable. As challenging as it might be to exist in mindful meditation, it is this above any other behavior that helps repair and strengthen your brain, quiets fear, and increases awareness. Meditation also decreases the harmful bodily effects of stress.

Today's PI

Sit in silence for five minutes twice today. If you can manage to sit for longer, go for it. Find a comfortable, quiet place on the floor or in a chair. Focus on your breath and the rhythm of your breathing. Pay attention to your thoughts as if observing from a nonjudgmental, third-person perspective.

When you complete each session, journal about where your mind took you. Create a section in your journal ("Where My Mind Wanders To") to keep track of this, and compare today's entry with previous ones to discover your mind's travel habits.

DAY 226

⚜

*We are not physical beings here on Earth for a spiritual experience.
We are spiritual beings here having a physical experience.*

—Anonymous

The body is a temple and your temporary vessel. You must care for it the best you can. Fortunately, most people have relatively long periods of good health. However, many take that good health for granted. Your health is only "good health," and it only contributes to overall happiness when you have the right relationship with your current state of health. When your body gets ill or experiences natural wear and tear, it's easy to assume the victim role or feel angry. While some emotional discomfort is to be expected around these issues, overly engaging in this type of perspective adds to your emotional stress, exacerbates your health problems, and decreases your happiness even further.

Growing old or getting ill is not for wimps. Whatever physical maladies you might have in your lifetime, remember that your body owes you nothing.

<u>Today's PI</u>
Reflect on what being a "spiritual being having a physical experience" means to you. Do you believe this is true for you? How can this perspective help you in times of physical malady? What aspects of your physical body can you be grateful for? Journal your answers to these questions, and share your insights on the website.

DAY 227

The problem is not that there are problems. The problem is expecting otherwise and thinking that having problems is a problem.

—Theodore Rubin

Every emotion is right. Happiness is not something you can simply turn on like a light bulb. While happiness is a valuable goal, happiness is not a moral obligation or even healthy all the time.

Sadness and other negative emotions are not signs you are broken or sick. Negative emotions actually ought to be embraced with the same amount of acceptance and room as happiness. Instead of pushing negative emotions away or using them as evidence that you or the world is negative, look for activities that can bring on positivity. Instead of trying to deny or change negative emotions, let them be. Then lead with your strengths, envision a positive future, and cherish your blessings, relationships, and progress.

Today's PI
"No emotion lasts forever. I do not have to change or control my emotions. They are my teachers, and I am resilient."

Utilize this statement (or a version of it that resonates with you) as a mantra and inspiration for meditation. Repeat the essence of this statement as you meditate for at least ten minutes.

DAY 228

When you judge another, you do not define them, you define yourself.
How people treat you is their karma; how you react is yours.

—Wayne Dyer

Other people's actions define them. If someone else is rude, sarcastic, or otherwise offensive, you are wise to leave their action in their laps instead of picking it up like the contagious infection it is. Spending time and energy returning perceived insults and seeking vengeance is the plague of the frustrated and unhappy. Too often people judge others by their actions but judge themselves by their intentions. People often have biased judgments of others. They either habitually hold others to higher standards than they hold themselves or perceive them as better. People often convince themselves that they are free from bias but believe others cannot be objective.

How you perceive others' behavior is seen through your own lens. When another's character flaws irk you, either you believe you are somehow unwaveringly exempt from those character flaws, or you dislike something about yourself that is being mirrored. Judgment and envy snuff out happiness like water poured over a flame. Focus on what you have, and see that your judgment defines you—not them.

Today's PI
Throughout the day, try to notice what your judgments are telling you about you. *Are you nurturing envy? Anytime you find yourself slipping into judgment of another, ask yourself if the trait you are criticizing exists within you.*

DAY 229

Gratitude begins where my sense of entitlement ends.

—Steven Furtick

People are entitled to certain freedoms, such as freedom of thought, speech, and religion and the pursuit of happiness. People are not entitled to other things, such as power, other people's belongings, or the fulfillment of each and every desire.

Life is tough. Entitlement (the wicked offspring of fear and insecurity) completely robs you of peace and resilience. Breath is guaranteed to no one. Life itself is a gift to be grateful for. Everything else is a bonus prize. Why do many focus on the things they want but don't have? They don't get enough gratitude from others, they don't make enough money, they aren't as wealthy or handsome or beautiful as someone else, and so on. This attitude breeds nothing but dissatisfaction and contempt. Like Furtick said—lose entitlement and gain gratitude.

Today's PI

Go all day without a sense of entitlement. Focus on seeing how all you have is more than what you are due and more than what you need. Allow gratitude to fill your heart like a wellspring. Create a list of those aspects of life you frequently take for granted. For example, I am grateful to have lungs that breathe, I am grateful to have legs that walk, and I am grateful for potable drinking water when I am thirsty. Don't stop until you have at least fifty items on your list.

DAY 230

With courage you will dare to take risks, have the strength to be compassionate and the wisdom to be humble. Courage is the foundation of integrity.

—Keshavan Nair

You can't be brave without being afraid. Without doubts, you can't have faith. Without the ego, you can't develop humility. An essential key to success in recovery is following this clear, simple rule—do the next right thing or the right thing next. It takes a massive amount of courage to take risks, live a life fully committed to recovery, extend love outward, and stand in your truth. There are no shades of gray with integrity. That's what makes it so difficult. White lies, small larcenies, manipulations, cut corners, and unfulfilled promises are just a few examples of ways fear and ego can divert you from the right path.

Today's PI

Use courage to overcome every instance of diversion. Anytime your ego, fear, or a self-serving voice tries to keep you from doing the next thing right or the next right thing, use courage to maintain integrity. Bring intention to every one of your experiences today by literally asking yourself, "What is the right thing to do? How can I do this thing rightly?"

DAY 231

Each generation imagines itself to be more intelligent than the one that went before it, and wiser than the one that comes after it.

—George Orwell

Throughout time and around the globe, inscriptions on ancient stone tablets and cave dwellings reveal warnings that younger generations are too spoiled and self-indulgent to survive, much less thrive. History teaches, however, that these predictions proved false. Younger generations were able to plant food, maintain clean water supplies, hunt, and invent vaccines, air conditioning, computers, and space travel. The current younger generation is *not* doomed, and the older generation is not foolish. Each generation has its own challenges to address. Use this wisdom to gain some humility and perspective. When you let go of self-righteous indignation, you open yourself up more fully to learning and connecting.

Today's PI

Write two letters. Neither will be sent. Write one to the older generation. Thank them for what they have done to improve your life and the lessons you have learned from them. Write one to the younger generation. Thank them for what they have done to improve your life and the lessons you have learned from them. These letters should be written as general odes of gratitude to those who have come before and those who are coming after, rather than being addressed to specific individuals. Did this open your eyes and heart with gratitude throughout your day? Write about your experience on the website.

DAY 232

Take your life in your own hands and what happens? A terrible thing: no one to blame.

—Erica Jong

People who see they have the choice to be the captains in their lives are happier than people who perceive fate or happenstance as throwing them about. Whichever of these perspectives applies to you, your life is nonetheless a story you write. If you think you're a puppet on a string, you aren't likely to pursue stretch goals or flourish. If you see you are a capable agent of change, chances are high that you're taking risks, achieving the impossible, and thriving. Even choosing the perspective that nurtures helplessness is a choice.

<u>Today's PI</u>

Take responsibility. Improve your overall level of happiness by imagining your life is a movie you write, produce, edit, cast, and star in. You can even revise your script at any point. You decide if the main character is in recovery and has integrity, courage, honesty, loving-kindness, spirituality, deep and long-lasting relationships, and purpose. If so, the main character will behave in those ways, overcome obstacles, and thrive in recovery.

DAY 233

Only after settling down one's mind can one obtain peace.
Only after obtaining peace can one think.
Only after carefully thinking can one attain a favorable end.

—Chinese Proverb

The single most powerful victory any person can ever accomplish is breaking through the sea of racing thoughts, because the mind is a mess. Even when fame and fortune are found, any victory lacks substance when there is no inner peace. One can only run for so long.

Today's PI

Practice mindful meditation. Use guided meditation or sit in silent awareness for forty-five minutes. Anchor yourself to your breath by focusing on the in breath and out breath. Pay attention to where the air enters and leaves. Focus on how your body moves with the breath, and when the mind wanders, gently bring it back to your breath and body without judgment. Don't worry if you cannot meditate for forty-five minutes. Try it anyway. It's perfectly OK to sit for five, ten, or twenty minutes. The goal isn't so much any one length of time. It's to settle the wandering mind and to be calm and at peace so you can find and sit in your power. Meditate in any comfortable pose, so long as your back is straight and you're not lying down. Practice until you can be with your breath for forty-five minutes.

DAY 234

Doubt everything or believe everything:
these are two equally convenient strategies.
With either we dispense with the need for reflection.

—Henri Poincare

An addict has an astute but not always helpful ability to think in terms of extremes. People, places, and things can appear either one way or the other. Shades of gray often cause enormous discomfort and are conveniently ignored. Packaging everything into the completely true or completely false is a way for memory and emotion to soothe the fear of not knowing everything. However, how you feel, what you remember, and what you want heavily influence your life experience. In accepting that life is gray and by approaching life in a curious way, you courageously counteract fear and remain open to possibility.

Today's PI

At this point in your journey, you might be feeling the benefits of prioritizing balance in your life. In doing so, you can release the black-and-white thinking that accompanies active addiction. Create an image, poem, song, collage, or piece of art that represents "living in the gray" or balance to you. There is no way to do this assignment wrong. Embrace your creativity!

DAY 235

⋆──⊰⊱─⊰⊱──⋆

No one's head aches when he is comforting another.

—Indian Proverb

Being of service must be part of a general mind-set to anyone seeking happiness. Acting in reasonably prosocial ways improves immune function and slows the aging process. People feel the raw joy that comes from doing something kind and generous as well as the positive experience of seeing themselves as the type who comforts others.

Giving increases social connections and fosters a more positive view of yourself and your role in the world. Giving helps put your own troubles in perspective. Reaching out a helping hand enables you to forget about the self with all its desires, attachments, angsts, and self-preoccupations. Best of all, giving yourself to others with addiction is an evidence-based way to strengthen your recovery.

Today's PI
The goal for today is to help another through an action of service. Nothing helpful can be too small. Help your family, friends, the world, strangers, or animals. At the day's end, journal about what you did and how you felt. Share it on the website when finished.

DAY 236

——⚜ ⚜——

Twenty years from now you will be more disappointed by the things that you didn't do than by the ones you did do. So throw off the bowlines. Sail away from the safe harbor. Catch the trade winds in your sails.
Explore. Dream. Discover.

—Mark Twain

Mark Twain was wise beyond his years. He lived before scientific studies proved people really do regret what they have not done more than what they have done, even when they've tried to do something but failed. Evolution requires organisms to react to fear more powerfully than to savoring life's delights. Modern humans inherited brains hardwired to focus on the bad stuff, but this doesn't need to dictate where you cast your attention. Since you are no longer in real peril when you throw off the metaphorical bowlines of fear and head for distant, unseen shorelines of hope and possibility, the only thing stopping you is yourself. A woman named Ilana Z. used to believe the voice that told her she just wasn't cut out for distance running. Then one mile became two, and two became five. Through action and grit, she worked her way up to marathons. I used to hear a voice saying, "You can't write." It's amazing, though, how writing silenced that voice.

Today's PI
What do you hear in your head that keeps you from casting out of the safe harbor? What would be at risk if you tried to chase that one improbable yet amazing dream?

DAY 237

A man should never be ashamed to own he has been in the wrong,
which is but saying...that he is wiser today than he was yesterday.

—Alexander Pope

Mistakes (and making amends) are not charged with such energy when people realize mistakes are teachers on the paths to wisdom. When you take responsibility for your misdeeds, you are essentially choosing to stand in your truth. However, you must do more than say the words "I am sorry" or "I was wrong." Making amends involves changing behavior. Amending yourself means making a change for the better. But while you should take responsibility and make amends, you also shouldn't ignore your accomplishments. Truth includes taking healthy pride in what you do right. You grow better every day by owning all your truth—the good and bad.

Today's PI

What do you have to be proud of today? What character traits and strengths do you embody that serve you and those around you well? Do not be boastful, but do look honestly at those positive aspects you can take meaningful pride in. List at least twenty sources of authentic pride in your journal, and share these on the website.

DAY 238

When men speak ill of thee, so live that nobody believe them.

—Plato

If you do not care about the public or private opinion of others, you are pro-tected from negativity dramatically swaying you. You recognize you cannot own what others say or perceive. Their perceptions are their business. All you can control are your actions. You live as if their slights are not true. On the other hand, if you are a people pleaser, have codependent tendencies, or live for approval, then exposure to negativity can easily turn your world upside down. Plato suggested you rise above the pain of ill words by living as if no one else believes them. Of course, ideally you will one day access your true inner self who is in alignment with who you want to be—full of unconditional love for others and yourself, without buttons so easily pressed by the approval of others.

Today's PI

Act as if no one believes what ill has been said by others or your inner critic. Any moment you feel ill spoken of, give yourself permission to believe the words are lies. Don't use this as an excuse to shrug off constructive criticism. Don't let this exercise blind you. At the day's end, journal about how you felt, and share it on the website.

DAY 239

I find that the more willing I am to be grateful for the small things in life, the bigger stuff just seems to show up from unexpected sources, and I am constantly looking forward to each day with all the surprises that keep coming my way!

—Louise L. Hay

Gratitude cannot be overemphasized. It can positively transform your life like nothing else. Many experience great awakenings of the heart, mind, and senses when embarking on recovery. Recovering addicts begin noticing minor joys and beauties they had neglected to appreciate for some time. As recovery lengthens, though, it's just as natural to adapt and forget to appreciate the small things. Good things lose their appeal unless people actively counteract hedonic adaptation. That is why you should return to gratitude often. It's one of the fundamental building blocks of happiness.

Today's PI

Focus on renewing gratitude through appreciating the small, often unnoticed things. Spend ten minutes in your home, yard, or place of work and simply notice things you haven't noticed before or else have forgotten about. The texture of the paint, the shape of the clouds in the sky, or the smell of cooking—nothing is too small. Appreciate how each of your senses allows you to experience your same world in a fresh way.

DAY 240

⚜

Of my own spirit let me be in sole though feeble mastery.

—Sara Teasdale

People are powerfully driven to direct what they do in their own lives (how, when, and with whom). Mastery matters. People need to become better at something, but not just anything will do. People are happier when they deliberately and persistently engage themselves in practice at something with substance. This explains why people create meaning in life, connect with a sense of purpose larger than themselves, learn and create new things, and connect with others. Mastery is only possible when you realize you can grow, cultivate your strengths and abilities, and improve.

Today's PI

Look back at your life's purpose from your imaginary great-great-grandchild's perspective. Close your eyes and take five long breaths. Imagine you successfully accomplished all you could have possibly hoped for. Reflect on what you did, what you mastered, and what you stood for. When this child describes you to a friend in less than a minute, what does the child say? Journal the child's less-than-one-minute spiel, and share it on the website.

DAY 241

*Go deeper than love, for the soul has greater depth,
love is like the grass, but the heart is deep wild rock
molten, yet dense and permanent.*

—D. H. Lawrence

Love is an act of courage—a deep and brave way of putting acceptance, gratitude, and joy in the world. To love is to appreciate that everyone is one and part of something more vast, powerful, and mysterious than people comprehend. Love is also to see the best there is—often when you are the only one who sees it. Love is also the fountainhead of happiness.

Today's PI

Practice loving-kindness meditation. Either follow a guided meditation, or sit in quiet practice for ten minutes. Focus your mind on love. Find the time to sit undisturbed, and center yourself with a few deep breaths. Once you are in touch with yourself in the present moment and anchored in your breath, begin. Feel love well up from deep within your heart and extend outward. Feel it cover the entire world in a warm, faint glow.

DAY 242

Vision without action is a daydream.
Action without vision is a nightmare.

—Japanese Proverb

Perhaps you're more familiar with this proverb said in other ways, like "The road to hell is paved with good intentions" or "Faith without works is dead." Phrased any way, the wisdom stands. If you see, feel, or intend it without *doing* it, you are doing little more than dreaming. In recovery fellowships, there is a common saying: "Knowledge avails you nothing." This saying also points out that positivity, recovery, faith, and so forth are verbs.

The second part of the Japanese proverb insists you plan. Planning (a form of harnessing one's thoughts and energy) separates action from blind impulse. Lack of impulse control leads to trouble. Vision and action are both needed, but neither one is enough on its own. You can gain that little bit of vision when you pause instead of react, and you can achieve more by simply moving (even slowly) to put your faith and intention into action.

<u>Today's PI</u>
Plan to act. Take a few moments to reflect on your current goals. These could be goals as they pertain to your recovery, relationships, health, profession, education, or anything else. Take out your journal and write down five actions you can take within the next six months toward these goals. Make sure at least one action is something you can do this week. Then get out there and live it!

DAY 243

Today I choose to live by choice, not by chance;
To make changes, not excuses.
To be motivated, not manipulated.
To be useful, not used.
To excel, not compete.
I choose self-esteem, not self-pity.
I choose to listen to the inner voice, not the random opinion of others.

—Anonymous

Today's PI

Today, we jump right into the PI. Replace the old quote on your mirror with today's quote, above. Sit in silence for five minutes twice today. Find a comfortable and quiet place. It can be on the floor, in a chair, or somewhere else. Focus on your breath and the rhythm of your breathing. Pay attention to your thoughts, as if observing them from a nonjudgmental third-person perspective.

After each session, journal about where your mind took you. Journal in the "Where My Mind Wanders To" section, and share your experience on the website.

DAY 244

When eating a fruit, think of the person who planted the tree.

—Vietnamese Proverb

The sun generously gives its energy to plants that convert that energy into food to grow. Thus the plants provide much of life with sustenance, whether directly or indirectly, in carnivores' cases. Those of us who plant seeds, tend the soil, harvest the bounty, transport the food, package it, store it, and sell it are similarly intertwined in the chain of sustenance giving we enjoy on a daily basis. Even if you simply buy food, the give is bidirectional: the money you earn to pay for sustenance involves countless others as well.

Today's PI

At every meal today, take a few moments to think about and send thanks to everyone and everything that made the nourishing food possible. Then, journal tonight for ten minutes, and pay close attention to how much connection you feel. See if giving thanks in this way throughout the day sheds light on the interwoven fabric that binds all life, the earth, the sun, and the universe together. Sages say everyone is connected. If you can see this through the food you eat, maybe you can see it in other ways too. At the very least, you can be grateful to so many people and things for helping keep you and those you love alive.

DAY 245

———❧ ☙———

The gem cannot be polished without friction,
nor man perfected without trials.

—Chinese Proverb

Of the many techniques to develop optimism and emotional sobriety, the most significant is to view every challenge as holding an opportunity. Hindsight allows you to see how trials and tribulations ultimately led to your growth and development. Looking backward, you see the wisdom in the old adage "That which doesn't kill you truly makes you stronger." In the heat of the moment, though, challenges can send you into tailspins, and the temptation to control or hide from these challenges is large.

Some people live in ways that focus on avoiding this type of pain. Perhaps you too play it safe in some way and avoid certain risks so that your world is insulated. In so doing, however, you stop living. Those who understand that growth comes from difficulties are actually grateful for and embrace challenges instead of shunning and hiding from them. In turn they live free from extreme fear of what the future has in store.

Today's PI
Write about the last three painful experiences you endured that led to the growth of your character in some way. What happened, how did you react at the time, and how have you changed as a result?

DAY 246

Teach this triple truth to all: A generous heart, kind speech, and a life of service and compassion are the things that renew humanity.

—Buddha

Many do not lack speech, but they lack the power of tact and conversational restraint. As a result, regrets most often come from words said in anger, fear, and reactivity. Through using the character strengths of prudence, wisdom, and love, you can spread renewal rather than destruction, behave with kindness, and avoid making agonizing amends.

Today's PI

Practice advanced "right speech." Filter everything you say through the following five-question criteria. At the day's end, journal for five minutes about how you felt not saying things you otherwise would have said, and consider whether this is an exercise worth incorporating in your daily life.

1. *Does it need to be said?*
2. *Does it need to be said now?*
3. *Does it need to be said now by me?*
4. *Is it kind?*
5. *Is it true?*

DAY 247

꙳⸺⸰⸱⸰ ⸰⸱⸰⸺꙳

There are two rules on the spiritual path:
Begin and Continue.

—Sufi Proverb

Life is complex. With all the choices, unknowns, and different ways of looking at the same thing, it's no wonder that many are flummoxed. Perhaps no life arena is more complex and confusing than spirituality. People can keep this topic very simple, however. At times, the most spiritual thing most do is not act out on an addiction—*begin*. Without recovery, there is no room for anything else, because addiction requires you put addiction first. It leaves no room for other gods. Essentially, addiction says, "I am your one and only god. Kneel before me." When addiction is active, no amount of chanting or praying can elevate you to a sacred space. Addiction silences and suffocates your spiritual core.

Be wary. Look around. It seems as if everywhere you look, people are promising to catapult you into a spiritual dimension of nirvanic bliss. People can also simplify spiritual advice. The greatest spiritual growth comes from repeatedly doing all the small things in the best way possible—*continue*.

Today's PI

Start or continue your spiritual practice in whatever form it takes for you by writing it down and sharing it with a trusted accountability partner. Begin and continue.

DAY 248

God, grant me the serenity to accept the things I cannot change,
Courage to change the things I can,
And wisdom to know the difference.

—Reinhold Niebuhr

Know thyself. How can you know yourself? Simple. Practice identifying your emotions. People who can identify how they are feeling are better suited to respond to stressful events instead of reacting like a puppet on a string. Knowing how you feel enables you to staunchly accept reality and improvise whenever and wherever needed. This is correlated with a deep belief that life is meaningful. Better still, know thyself because it just might help keep you balanced—and sober.

Today's PI

Acknowledge reality resolutely using the serenity prayer. Accept that how you're feeling is how you're feeling. Work with your emotions instead of trying to push them away or change them. Accepting these emotions enables you to improvise on the fly, but it also minimizes unnecessary suffering. Keep your journal on you all day, and find space after each emotionally charged situation to jot down how you felt, what your inclination was, and what you did. Also note how you applied the serenity prayer or how you could apply it more fully next time around. Reflect on whether your reactions (feelings and actions) revealed anything about how you pursue wisdom, approach personal growth, give to others, and derive strength from being part of something larger than the self. Share your insights on the website.

DAY 249

Tell me to what you pay attention and I will tell you who you are.

—Jose Ortega y Gasset

Your thoughts help define you, so exercise caution in what you actively think about. Your thoughts become your actions. Your actions become your habits. Your habits become your character, and your character shapes your destiny. Fear of not being or having enough drives people to look around and find evidence supporting or refuting that they aren't enough or don't have enough. One method people use to do so (in vain) is comparing themselves to others. Since people are all essentially equals and because judging your insides on someone else's outside is an exercise in futility, comparing yourself to others is a submission to fear, and it leads only to envy or superiority—neither of which is beneficial.

<u>Today's PI</u>
Practice avoiding overthinking or engaging in social comparisons. Every time you find yourself comparing yourself to others, say or shout to yourself, "Stop! What I would really like to be doing right now is _____." Fill in the blank with an activity you can do in the moment, such as admiring the clouds, starting a task, or calling a friend to ask about his or her day. This form of intentional distraction can help when you are in fear or self-criticism mode, have cravings, or experience any emotion not worth acting on.

DAY 250

✦━━━━✦

The secret of happiness: Keep smiling at your fate, and your fate will smile back at you.

—Vadim Kotelnikov

As far as humans know, we are the only animals on Earth who plan for the future. You could say we live in moments we create simply by asking ourselves, "What's next?" The act of thinking about the future starts the planning process, which feeds back to shape your thinking and influence your motivation and feelings.

Start with gratitude for the blessings that have yet to come. While there is no link between wishful thinking and results, it can't hurt. Wishes don't fill bellies, but intention is still a powerful force. Look toward your future with openness and optimism. This might very well strengthen your ability to find joy in tomorrow, and it might enable you to discover contentment, serenity, and hope in today.

<u>Today's PI</u>
Prospect. Be forward looking. Be grateful for all you will have. Smile for the blessings of the future. Smile for your ability to influence your fate in becoming the best of all possible versions of yourself. Smile in knowing you can't simply will the brightest future possible by doing nothing but smiling.

DAY 251

When you see a good man, try to emulate his example, and when you see a bad man, search yourself for his faults.

—Confucius

A variety of disciplines reveal that when you see something you dislike in another, it is often because you are triggered by your own "stuff." Similarly, when you see "good" and internal beauty in another, it's also because you recognize something good within you. Whether you see someone use a certain strength or accomplish something extraordinary, the virtues you see in others exist within you as well. You must only access and practice those strengths to bring their benefits to fruition in yourself. If you can spot it, you can claim it.

Today's PI

When you judge, look for opportunities to learn. When triggered into judgment by someone else, be curious. How does that trait show up in you? Cut yourself and the other person some slack with compassion and kindness. Recognizing the good in others mirrors the gold in yourself. In place of envy, create space for abundance and ambition. Allow for success in everyone, and make sure you live according to standards you set for yourself. Journal tonight about your experience, and share your insights on the website.

DAY 252

There will be a time when you believe everything is finished.
That will be the beginning.

—Louis L'Amour

Getting sober is not the end. It's the start of a long process. Sadly, too many with a bit of recovery time feel as if they can take it easy. Complacency is enticing. It lures and hypnotizes with promises of rest and relaxation. It includes thoughts such as "I got this." This is simply delusional. Addiction grows stronger every day with or without your participation. Complacency is stagnation. It leads to neglecting opportunities for growth and eventually to relapse. Each moment you fail to wholeheartedly devote yourself to your recovery program, you grow more vulnerable to relapse. You must remain vigilant against the tyranny of complacency, compulsion, and addictive patterns of any kind. There is no holiday from the ominous threat of relapse. Perhaps that is why addicts continue to celebrate milestones of recovery.

Today's PI

Focus on your recovery. How vigilant or complacent are you today? Spend a few moments journaling about any areas in your life where you currently see addictive behaviors, thinking patterns, or attitudes cropping up. The strongest recovery programs are founded on awareness and continued self-reflection. Be brave today, and take an honest look inward!

DAY 253

⚬⚬⚬

Comedy is tragedy plus time.

—Carol Burnett

In addiction recovery fellowships, members insist on humor. Rule number sixty-two is to not take oneself too seriously. Twelve-step meetings are the only places you can find people laughing heartily about failed suicide attempts. Doing so is not evidence of moral baseness. It's a way members support one another. Members know that if it isn't funny, it's too real. The dark desperation that leads to suicidal thoughts (let alone attempts) is severely wretched. A joke is often the quickest way to briefly turn on a light when your world is engulfed in darkness.

Repatriated prisoners of war from the Vietnam era have said making light of the intolerable was more helpful than religion. From naming their horrific POW camp the "Hanoi Hilton" to scratching the note "Smile. You're on *Candid Camera*" on the wall of a decrepit shower stall, POWs found temporary mental escape from the prison walls. "Believe it or not," one survivor recalled, "even under the almost worst of conditions over there, under the right circumstances, we could laugh."

Today's PI

My dear friend George Joseph and the online shoe store Zappos inspired this PI. Create some fun and maybe a little weirdness. Aristotle said the unexamined life is not worth living. This says the "unfun" life isn't worth living—so have fun today. Make the journey entertaining, amusing, and joyous. What can you do to liven up a meeting, your work, or your home?

DAY 254

Addiction is the one disease that cannot be managed alone.

—Benton Yale

As a physician and recovering addict, I fully agree with this quote, although I cannot actually think of a single disease that supportive relationships wouldn't aid. I wish I could write everyone a prescription for supportive relationships. They reinforce personal responsibility, promote service to others, increase meaning and purpose, and are free of charge. All over the world, only one illness offers afflicted people such an abundance of positive communities. Addicts are fortunate to have this international web of people who are ready to lend a hand irrespective of race, sex, nationality, or socioeconomic level. Positive communities (church groups, support groups, etc.) lessen their members' troubles and enhance their resilience.

Today's PI
Reach out to a peer or friend in recovery. Remind yourself that your recovery and happiness are bolstered when others are part of the equation. If possible, spend some quality time with that person today. If not, schedule a date within the next week when you can enjoy each other's company.

DAY 255

In the long run the pessimist may be proved right,
but the optimist has a better time on the trip.

—Daniel L. Reardon

Pessimists have an extremely easy time defending their views. It's not difficult to discover harsh realities—terrorism, cyber warfare, political discord, and more. Finding evidence of the sordidness in human nature and the limitations of rationality is quite effortless.

Born pessimists (those whose natural instincts are to be dubious and doubtful) must work harder to find evidence of a better world. Except for the naturally sunny, shiny, happy people, most find that optimism, hope, and faith are often difficult propositions to embrace.

<u>Today's PI</u>
Focus on what is right. While you're at work and otherwise engaged in daily affairs, be prudent. Don't overuse the strength of optimism. When the risk of failure is high, use a skeptical eye. But for this PI, look forward to the future with hope; visualize it unfolding in the best possible way. See the good in yourself and others. When negativity bubbles up, tell it you're busy endorsing the optimistic candidate today. Practice optimism today in all things.

DAY 256

The greater the sinner, the greater the saint.

—English Proverb

Turning your life around is no easy feat. Other people scoff at how addicts celebrate milestones of not committing lascivious acts such as consuming exorbitant amounts of mind-altering substances or food, gambling away savings and homes, committing adultery, having meaningless sex and sometimes even paying for it, and engaging in other behaviors people "shouldn't do" in the first place.

Addicts aren't smug for using this proverb, however. When they choose the right action against the odds, they exercise more freedom than if they had no experience in or any gravitational pull toward the "dark side." In that vein, they should celebrate how well they behave regularly, and it is completely healthy to accept that they are now more saintly than they would be had they not consciously chosen the right action. Of course, addicts aren't necessarily saints. They simply behave with more piety now than they once did.

Today's PI
List twenty accomplishments or aspects of your life (e.g., your professional life, physical health, material possessions, relationships, spiritual connection, emotional well-being, etc.) you would not have if not for recovery. Allow yourself to reflect with genuine (but not excessive) pride on the work you have put into your recovery that has engendered these positive achievements in your life today.

DAY 257

We are not so sensible of the greatest health as of the least sickness.

—Benjamin Franklin

Bad things are by definition "unfavorable," and venting is perfectly natural. Holding things in is not good, but neither is dwelling on the negative. Complaining is almost never a useful reaction, but it can be one of the most automatic. When you have complained for years, it becomes a subconscious habit. Most aren't even aware when they are complaining.

A major issue with this automatic complaining habit is that you can almost always find (or create) what you look for. Your attitudes shape your experiences, so when you view the world in a negative, hostile, or aggravating manner, you typically come out feeling negative, hostile, and aggravated. Complaining also circulates negativity to others. (It's contagious.) Humans feed off others' thoughts, emotions, and opinions. When you engage in negativity, you are likely to cultivate and attract others in similar states of mind.

Today's PI

Counteract the complaining habit by wearing a rubber band on your wrist all day. Anytime you find your mind wandering toward negativity or complaints, or anytime you hear yourself voicing complaints out loud, snap the rubber band. This should not be a physically painful experience, but it should serve as a small sensory reminder of your decision to abstain from complaining for today.

DAY 258

—⊰✦⊱—

A good listener is not only popular everywhere, but after a while,
he knows something.

—Wilson Mizner

Cultivating listening skills is extremely challenging. As Bette Midler once said, "But enough about me; let's talk about you. What do *you* think about me?" Sadly, listening to others is a lost art. If you observe conversations, you might notice that many people merely wait for their turns to speak, or even worse, they don't even wait at all! When we are listening to ourselves while others speak, we seem to know exactly what they mean and what they're going to say before they finish talking. Fortunately, cultivating listening skills can increase your well-being. Lead with curiosity, practice mindfulness, and use conversations as opportunities to give. You'll benefit from escaping the chatter in your mind, and you'll be nurturing social connections with others.

Today's PI
Listen, listen, listen. Resolve to wait five seconds after the other person has finished speaking before you open your mouth. Allow that person's words to sink in rather than jumping to formulate what you are going to say next. Allow yourself to be in the role of student, and practice gratitude for what you might learn.

DAY 259

✦✦✦✦

The difference between "involvement" and "commitment" is like an eggs-and-ham breakfast: the chicken was "involved," but the pig was "committed."

—Anonymous

There is a tenet in traditional recovery fellowships that encourages more "piggish" than "chickenish" behavior. Half measures avail people nothing. Living a life in recovery full of growth, integrity, and happiness requires that you commit yourself wholeheartedly. Anyone can dabble, but in order to fulfill your potential, you must dig in, cover yourself, and leap into the chasm of your new life with complete abandon. Commit yourself body, mind, and soul.

Commitment, however, can have a dark side. Life is truly a journey, and if you're lucky, you receive feedback throughout it. Goals are one construct wherein feedback and support are especially helpful. The feedback of experience or others often reveals that the best pathway to achievement and happiness is in fact dropping a goal. Think of the mountain climber who can't drop his or her goal of reaching the summit and either dies or suffers from frostbite, losing fingers, toes, ears, and nose.

Today's PI

Looking back at your day-one goals, have you dropped or changed any? If so, was it due to feedback or experience? What have you learned about yourself along the way? Post your answers to these questions on the website.

DAY 260

✦━━◦❃◦ ◦❃◦━━✦

The essence of all beautiful art, all great art, is gratitude.

—Friedrich Nietzsche

Music is therapeutic. Most people intuitively know how certain songs enhance or change their moods. However, most people wouldn't agree that art is therapeutic too. How many people have playlists of images on their phones or MP3 players? Yet art isn't for an elite few, and it isn't just "pretty." There is nothing wrong with "pretty," but art isn't simply eye candy that gives us a reprieve from all the bad stuff. Admiring a beautiful piece of art doesn't cast a person into a delusional state where he or she loses sight of the actual harshness of reality. The brain's negativity bias makes good stuff slide off, but it makes bad stuff stick like glue. People are not in any danger of forgetting about everything they can possibly worry about—snakes, spiders, and how they compare to others. With enough insight and practice, however, art enables you to align with your most authentic self by offering clues about what is happening inside the body, mind, and soul.

Today's PI

How can art (especially beautiful art) be therapy? You decide. Visit a museum today, or pull up a few fine art images on the web. Write about what you uncover on the website.

DAY 261

❧ ⬦ ⬦ ❧

*I find television very educating. Every time somebody turns on the set,
I go into the other room and read a book.*

—Groucho Marx

Physical activity can keep the brain fit and help maintain a mental edge. Even six short months of exercise can increase attention, memory, and decision-making ability by nearly 20 percent. Exercise increases blood flow to the brain, brain volume, and the level of chemicals involved in the production of new nerve cells. Brain exercise, such as reading and engaging in hobbies, can also delay and prevent memory decline, whereas watching television more than seven hours a day can cause mental decay.

Besides exercise, you can keep your brain fit and alert via other people, food, and laughter. Strong community involvement and interpersonal relationships sharpen cognitive skills. So does proper nutrition consisting of whole foods, macronutrients, and micronutrients. (These provide the building blocks for brain chemicals, neuron growth, and the repair that your brain and body need to stay strong.) Laughter also increases blood flow to the brain.

Today's PI
Discover a mentally stimulating hobby you enjoy, and begin to master it. Avoid the television completely today. Use the time you save to practice a healthy brain-enhancing habit.

DAY 262

Gratitude is when memory is stored in the heart and not in the mind.

—Lionel Hampton

You might have heard your inner critic say, "Life is unfair," or, "I was wronged." In reply, ask yourself how you want to spend your days and fill your heart. People are hardwired to look for and react to negativity. You need to use your intention to overcome this inclination. Life is sweet when gratitude fills your heart. Tomorrow is promised to no one. Gratitude allows you to accept this fact and appreciate every moment. Life is hard when anger, resentment, or revenge fill your heart. Gratitude will fill the heart and push out fear and negative emotions. This program spends one day a week on gratitude because it's such a powerful tool for flourishing in recovery. Gratitude allows you to cultivate joy and fulfillment, opens up your heart, attracts others to you, boosts your mood, empowers you, and elevates your spirit. Very few enlightened souls are able to access gratitude all the time, but setting your intentions to look for and foster gratitude will move your heart and life in a positive direction.

Today's PI

Make a list of at least twenty things you are grateful for. Who in your life has helped you and how? Include material successes, physical comforts, health, relationships, positive emotions, past experiences, and feelings of hope for the future.

DAY 263

❦

Far and away the best prize that life has to offer is the chance to work hard at work worth doing.

—Theodore Roosevelt

For many, *work* is a four-letter word. People generally view work in one of three ways. One, it's a job—a way to collect a paycheck and nothing more. Two, it's a profession—a way to advance, but it's still a grind. Three, it's a calling—a way to engage in a passion, and something that would be done for free. Wherever you might fall, don't fret. Anyone can reframe a job into a calling. Janitors and street cleaners who see they're making contributions to individual wellness and communal beautification enjoy what they do, grow from their work, and experience more happiness and longevity than doctors, lawyers, and CEOs who don't appreciate how their work could be aligned with a higher sense of meaning and purpose.

Today's PI

Rewrite either your "job description" into a "calling description," or your "family role" into a "calling role." Describe all the ways you help others and the world around you through what you do. Be specific. Give three to five examples of how you contribute. If you are not currently employed and wish to be, write a description of your calling. When/if you do resume working, refer back to this calling statement to create greater meaning in your professional life.

DAY 264

A man's memory may almost become the art of continually varying and misrepresenting his past, according to his interest in the present.

—George Santayana

Your memory makes you. You simply couldn't manage without remembering the what, where, why, when, and who in your day-to-day life. Your memory also shapes you. Past experience informs present decisions and future planning.

People, though, are strangers to themselves. The passage of time erodes how accurately people remember everything, and present feelings powerfully influence how people recall events. This makes history more fluid than fact. To make matters worse, events are imperfectly stored in bits and pieces in the brain. People remember previous experiences like archeologists. They construct complicated and coherent stories based on very limited data, then articulate these stories like messy storywriters. These are imperfect (at best), often non-linear, and sometimes completely fictional. While people would like to think these dynamic reconstructed narratives are nonfiction, they are just stories. Incredibly, even when people are aware that the mind automatically creates stories, they will still vigilantly guard and protect their narratives as if their lives depended on it.

People's pasts may change, but don't go so far as to fabricate a delusional world that disregards or denies reality. Instead, give yourself permission to be a messy, imperfect student and a traveler of life and the world at large, doing the best you can with the tools you have at the time.

Today's PI
Journal and share your thoughts on today's reading on the website.

DAY 265

There is never a better measure of what a person is than what he does when he's absolutely free to choose.

—William Bulger

Perhaps there is no greater paradox than the one that exists between one's power and powerlessness. On one hand, willfulness erodes the ability to connect with others, to achieve viable goals, and to experience equanimity. People get themselves into trouble when they try to "run the show." On the other hand, passivity disguised as reasonableness robs people of autonomy, mires them in complacency, and makes relapse more likely.

To flourish in recovery, people must be self-directed and in control of personal behavior. They must give up willfulness but not will. Living in recovery gives people the precious opportunity to rebuild trust through living in alignment with their values and practicing integrity in all affairs. Integrity does not require public attention or accolades. It exists unwaveringly within everyone, and it's a powerful determinant of self-respect, self-efficacy, and trust.

Today's PI

Before each action today, ask yourself, "Is this in line with my integrity?" Do not waver from your commitment to act in line with your values and integrity today. At the end of the day, reflect on what you have experienced by bringing this mindful intention to your actions.

DAY 266

✦⋯✦⋯✦⋯✦

To love deeply in one direction makes us more loving in all others.

—Anne-Sophie Swetchine

Just as secrets in one area erode the fabric of integrity, love in one area infuses your entire life with light. The order to love is vast and might be overwhelming. Love is hard to define. For those who have not yet learned what it means even to love themselves, the command to love can be overwhelming because love itself is overwhelming. How does one love, then, and how does one love better? The answer is simple but not easy—start with one thing. How do you eat an elephant? With a spoon. Slowly but surely, you'll win the race like the tortoise. Don't try to love everything perfectly. Begin at one.

Today's PI

Focus your love on just one thing. Choose a person, place, idea, or thing to send intentions and feelings of one or more of the following: acceptance, intimacy, passion, commitment, respect, gratitude, kindness, compassion, and attachment. Journal tonight for five minutes about the experience. Were you able to keep your love compartmentalized to that one thing? Did you find your love expanded itself? Did it feel good to practice this?

DAY 267

It is not the strongest of the species that survive, nor the most intelligent, but the one most responsive to change.

—Charles Darwin

Do you like change? Most people don't. It challenges comfort and safety, and it leads to fear. Some embrace change. They're the ones who appreciate, accept, and welcome the truth of reality. Change has the potential to make people temporarily uncomfortable, but to deny change and fail to respond appropriately is to decay. Change is the only constant. Accepting that truth and learning how to adapt resiliently will enable you to respond better when change happens, and it will also lead you to thrive. Think about this: "Normal" is only a setting on a washing machine. The normal you have now is simply a transition between the past "normal" and the future "normal." So build resilience. Welcome new experiences. Create change.

Today's PI

Create and embrace small change. Attempt to engage in all your routines in new and different ways. Apply soap first instead of shampoo while bathing. Brush your teeth with a different hand. Take a different route to work. Order a new entrée at your favorite restaurant. Sleep on the opposite side of the bed. Find opportunities throughout your day to do things differently, and share your experience on the website.

DAY 268

—⸙⸙—

A work of art is a confession.

—Albert Camus

Do you know your beliefs and thought patterns? You should. By permeating every experience, they create your life. Thought patterns are easy to ignore, but you can discover them through mindful awareness or through crafting art, because they're hidden in your imagination as well.

Even if you loathe drawing and have no experience in ice sculpting or any formal art instruction, using the character strength of creativity by engaging in artwork can often help alleviate negative emotions such as guilt, regret, or torpor. More than a coping skill, art can teach you what you believe. Only by knowing your beliefs, mind-set, fears, and resistance to change can you grow and evolve into the best version of yourself.

Today's PI

Create an art box. The objective is to decorate a box full of art materials that will be ready when you need insight, struggle with challenging feelings, or simply want to create. Decorate the box however you're moved to after today's reading. In this box put some paper and pen (journaling), crayons and construction paper (drawing), model clay (sculpting), magazines, glue, and scissors (collage), and other items so you are ready to create when needed.

DAY 269

I would maintain that thanks are the highest form of thought, and that gratitude is happiness doubled by wonder.

—Gilbert K. Chesterton

Hedonic adaptation describes the way people get used to both good and bad "stuff." Over time, hurts lose their sting and sweetness loses its charm simply because humans adapt. We like the good stuff, so how can we maintain the pleasure of "good" things over time? The rate at which new homes, new jobs, promotions, marriages and partners, financial gains, and other favorable events lose their mood-boosting strengths depends on an individual's ability to experience gratitude.

Today's PI

Count your blessings. Make a list of twenty things you are grateful for. Notice anything new on the list. Look through your gratitude journaling entries over the last nine months, and notice if this (roughly) weekly gratitude practice has thwarted hedonic adaptation in your life. Pay attention to specific areas (material things, relationships, work, etc.) to determine if it has had a more pronounced effect on certain things. Then determine if the effects are related to what you choose to put on your gratitude list. Reflect on what you found. Did you gain any new insight? Share your thoughts on the website.

DAY 270

Hurt no one, so that no one may hurt you.

—Mohammad

Despite what you've heard, humans aren't selfish, evil, or wretched to the core. Study after study confirms that compassion is deeply rooted in human nature. It has a biological basis in the brain and body, and it's also communicated through facial expressions and physical touch. Compassion strengthens social bonds and enables communities to thrive. It overwhelms selfish concerns and motivates altruistic behavior. As with intelligence, evolution has selected the trait of compassion. Even Charles Darwin argued that humans' strongest instinct is compassion.

Studies reveal that compassion contributes to human happiness. Fortunately, research also reveals that you can strengthen your compassion. People are twice as likely to help others in need when they have been practicing the development of compassion. If you aren't naturally very compassionate, you can improve by volunteering your time (which can enhance your happiness and longevity) or donating money (even in small sums) to those in need. Being kind can make you happy, just as being happy can make you kind.

Today's PI

Reflect on anyone in your life (or a group) that might be suffering. Approach your reflection with a peaceful and action-directed mind-set. Then do one thing today to help that group or person. Journal about your experience, and share it on the website. What did you do and for whom, and how did you feel?

DAY 271

It doesn't hurt to be optimistic. You can always cry later.

—Lucimar Santos de Lima

The mind is a mess. To be human is to have a mind that sometimes races, obsesses, and worries. Often waves of fear sweep people away and cast them into an ocean of despair. In the past, addicts used drugs, food, sex, gambling, and more to minimize or quiet this messiness. Whereas those were self-destructive habits, you can now try a novel strategy for rising above the noise—making time for it later.

Today's PI

When you have the urge to ruminate and obsess, make time later to sit and stew. Plan a messy mind date. In response to anxiety and fear, tell them you will create space to do nothing but sit in them later. Inform them that at this moment you're busy. Then, at the predetermined time, have the date with worry. Allow yourself to obsess and feel whatever difficult emotion you were putting off until that time. You will likely find the obsession is either gone, forgotten, or decreased. You might even discover you remain too busy to address it, and therefore have allowed it to pass.

DAY 272

The glory of friendship is not the outstretched hand, nor the kindly smile, nor the joy of companionship; it is the spiritual inspiration that comes to one when you discover that someone else believes in you and is willing to trust you with a friendship.

—Ralph Waldo Emerson

One of the greatest gifts humans receive is friendship. When you know someone calls you his or her friend, do you feel the same inspiration Emerson speaks about? Yes, the outstretched hand, the help, the happiness, the joy of companionship, and other benefits are real. Emerson is correct, though, about the uplifting, divine, and spiritually inspiring aspect of being someone's friend.

In order to be a friend, we must be worthy of a friend. In order to trust others, we must practice trustworthiness. In order to be gifted any of these, we must give unconditionally. Start with the person in the mirror. To be anything to anyone else, first you must be that thing to yourself. Begin by being your own best friend. Treat yourself as a good, loyal companion would. You can then treat others in kind, which will enhance your worthiness of friends.

Today's PI
Practice being your own best friend. Only say nice things to yourself, and treat your body as the sacred temple it is by getting enough sleep, sunshine, fresh air, exercise, and nutrition. Expose yourself to other good people who treat you in kind.

DAY 273

You can spend all your time making money.
You can spend all your love making time.

—The Eagles

Rock bands are known to wax poetic. Those two lines of text are rich in meaning. They also happen to be extremely applicable to authentic happiness. The statement is true: you can spend all your time making money. How can you be blamed? It's your right to spend your time however you wish. You'll have lots of company; scores of people are in the rat race. Chances are high, though, that you'll feel totally alone anyway.

On the other hand, can you actually use your love to make time? Is time made in that way? What the Eagles could not have known at the time they wrote the song was what science tells us today. Experiences do create more happiness than money or objects. Therefore, if the band meant that you could use your time wisely to make memories with a loving heart and loving intention, you can actually create something intangible such as time.

Today's PI
Use your money or time on something love enhancing. Purchase a gift, donate to charity, or send love out into the world. The specifics don't matter here as much as your intention to love.

DAY 274

—————8o 8o—————

A man too busy to take care of his health is like a mechanic too busy to take care of his tools.

—Spanish Proverb

When everything is going exceptionally well with health, fitness, and more, happiness and relapse prevention can feel effortless. However, even the best life includes sadness and hardship. When you experience valleys of turmoil and must do the heavy lifting to thrive in recovery, doesn't it seem as if any good habit weighs a million pounds? People with active hobbies and a social lifestyle have merely a 5 percent lifetime incidence of being chronically ill, as opposed to over 80 percent incidence in unfit people who tend to be isolated.

"Fake it until you make it" is rooted in wisdom, and science validates it. Exercise increases feel-good chemicals, and when combined with other people, you have one powerful antidote for sadness and hardship.

Today's PI
Get at least thirty minutes of exercise. If possible, find an activity you can start doing with other people. Join a gym, start karate lessons, or join a walking, running, biking, or swimming club.

DAY 275

Competition brings out the best in products and the worst in people.

—David Sarnoff

Human happiness is a specific form of achievement—one pursued for its own sake and not for external awards such as power, fame, or money. What is achievement, then? It's peace of mind knowing you did the best you could in pursuing meaningful goals. The flavor of achievement most often portrayed in the media is glory—not one that enhances well-being. Not all achievement pursued for external gains is bad, though. Success can lead to happiness, help fulfill your potential, and assist in your recovery.

Likewise, there's nothing wrong with healthy competition. Though if you're driven to beat others because you feel they're threats to your happiness, and if you choose to see a fixed world with finite resources, the power of fear (the fear of having no power) has seduced you. You're more likely to behave unethically and self-destructively, such as by insisting on being right. Some become so preoccupied with being right that they cause unnecessary strife in their important relationships. Being right might feel good in the moment, but it is not what sustainable happiness is built upon.

Today's PI
Release any compulsions to be right or to be ahead of the rest of the pack. The only thing you can truly be the best at is being you. Allow that to be enough for today.

DAY 276

Don't blame God for creating the tiger;
thank him for not giving it wings.

—Ethiopian Proverb

Imagine you and a thousand random people are gathered in a giant circle. Everyone is then instructed to throw their problems in the middle of the circle. You should feel relieved. Your problems are now gone. They exist only in the middle of the group and adjacent to one thousand other sets of problems. The group members are then told to go in the middle of the circle and grab a set of problems.

Which set of problems would you choose? As it turns out, most people report they would grab their own problems right back. As much as people complain, the bottom line is that things can always be worse. If you chose someone else's problems, you would have to manage someone else's partner, health, children, family, and job. In sum, this can appear downright dreadful. Your problems often lose much of their disruptive power when you think about them in perspective.

Today's PI
Write a letter of gratitude to your parents, teachers, bullies, or any other sources of "past pain" who contributed in some way to helping shape who you are today. This PI is not for sending. It's for you and your journal.

DAY 277

———⚜ ⚜———

How many slams in an old screen door? Depends how loud you shut it.
How many slices in a bread? Depends how thin you cut it.
How much good inside a day? Depends how good you live 'em.
How much love inside a friend? Depends how much you give 'em.

—Shel Silverstein

Even though bad stuff happens, people tend to share the best thing that happened to them with someone else 400 percent more often than they share the bad stuff. Think about what an honor it is to hear another person's good news. Out of all the billions of humans, that person chose to share it with you. When someone entrusts you with good news, it's an opportunity to foster trust within the relationship by sharing joy. However, it's also an underestimated moment of vulnerability. You can do sizeable harm if you do not respond to good news mindfully.

Today's PI

This comes from Chris Peterson's 2013 book, Pursuing the Good Life: 100 Reflections on Positive Psychology: *"When someone relates good news, respond without using the word* but. *The generalized version of this intervention is to go through an entire day without using the word* but *or any of its close cousins like* however, whereas, yet, then again, *and* on the other hand." *Today, have a Chris Peterson "but" free day!*

DAY 278

First say to yourself what you would be;
and then do what you have to do.

—Epictetus

Human beings cannot completely do away with negative thoughts, doubts, or fears. These are simply part of the human experience. While these are part of life, they do not need to rule over the best of your nature. The experience of your life is under your control to a large degree. How you direct your attention and behaviors will determine your character and forge your legacy as you aim to live the best life possible in recovery. It's far easier to create positive thoughts and affirmations than it is to act on them. In fact, sometimes visualization can make your goals more unlikely. So make sure you listen to the wisdom of William James, the founder of American psychology. He said, "Thinking is for doing."

Today's PI
Identify one major thing you want to improve or create in yourself. Write it down in your journal so you can refer back to it frequently. Then practice making it so every day for the next ninety days.

Here are two examples:

1) For the next ninety days, work on stopping yourself from interrupting people when they speak.
2) For the next ninety days, work on avoiding self-critical talk.

DAY 279

*In times of quietness our hearts should be like trees,
lifting their branches to the sky to draw down strength, which they will need
to face the storms that will surely come.*

—Toyohiko Kagawa

There is a rhythm in your body and world that must be obeyed, lest you fall victim to exhaustion, depression, relapse, and disease. Your batteries must be recharged by purposeful and intentional renewal. Too often the worst kind of misery is found when you are alone in a quiet room. Yet, when you can transform those quiet moments into opportunities to rest and recharge, you increase your ability to refill your life's capital.

Today's PI

Breathe, rest, relax, and renew. There are not enough of these days in life, and hopefully you take more than this day to recharge your batteries. Even if today is a workday, put off extra projects and demands because of the prior commitment you have to yourself. Try fitting in a nap or engaging in another purposeful form of rest, such as meditation or spending a brief period of time simply enjoying some relaxing music.

DAY 280

There is no repose for the mind except in the absolute; for feeling,
except in the infinite; for the soul, except in the divine.

—Henri-Frédéric Amiel

Chances are high that you consider your life to have a spiritual dimension. Most people throughout time and across cultures have considered that humans are biological animals with an ill-defined stream of consciousness and metacognition that can seem alternately weird and awesome. This "spiritual" nature is impossible to measure and dreadfully awkward to vocalize, but when applied, it enhances human happiness. Spiritual practices are correlated with better health, longer life spans, more satisfying relationships, better moods, and even more continuous recovery. Some spiritual practices, such as meditation, enhance the size of brain areas responsible for joy and rapt attention.

Today's PI
Spot the divine. Look for evidence in your daily life that lifts you up, inspires you, or connects you to something larger than yourself. Reflect and journal tonight. Did you feel more awe than usual? Did you notice "beauty" any differently? Did you feel humble with more depth?

DAY 281

People use drugs, legal and illegal, because their lives are intolerably painful or dull. They hate their work and find no rest in their leisure. They are estranged from their families and their neighbors. It should tell us something that in healthy societies drug use is celebrative, convivial, and occasional, whereas among us it is lonely, shameful, and addictive. We need drugs, apparently, because we have lost each other.

—Wendell Berry

Every addict has his or her own metaphorical recovery bank account. By developing good habits, you make deposits into this symbolic reservoir. In times of trouble, you'll have a reserve of resources. Beware, though. While you can nurture strength of spirit to shield you in times of sudden misfortune, you cannot cease from depositing assets in your recovery bank if you wish to maintain it long term. The phone that weighs a million pounds when you're feeling hopeless can be lightened by using it when the sun is shining and things are going your way. As an Aesop fable illustrates, "We must make friends in prosperity if we would have their help in adversity." Fellowships, therapists, and other forms of help will seem out of reach if you wait until you're full of woe to reach out.

Today's PI
Place five distinct credits into your interpersonal recovery bank account. Make phone calls to supportive allies of your recovery, attend a support group meeting, participate in service work, or practice meditation. Do something today to strengthen your interpersonal recovery support structure for tomorrow.

DAY 282

Don't be afraid to fail. Don't waste energy trying to cover up failure.
Learn from your failures and go on to the next challenge.
It's OK to fail. If you're not failing, you're not growing.

—Anne Sullivan

When you don't risk, you stagnate. It's far easier, though, to avoid the pain of failure than to use the strengths of bravery and perseverance when fears, doubts, and insecurities plague you. Many seek to protect themselves from the pain and shame of perceived "failures" (which are really "growth opportunities") through perfectionism. Instead of actually making them perfect, however, perfectionism is an exhausting exercise in futility that moves people away from their authentic human natures. Releasing yourself from perfectionistic ideals gives you space to risk, to sometimes fall, and to sometimes fly—all within the life-enhancing framework of authenticity.

Today's PI

"I give myself permission to be imperfect."

Write this simple statement down on a piece of paper, and place it on a mirror, computer, bedside table, or anywhere you will see it frequently. Allow these words to sink in each time you see the note or find yourself slipping into perfectionism.

Jason ZW Powers, MD, MAPP | 285

DAY 283

He is a wise man who does not grieve for the things which he has not, but rejoices for those which he has.

—Epictetus

One of the most frequent mistakes people make is failing to quiet craving minds. People want what they want when they want it. What's worse, when they get it, they want something else or more. The never-ending craving mind adapts to everything and is always searching for what you lack. Fortunately, human beings are remarkably adaptive in both directions. People can just as easily adjust to sleeping on floors as to eating off silver spoons. Yet many get bent out of shape when removed from their comfort zones and forced to change plans, adapt to circumstances, drink a different cup of coffee, make different meetings, or experience anything other than how they want it to be. Nonethless, people can learn to quickly adapt to what is before them, even when their craving minds find reasons to be unhappy.

Today's PI

Choose to work your adaptive muscle by seeking out novelty. Be curious and explorative throughout your day. Engage in your day-to-day routine differently. Enable yourself to break patterns of continual dissatisfaction with "what is" by seeking and living in the small renewing possibilities of what can be.

DAY 284

Expectations have been inflated to such an extent that people think the perfect choice exists.

—Renata Salecl

Freedom to choose is the keystone of both democracy and the free market. It influences demand and drives competition. While some choice is good, more choice isn't better. Humans have been overdosing on choice. Too much overwhelms our ability to enjoy the decisions we make. We end up fretting about the positive attributes among all the options we didn't choose and fail to enjoy what we have. We want more than any one option can provide. In this way, even good decisions can feel like bad ones.

Today's PI

Protect yourself from what Barry Schwartz calls the "tyranny of choice." Follow his suggestions. Examine the time you've spent on prior decisions, and decide if the work is worth the gain. Some choices (finding a mate) will naturally require a higher degree of investment than others (purchasing a shirt). Determine a set of "good enough" criteria for yourself in any situation beforehand, and once those criteria are fulfilled, stop. Set your expectations low, but keep high expectations with performance goals. In other words, do your best. Anticipate hedonic adaptation. Assume you'll get used to stuff. Practice gratitude. Nothing else counteracts hedonic adaptation quite as well.

DAY 285

You only live once, but if you do it right, once is enough.

—Joe Lewis

According to some, Joe Lewis was the greatest boxer of all time. As a world champion, Lewis knew a thing or two about doing things right. You can begin doing things right even if you've failed in the past. Recovery often catalyzes such major personal change that addicts experience what the Nami (the alien race from the movie *Avatar*) referred to as universal law: all people are born twice (biologically and authentically). What are you doing with your second chance? If you sit in the shame and guilt of the past, that's what you get. If you create worthy goals and stay mindful, you get a chance to do things right. You'll get opportunities to be of service to others, to love instead of hate, and to listen instead of talk.

Today's PI

Share your good stuff with a gratitude partner, and listen attentively when that partner shares with you. Specifically, share about those areas of life where you're both flourishing. How are you living life to its fullest potential? What character strengths are you utilizing on a regular basis? What areas of your life are filled with hope and/or love?

DAY 286

—⸙ ⸙—

The only problem with instant gratification is that it takes too long.

—Carrie Fisher

Addiction is not a pleasure-only illness, but the pleasure factor cannot be denied. People try to make themselves happy through hedonic pleasures such as those caused by drugs, ice cream, or sex, but as addicts are well aware, these don't lead to authentic happiness. You can still experience maximum pleasure in recovery. The key is to savor your positive experiences. Savoring enables you to appreciate the present, past, and future. It maximizes pleasurable experiences and enriches your repertoire of positive memories. While gratitude is a form of directing attention to what is good in your life, savoring is a way of intentionally basking in past, present, and future sweetness.

Today's PI

Identify one thing in your life that is truly life enhancing and that brings you healthy joy and helps you flourish in your recovery. Then do it! Savor the experience. Deliberately and mindfully attend to it. Lose yourself in each moment. Immerse yourself through your senses, and let go of your thoughts. Journal about your savoring PI. Reflect on whether doing it intentionally brought about any discernable rewards and if there were any surprises.

DAY 287

Happiness is not a destination, it is a by-product.

—Eleanor Roosevelt

Happiness isn't an end point. It can't be pursued directly, and it isn't controllable. If you try to hold on to happiness, it will quickly disappear. Science teaches that tangible strategies increase durable happiness. Happiness results from right action. Waiting for happiness to happen to you is like holding your breath in order to breathe. Happiness is complex, though, and hard to define. It's a dynamic state that fluctuates within the one individual and between the many individuals. No one is happiest spending all his or her time alone, looking at the mirror, only contemplating his or her own navel. Happiness also shifts with age, life experiences, and environments. While health matters, your relationship to the health you have is more important. Remember that after your basic needs are met, money has decreasing influence. Altruistically spending time and money on experiences with other people is time and money best spent. Most importantly, be mindful and present.

<u>Today's PI</u>

There are no finish lines in recovery or happiness. Happiness in recovery is the by-product of living the best life you can. A common thinking error is, "I will be happy when _____." Fill in the blank with what you are waiting for to be happy. Challenge yourself to honestly reflect on whether this blank would really give you the genuine happiness you seek. Journal about your insights, and share them on the website.

DAY 288

If you want to work for world peace, go home and love your families.

—Mother Teresa

When you treat your family with anything less than peace, you rob the world. Working on world peace when your family is in chaos is like trying to swim in sand. You might flap around like crazy, but ultimately you won't get anywhere, and you aren't really swimming. Be the change you want to see in the world. Whether it is world peace, justice, or recovery, you must start with yourself and your closest circle. Afterward, you might expand outward.

Mother Teresa knew this, of course, and made peace her way. She also recognized that unless you start at home and in the mirror, any attempts to change the world will be for naught.

Today's PI
Prioritize your "inner circle." This might include your closest friends, immediate family, most central recovery supports, or others. Show those important people what they mean to you through your actions today. Go out of your way to be generous, compassionate, loving, and available. Consider going above and beyond by offering an unexpected gift of your time, talents, or treasures to someone you cherish.

DAY 289

We should never pretend to know what we don't know, we should not feel ashamed to ask and learn from people below, and we should listen carefully to the views of the cadres at the lowest levels. Be a pupil before you become a teacher; learn from the cadres at the lower levels before you issue orders.

—Mao Tse-tung

Sometimes the amount of time one has in recovery is worn like a peacock feather. Staying sober for a long time is remarkable, but it doesn't protect you from experiencing life on life's terms. Remain open to new perspectives with the understanding that you don't see your blind spot. Use your character strengths of humility and perspective to do this. You must remember your own inability to see the forest for the trees, no matter how enlightened you might think you are. Ignorance is simply what you don't know that you don't know. However, pride often prevents people from asking for help. No matter how much or how little time you have in recovery today, ask for help, and then listen whenever you can. These two acts separate foolishness and suffering from empowerment and growth.

Today's PI

Journal about one or two issues you are dealing with, and then look for three others whose counsel you can seek. Remain open to their feedback, and allow yourself to truly hear their words. Ultimately you will decide your follow-up for yourself.

DAY 290

⚜

Pessimist: One who, when he has the choice of two evils, chooses both.

—Oscar Wilde

Optimism is a choice to foster a positive mental state of mind. While optimists choose to enjoy their lives, pessimists look for evidence that they should fret. Optimists extend love and trust to others. Pessimists "know" they will be burned, deceived, and left. In general, optimists feel better, have more friends, are more resilient, live longer, and are happier than pessimists. Optimism in the right amounts, with just a splash of cynicism, can enable you to find the best in what happens even when things don't happen for the best.

Today's PI

Anyone can learn to be (more) optimistic. One simple strategy is to repeat the follow mantra ten minutes twice a day every day, until every cell in your body feels it:

Everything is going to work out.
I am trusting and trustworthy.
I can find the best in any situation.

DAY 291

———◦◦◦◦———

Some say a cup of chamomile tea or a warm bath can induce relaxation,
but gratitude is the great wooer of sleep.

—Elizabeth Yates

Have you ever tried gratitude as an antidote for insomnia? As it turns out, racing minds and disturbed hearts can be made still with an attitude of gratitude. Gratitude is amazing. It can also help you nurture supportive relationships, conquer stress and trauma, bolster positivity, and encourage virtuous action.

An incredible truth is that everyone has something to be grateful for, and when you put your thoughts on those positive things, you cannot also focus on whatever is dragging you down. This does not mean you live in a delusional world where everything is peaches and cream. This means you have a science-substantiated tool at your disposal that can decrease stress and toil.

Today's PI
Make a mental list of twenty blessings in your life. As you fall asleep tonight, focus on the contents of that list. Repeat each blessing in your mind until you have all twenty memorized.

DAY 292

If you tell the truth, you don't have to remember anything.

—Mark Twain

Trustworthiness is one of the most vital virtues you can cultivate. As Twain indicates, honesty is freedom. A cliché often heard in fellowships illustrates this idea: "We are only as sick as our secrets." You must, however, spare harm with inconsiderate or unnecessary disclosures of brutal truths. Even an ugly bride on her wedding day should be told she looks radiant and beautiful. Where brutal honesty is key, though, is in your actions and within yourself. One lie makes the subsequent lie easier to tell, until you cannot discern the true from the false.

<u>Today's PI</u>
Write freehand in your journal for ten minutes. Start writing out what you are keeping hidden from the world, such as any fears, forbidden desires, or doubts. Then decide which one(s) you can unveil or stop and which ones you need help with. Writing alone might be powerful enough to permanently leave behind whatever it is you are keeping hidden. In any case, destroy what you wrote. This exercise is for you and you alone in this time and space.

DAY 293

In its famous paradox, the equation of money and excrement, psychoanalysis becomes the first science to state what common sense and the poets have long known—that the essence of money is in its absolute worthlessness.

—Norman O. Brown

Solomon, the very wealthy and powerful king, said, "Ashes to ashes, dust to dust," upon discovering that money and power alone added nothing to his happiness. Despite studies that confirm his insight, many are still drawn to the allure of external and materialistic goods. Does this resonate with you? By venerating these things, you risk shutting out community and social priorities and experiencing poorer health, less life satisfaction, less happiness, and less pleasure than when you value love and social ties most. In any case, you can enhance your emotional equanimity and overall well-being at any time by placing less emphasis on material goods, power, and prestige.

Today's PI

Try not to spend a single cent. If you are unable to do so today, try again tomorrow. Utilize this practice to enhance your mindfulness about material pursuits. Focus your energy instead on fostering love, social relationships, and other peoples' character strengths. Reflect tonight on what you value most in your life today. What would you like to value most? Were there any surprises in this activity?

DAY 294

One cannot think well, love well, sleep well, if one has not dined well.

—Virginia Woolf

Food is fuel. Not all food is created equal, though. The type of fuel you choose to put in your body can either significantly aid or devastatingly hinder your ability to flourish. Proper nutrition can help you achieve and maintain optimal energy levels, sleep quality and duration, emotional well-being, and mental clarity. Virginia Woolf's recommendation to "dine well" doesn't limit people to eating a five-course meal at a five-star restaurant. Instead she asks people to be moderate. Eat enough to nourish the body and sustain energy without overdoing it and leaving yourself stuffed and lethargic. You benefit from making choices that both delight your taste buds and provide the balanced nutrients your body and brain crave to thrive.

Today's PI

Aim for a colorfully mixed plate at each meal. Different-colored foods typically hold different sets of nutrients. Green spinach and orange carrots offer unique contributions to your overall nourishment, as do brown rice, yellow bananas, and red tomatoes. Throw some berries in your cereal, add a side salad to your normal lunch, and aim for lots of colorful veggies with dinner. Savor the taste of your food while simultaneously practicing gratitude for the nourishment it brings.

DAY 295

Happiness grows at our own firesides,
and is not to be picked in strangers' gardens.

—Douglas Jerrold

As ancient as the Old Testament, the habit of coveting your neighbor's "fruit" has long been recognized as an unworthy pursuit. While coveting might not necessarily be sinful, it won't enhance human happiness either. Happiness grows at home, where you are, where your support is, and within. Why compare yourself to others anyway? The answer is that if you can maintain your value by matching the outward appearances of those around you, you will feel you fit in and deserve a place at least as much as the people next door. A survival instinct, fear of abandoment, ultimately drives this thinking and causes you to stay vigilant for external signs that you fit in more than others. True and lasting happiness, however, comes when you identify your own internal values and make daily choices in accordance with them.

Today's PI

Focus in on your values, and foster alignment with them in your daily choices. Following is a list of values. Go through the list, and write in your journal those values that deeply resonate with you. Don't overthink it. Just write the ones that bubble to the surface as a clear part of your value system. Once complete, review your list, and write down any themes in your values. For example, if you value family, compassion, and community, a theme could be "relationships." Write down examples of how your behavior matches these value themes, and then think of at least one daily chore you can add to that list for each value theme.

Accountability	Excellence	Piety
Accuracy	Excitement	Positivity
Achievement	Expertise	Preparedness
Adventurousness	Exploration	Professionalism
Altruism	Expressiveness	Prudence
Ambition	Fairness	Quality
Assertiveness	Faith	Reliability
Balance	Family	Resourcefulness
Being the best	Fitness	Restraint
Belonging	Focus	Security
Boldness	Freedom	Self-actualization
Calmness	Fun	Self-control
Carefulness	Generosity	Selflessness
Cheerfulness	Grace	Self-reliance
Commitment	Growth	Sensitivity
Community	Happiness	Serenity
Compassion	Hard work	Service
Competitiveness	Health	Shrewdness
Consistency	Helping society	Simplicity
Contentment	Holiness	Spontaneity
Continuous improvement	Honesty	Stability
	Honor	Strategy
Contribution	Humility	Strength
Cooperation	Independence	Structure
Correctness	Ingenuity	Success
Courtesy	Inner harmony	Support
Creativity	Inquisitiveness	Teamwork

Curiosity	Insightfulness	Temperance
Decisiveness	Intelligence	Thankfulness
Dependability	Intuition	Thoroughness
Determination	Joy	Thoughtfulness
Diligence	Justice	Timeliness
Discipline	Leadership	Tolerance
Discretion	Legacy	Traditionalism
Diversity	Love	Trustworthiness
Economy	Loyalty	Truth seeking
Effectiveness	Making a difference	Understanding
Efficiency	Openness	Uniqueness
Elegance	Order	Unity
Empathy	Originality	Vision
Enthusiasm	Patriotism	Vitality
Equality		

DAY 296

✦──✦✧✦──✦

The most powerful weapon to conquer evil is humility. Evil doesn't know how to employ it, nor does it know how to defend itself against it.

—Vincent de Paul

Humility doesn't counteract evil by eliminating your critical thinking. Indeed, you can learn from mistakes while maintaining humility more easily than while festering resentment. Resentment blocks broad and creative thinking. It's the poison people drink in order to hurt others. On the other hand, humility releases people from the need to retrieve what they think has been lost, relieves them from the need to justify themselves, and liberates them from fear and ego. Humility actually prepares people for change. It allows them to see themselves in the greater context of the universe without ever having to engage in false self-deprecation or boisterous pride. Humility allows people to see others as equals and creates a benevolently even playing field for all.

Today's PI

Either engage in or make solid arrangements to engage in service work with individuals whom you might have considered "below" you. These could be people of differing socioeconomic status, age, or ability. Fulfill this PI commitment within the next two weeks with an open, humble, and compassionate heart. Look for the similarities between you and the human beings you choose to serve, and look for the valuable lessons they can teach you when you allow yourself to take on the role of student. When you complete this activity, reflect on any insights gained, journal these, and share them on the website.

DAY 297

━━◦⟡◦ ◦⟡◦━━

Knowing yourself is the beginning of all wisdom.

—Aristotle

Everyone has a *literal* blind spot. There is an area in the eye where you cannot form any images, and instead of seeing a black hole, your brain fills in the gap using imagination. Everyone also has a *figurative* blind spot. A person is limited by only one set of eyes, a biased memory, and his or her primarily emotional judgments. While self-knowledge comes from within, people have tricky biases that can prevent them from noticing fundamental truths about themselves. People risk never becoming aware of this figurative blind spot when not open to learning about the entire self. Full cups have no room for more liquid, and full minds have no room for more learning.

Today's PI

Ask five close, supportive friends to write a list of three of your most defining virtuous characteristics and three reasons why they chose you as a friend or coworker. Before you get their feedback, make your own list to compare. If there are any major differences between your list and your friends' lists, use the character strength of curiosity to help shrink your figurative blind spot. Journal about any insights you gain, and share them on the website.

DAY 298

❦❦

When people see my images, often times they will say, "Oh My God!" Have you ever wondered what that meant? The "oh" meant it caught your attention, makes you present, and makes you mindful. The "my" means it connects to something deep inside your soul. "God" is that personal journey we all want to be on, to be inspired, and to be connected to a universe that celebrates life.

—Louie Schwartzberg

In this moment, you get the present. The present is the first and last gift you are given—always right now. The people around you, the beauty of nature, and everything else will never be as they are in this moment, in this time, and in this place.

Today's PI

Are you grateful you have eyes to see the beauty of nature, a brain to interpret its signals, and a heart to feel its beauty and pleasure? Spend some time in nature appreciating its beauty and life-giving grace. If you can create an appropriate space and clear the time, spend twenty minutes in reflective meditation while in nature. Journal only if you're inspired to do so, but wait until after you've spent at least twenty minutes meditating (sitting, walking, etc.) in nature.

DAY 299

A great attitude does much more than turn on the lights of our worlds; it seems to magically connect us to all sorts of serendipitous opportunities that were somehow absent before the change.

—Earl Nightingale

When you cannot control anything else in the world, you can still control your attitude. People are powerless over addiction, people, places, and things. People do not cause the sun to rise or set, and they're not in the outcome business. You can change your behavior and work as diligently as possible. What you cannot do is manipulate the outcomes. That is up to a power greater than yourself.

What are you not powerless against? You do have free will, and you are happiest when self-directed. You owe it to yourself to take full advantage of the power you do have. You can control your attitude, even when you experience emotions you want to change.

Today's PI

Spend time journaling about when having a positive attitude has helped you in the past week, the past month, and the past six months. Look for specific examples as well as general patterns. Are there any growth opportunities that surface where you recognize you could have chosen to operate with a more positive attitude? Use your exploration of past attitude choices to bolster your attitude this coming week.

DAY 300

~—⁂ ⁂—~

*You come to love not by finding the perfect person,
but by seeing an imperfect person perfectly.*

—Sam Keen

In the West, reverence for beauty and perfection reigns supreme. Airbrushed and computer-altered magazines rob people of viewing the authentic. "Perfect" beauty is valued more than the real, and people often lose sight of the fact that nothing is perfect, nothing lasts, and nothing is really finished. In the East, the highest valued aesthetic is not beauty and perfection. Instead, experiences that elicit spiritual connections with a sense of longing and melancholy are highly prized. This concept (known as *wabi-sabi*) is not a love of the ugly, grotesque, or twisted. It is an appreciation of the candid honesty of natural objects and processes—the unassuming, unambiguous, modest, and intimate. In love, when people expect perfection and focus only on their wants, they can easily become disillusioned with their mates or other close relations. In applying wabi-sabi to loving relationships, what you essentially do is shift your focus from what's not perfect to what's right. Wabi-sabi requires mindful appreciation of the unique and hidden beautiful imperfections in all things.

Today's PI

Journal for three minutes today about the wabi-sabi in your mate or close relations. Look for opportunities to love others for their perfect imperfections.

DAY 301

The human understanding when it has once adopted an opinion (either as being the received opinion or as being agreeable to itself) draws all things else to support and agree with itself.

—Francis Bacon

Most often, emotions and memories contribute the lion's share of daily experiences. Thoughts and emotions aren't directions, commands, or absolute truths. However, people heed and follow them as if they were real, wise, and true. Beliefs and feelings infuse experiences with stories, which become realties and yield power. People, after all, often believe the stories more than the facts, but reality comes first. Thoughts and emotions cannot replace the laws of gravity. However, when thoughts and emotions are treated like wise and absolute masters, they can frighten, threaten, and demean: *I am a failure! They don't want me here! She is after my husband!* These are a few ways storytelling enslaves people and casts them into preventable agony and despair.

Today's PI

Be mindful of your storytelling. When you have an emotion or thought, ask yourself how true, relevant, useful, demeaning, exaggerated, or nonsensical it is. Tell yourself you're making up a story, and if you can't determine its validity, ask for input from others. See how many times your storyteller is true or false. Replace untrue, negative, and degrading stories with positive ones. Change "I'm a fraud" to "I'm authentic."

DAY 302

—⟡—

When we honestly ask ourselves which person in our lives mean the most to us, we often find that it is those who, instead of giving advice, solutions, or cures, have chosen rather to share our pain and touch our wounds with a warm and tender hand.

The friend who can be silent with us in a moment of despair or confusion, who can stay with us in an hour of grief and bereavement, who can tolerate not knowing, not curing, not healing and face with us the reality of our powerlessness, that is a friend who cares.

—Henri J.M. Nouwen

The problems we experience in life are like figurative onions. When you eat onions or experience difficulties in life alone, you cry more than when you eat them with others. Having a support system, communicating openly, and sharing emotions equally with genuinely supportive people decreases stress and increases happiness, and that means better health.

Today's PI

Reinforce your connection with your support system. Reach out and communicate. Challenge yourself to share a sorrow or current difficulty with one of your trusted allies. Be brave, honest, and compassionate with yourself. Allow the friend to share your burden with you.

DAY 303

It takes a clever man to turn cynic,
and a wise man to be clever enough not to.

—Fannie Hurst

The negativity bias is a hardwired neural phenomenon that directs people to look for and react more robustly to bad and frightening stuff than good stuff. With that in mind, businesses such as the media take advantage of what will capture their clients' attention (as any profit-driven business would). The media are not alone, and evidence of what is wrong, bad, deteriorating, and misplaced can be found in every corner, from sociology to cultural anthropology, from the political left to the right, and from religious organizations to watercooler chatter. If you are not mindful of the mind's mind of its own, you can easily feed off the negativity like a hungry leech at a bloodletting.

Today's PI

Instead of blindly looking for the bad and negative, focus your energy and thoughts today on all that is right in your life and in the world around you. Resolve to choose to disengage from any negativity-increasing external situations, such as watching most news programs, gossiping, complaining about the political infrastructure, or engaging in cynical conversations about your workplace. Spend today focused on staying in the positive. Journal tonight about your experience. Reflect on whether you have an easier time hunting for the good stuff now than when you started this guide.

DAY 304

What is the difference between a drunk and an alcoholic?
The alcoholic needs to go to those meetings.

—Anonymous

Someone doesn't necessarily have to be an addict to help an addict. Nonetheless, knowing the hell of addiction and the sweet road of recovery rapidly catalyzes trust between two addicts. In groups this leads to several benefits. Recovery fellowships are resources of social interactions, supportive group members, and a sense of belonging to something larger than the self. Robust social lives assist in breaking the literal and figurative isolation so typical of addiction and can enhance your overall well-being. Traditional recovery fellowships have many effective techniques for happiness. It is no wonder that they are wildly popular.

Today's PI

Find a fellowship meeting to attend in the next seven days. If you already attend one regularly, pick a new one where you will be a stranger. Observe how the different rhythms of different fellowships provide the same basic elements of recovery and happiness. Then try to expand your group participation to something outside of recovery. Join a volunteer organization, networking group, running club, hobby and enthusiast group, or other community where your interests lie and where you can reap the benefits of increased happiness, fun, and social connections.

DAY 305

Patterns persist. Persistent patterns persist persistently.

—Alan Fox

Who are you? While you might look at your intentions, feelings, thoughts, or words to answer that question, these areas are deceiving. Instead look at your behaviors. Actions reveal your true identity. People are what they repeatedly do. The best predictor of future behavior is current behavior, and most people intuitively prospect accordingly. People will generally know who you are and what you want through observing what you do and the company you keep. Your intentions, therefore, are inconsequential. Your words generally reveal only your integrity, because most people have pretty good lie detectors.

Today's PI

Recognize your own patterns or habits, and expect them to persist. Make a top-ten list of your habits. Continue doing those healthy, positive habits, but change the habits that aren't healthy or positive. Good habits are easily broken, so reinforce those as often as possible. Bad habits, however, are hard to break and easy to start. Therefore, do one of two things. One, avoid bad habits and any temptation to continue engaging in them, or two, intentionally try to change them. Journal tonight about what you plan to change, how you plan to do it, and how you plan to refer to it throughout the next thirty days.

DAY 306

We never know the wealth of water till the well is dry.

—English Proverb

Positive recovery is a balanced approach to helping addicts, their loved ones, and those who serve them to flourish in recovery. While you apply yourself intentionally to pursue happiness effectively, you cannot afford to take happiness for granted—that is, you can help yourself by enriching the value you give to happiness. Happy people place a high value on happiness and appreciate its fruits. The cynic will dismiss this perspective as fundamentally obvious or flawed. The optimist will embrace the challenge to value happiness more today than yesterday and more tomorrow than today.

Think of valuing happiness as the preparation stage enabling you to fully capitalize on the doing stage. People do what they value, so when you value happiness, you will naturally make time for close relationships and social networks, nurture your and others' character strengths, and train yourself to be optimistic (with a healthy dose of pessimism). Additionally, you will engage in meaningful endeavors with integrity, practice mindfulness, take care of your body, mind, and soul, achieve valuable goals, and practice love rather than hate.

Today's PI
Recommit to happiness and acting on all the guidelines that lead to it. Journal for five to ten minutes about why you choose to value happiness.

DAY 307

Advances are made by those with at least a touch of irrational confidence in what they can do.

—Joan L. Curcio

Life is full of thin lines. Self-efficacy ("self-esteem") contributes to resilience, hope, and achievement. Yet self-absorption, grandiosity, and narcissism tip the scale of valuing oneself from healthy pride to alienation, disconnection, and despair. However, Curcio's quote is also correct. Without sometimes irrational beliefs in your ability, you are less likely to take brave risks or be curious, and thus you are less likely to achieve your full potential. You must be willing to suspend self-doubt long enough to challenge yourself outside your comfort zone. In doing so, your confidence in your abilities and yourself grows. Recovery is similar in that it begins with the belief that you can handle this. Despite the odds that most will relapse in the first year, the fact that scores of people successfully maintain good, long-lasting recovery serves as a testament to how powerful a slightly irrational belief in the self can be. Whenever you must rise to a seemingly improbable challenge, tell yourself, "Yes, I can do it!"

Today's PI

Journal about what you believe yourself to be capable of doing. Allow yourself to engage in dreams that initially might seem to be irrationally outside of your grasp. Remove the barriers in your mind. The resilience and capability of the human soul is vast. Exercise hope and optimism, and envision you at your very best. Don't be as crazy as the person who jumped off a tall building thinking he could fly; be as crazy as those who made flight possible.

DAY 308

Happiness depends more on the inward disposition of mind than on outward circumstances.

—Benjamin Franklin

Again, for the majority of jobs, money has an indirect relationship with happiness, productivity, and job satisfaction. Numerous studies clearly demonstrate that once a person is paid in the neighborhood of fair, mastery (getting better at something), autonomy (being in control of oneself in tasks), and purpose (doing something with meaning and value) are what make him or her more successful and happy. Like most people, though, you probably do not think you are like most people. The ego tricks you into pursuing money, power, and other conspicuous symbols that people assume reflect value in relation to others.

Today's PI

Reflect on the following: most people would rather work at a job making $90,000 when all others make $70,000 instead of making $100,000 when all others make $150,000! Be honest when picking the scenario you would prefer. Even though comparing oneself to others is a natural human tendency, you can decide to start measuring your own self-fulfillment and sense of life satisfaction for yourself. Your right to be happy does not depend on how rich, famous, and beautiful you are as compared to others. Nobody is more special than another, so nurture a happy "inward disposition."

DAY 309

It is a wise person that adapts themselves to all contingencies; it's the fool who always struggles like a swimmer against the current.

—Anonymous

The only constant in the universe is change. By being open to change, you flow with eternity. Water doesn't struggle with conformity. It simply adjusts itself to any vessel it inhabits. Adaptation is not weakness. Water can move mountains. Water's flexibility is its greatest source of power. Likewise, of the many characteristics of happy people, there are three that contribute to immense personal power: adaptability, resilience, and tolerance.

Openness is not blind conformity, and adaptation is not ignorance of who you are and what you value. Choosing to adapt does not mean changing your values. It simply calls forth practical wisdom to remain malleable and humble. It allows you to accept the "what is." This wisdom enables you to live the best life possible in recovery.

Today's PI
How often do you find yourself struggling against the flow of life? How often do you practice acceptance of the inevitable and choose to adapt to the unavoidable? Sit in quiet reflection or meditation on your water-like, happy characteristics for ten minutes, and then journal tonight about times when you adapted easily and powerfully to given circumstances.

DAY 310

⸻ ❧ ❧ ⸻

Nothing is more likely to help a person overcome or endure troubles than the consciousness of having a task in life.

—Victor Frankl

Victor Frankl observed that prisoners of concentration camps who could identify meaning in their lives and who viewed each experience in life as a challenge from which to learn and grow gracefully endured the extreme hardship. These hardy people didn't think life owed them anything. They looked for what life expected from them. They made meaning in life rather than waiting around for it, and they fulfilled their purposes by acting accordingly.

Apply the lessons from these resilient survivors in your recovery, and perhaps you can overcome your troubles too. Happiness does not create a purpose in your life. Having a purpose creates happiness.

Today's PI
Make a list of the top ten priorities in your life. What resides atop your hierarchy? Ask yourself, "Am I living in alignment with my stated priorities?" If you decide to make any changes in your behavior, journal about them. What can you specifically do today and tomorrow to narrow the gap between what you say and what you do?

DAY 311

Be who you are and say what you feel because those who mind don't matter and those who matter don't mind.

—Dr. Seuss

Standing in one's truth requires knowing what one's truth is. Most people spend so much time and energy fitting in, trying to impress, and ignoring their inner voices, they are not even aware of who they are and what their truths are. Some others know their truths but are afraid to speak, or they have been overly conditioned to go with the flow. Dissenting opinions are unpopular. Rather than speaking up, people play it safe in silence. Self-censorship causes people to be short of integrity. Worse still, being concerned with abandonment by those who matter the least does not enable you to see who truly has your back. Those who don't mind when you speak your truth are the ones you should be most concerned with, because they are your support.

Today's PI

When was the last time you fearlessly expressed who you are and what you think in the face of fear? Reflect on how it felt to live true to your integrity in the face of conflict or challenge. How did this experience help you? If you cannot recall an experience where you engaged in this way, spend some time journaling on a situation you can anticipate in the near future where you will likely have an opportunity to speak your truth. Visualize how that will feel. What do you need to do in order to prepare yourself for this brave step?

DAY 312

———⚙⚙———

Gratitude bestows reverence, allowing us to encounter everyday epiphanies, those transcendent moments of awe that change forever how we experience life and the world.

—John Milton

Gratitude is a feeling and an unpretensious state of mind. It transforms the good stuff into appreciation with a warm acknowledgment of humility. Gratitude improves your mood, and it improves the overall well-being of all those around you. It has a ripple effect from your body to your soul to other people and their souls. Gratitude improves your altruism, health, and success. Too often, though, people overlook the little things in life. Millions of people don't have faucets to deliver drinkable hot and cold water. Millions of people do not have enough food to eat, homes to call their own, or anything besides their legs to get around. There is so much in this world to rejoice in. Everywhere you look, you can just as easily count joys instead of woes and friends instead of foes.

Today's PI
Make a gratitude list. Focus at least some of the list on sacred, transcendent, or sublime blessings in your life, such as connections to others, love, and hope.

DAY 313

꘎꘎꘎

As one man's meat is another man's poison, so one man's rubbish is another man's treasure.

—William and Robert Chambers

Don't wait for spring. Clean your clutter now. Living near the Gulf of Mexico, hurricanes and I are not strangers. Ike was especially familiar. Ike gifted me (and much of Houston) with flooding and downed power lines. With winds so fierce they uprooted trees and rooftops with ease, Ike wasn't selfish with its blinding force. Like my neighbors, I had to discard mountains of stuff ruined by rain and wind. I lost an entire garage full of stuff. There was so much stuff to throw away, in fact, it took months before the city could clear everything. Surprisingly, my family and I didn't miss a single thing. Had I cleaned it out and donated its contents to people in need, I could have capitalized on the benefits of giving. Had I cleaned the yard and house of clutter before Ike forced the issue, I could have avoided unnecessary strain. Research reveals that cluttered homes interfere with mental clarity, create stress, and cause irritability.

Today's PI

Look around your home, community, and work space. Clean the clutter. You're probably ignoring useful resources others can use. Neatly package and donate your clutter before an Ike visits you.

DAY 314

Time is too slow for those who wait, too swift for those who fear,
too long for those who grieve, too short for those who rejoice,
but for those who love, time is eternity.

—Henry Van Dyke

Everyone has the exact same amount of the most valuable commodity in life—the present moment. Time is a currency (a resource), and it's not as fixed as you might think. Until your body passes from this world, you are gifted with twenty-four hours to live each day. Those who appreciate the value of time spend it wisely. Those who value themselves don't waste precious minutes opening false doorways to happiness. Skipping out on recovery work because you get too busy with other stuff makes that stuff disappear. Spending time and money with family and friends on passions and experiences brings happiness. In contrast, some spend too much time working and making enough money so that, one day in the future, they will have enough cash to spend time with loved ones or to engage in meaningful experiences. They ignore, however, that an enormous drawbridge is retracted and blocking their way. They are doomed to crash. They must stop, wait, and proceed only when the time is right.

Today's PI

Spend one more hour than you normally would with family or friends or in a passionate, meaningful endeavor. Journal about what you did, how you felt, and any insights gained. Share it on the website.

DAY 315

When I managed my drinking I was not enjoying it, and when I drank to enjoyment, I was not managing my life very well.

—Klebo Price

When drugs or behaviors robbed you of volition, they filled your head with lies. Telling you that you had no problems, they were like friends who stole your stuff and helped you look for it. Like a parasitic plague, substances and addictive behaviors erode bodies, minds, and souls from the inside out. For many, the voice of addiction never fully ceases whispering lies and trying to convince them that it wasn't so bad. For all addicts, though, addiction never goes away. There is no cure. However, addicts don't enter and maintain recovery merely to hide out against any wisp of a threat. They do so to flourish. Preventing a relapse is key, but so too is living in balance between fulfillment of desire and succumbing to craving.

Today's PI

Discover. Reflect on the past three months. Journal about ways in which any desire overpowered healthy balance. Where did you experience cravings for more pleasure, money, or power? Where have you overindulged or acted on an addictive tendency? Use curiosity and bravery, and take an honest look.

DAY 316

———✦❊ ❊✦———

When you do things from your soul,
you feel a river running through you, a joy.

—Rumi

Spirituality is strange. Both a source of inspirational transformation and a never-ending search for the sacred, it's neither completely within oneself nor exclusively external. In addition, the more you find, the larger you grow. You're like an enormous tree that spreads its roots deep into the earth. The search itself catalyzes growth, connection, and shelter from the storm. Coincidentally, trees and other natural objects inspire, protect, and ground many in the spiritual realm. A tree does not plan on becoming a tree later; it is a tree today. Living in the present is spiritual, and living for tomorrow is absence. Think about humans. You are not a human "becoming." You are a human being. When you live in the moment, you give yourself the best opportunity to get out of your own way. You allow yourself to operate as a vessel that can be filled up with the river of God, a life force, a universal energy, or any other mysterious essence that guides, transforms, and fills you with joy.

Today's PI

Sit in quiet meditation for twenty minutes. Imagine you are a vessel filled with your thoughts, fears, desires, and ambitions. Once you hold that image, visualize the entire vessel emptying onto the floor at your feet. As you meditate, allow whatever comes back into the vessel to flow right back onto the floor in front of you.

DAY 317

———✦———

Appreciation is a wonderful thing;
it makes what is excellent in others belong to us as well.

—Voltaire

Count your blessings and flourish. Include others' wins as well, for there is enough joy to go around. Like love, joy is an inexhaustible resource. You choose whether or not to see the positive in life. A friend's promotion or windfall does not mean you're less than that person, unless you deem it so. Gratitude adds perspective. If you notice the great stuff around you, it's easier to notice the great stuff within too. Gratitude helps you realize what you have. This can lessen your need for wanting more all the time. Gratitude improves health, strengthens relationships, reduces stress, and increases overall well-being.

Today's PI

Make a list of or reflect on three of your loved ones' recent accomplishments. Also note how each person's achievement added to your life. Were you in awe, grateful for their successes, happy, proud, and so forth? At some point today, reach out and communicate these thoughts to them. Journal tonight about how you felt both during and after today's PI.

DAY 318

The thing that is really hard, and really amazing, is giving up on being perfect and beginning the work of becoming yourself.

—Anna Quindlen

Sometimes people try so hard to be perfect in all things that they forget to be themselves. Worse still, they forget who they are. Perfectionism is as futile and frustrating as herding cats. No one will ever be "perfect." That ideal doesn't even truly exist. "Perfection" is an idea, and it can vary from person to person, moment to moment, and culture to culture. Ideas of perfection obstruct people's ability to appreciate opportunities to grow. Accepting yourself for your perfect imperfections is a major component of compassion and self-love. Waiting for perfection in exterior circumstances or expecting it in others is oftentimes a misguided attempt to keep yourself emotionally guarded or safe, but it is nonetheless delusional.

Today's PI

Focus only on doing the best you can. Today, be the best version of yourself you can be. Try to be no more and no less than your authentic self, but be 1 percent better than yesterday in any way you choose: physically, emotionally, relationally, or spiritually. Be aligned with your values, and lead with your strengths. Reflect tonight on where you were able to accomplish that 1 percent improvement. Share it on the website as well.

DAY 319

*I challenge anybody in their darkest moment to write what they're grateful for,
even stupid little things like green grass or a friendly conversation with somebody
on the elevator. You start to realize how rich you are.*

—Jim Carrey

Many addicts say that even their worst days in recovery are better than their
best days during active addiction. While escape and many fun times could be
had acting out, a recovery lifestyle is much better than active addiction.

When people make recovery their primary purpose, they typically become
aware of secondary (luxury) problems in their lives. If recovery is not their
primary purpose, there won't be many secondary problems to worry about,
because addiction's problems are deadly serious.

<u>Today's PI</u>
*Write out a list of twenty-five things you are grateful for. Consider stretching your list today to
include gratitude for those "problems" you experience in recovery that wouldn't be possible if you
were still using and/or acting out.*

DAY 320

⋯⋯⋯⋯

It is the paradox of life that the way to miss pleasure is to seek it first.
The very first condition of lasting happiness is that a life should be full of purpose,
aiming at something outside self.

—Hugo Black

Addicts are often strangers to themselves. It is no wonder that they are enigmas to outsiders. Addicts are said to be egomaniacs with inferiority complexes. Yet many are people pleasers who claim not to care what others think.

Addiction is comically described as a disease of "first thought wrong." Yet addicts are supposed to "think, think, think" to "play the tape forward." In addition, addicts are encouraged to practice nonjudgmental thoughts, love, and tolerance of everyone while "sticking with winners." How are addicts supposed to know who the winners are without judgment? Life is full of paradoxes and shades of gray.

Today's PI
Reflect on the paradoxes in your life and journal about them. What challenges do you face when attempting to live by them? What benefits come your way when you do live in accordance with paradoxical truisms?

DAY 321

Aerobics: a series of strenuous exercises that help convert fats, sugars, and starches into aches, pains, and cramps.

—Anonymous

Laughing burns 1.3 calories per minute and is a good way to get the abdominal muscles toned. This fact reveals that the simple act of laughing is enough to constitute physical activity without even applying conscious effort. However, like with many things that are positive and foster sustainable happiness, exercise benefits only those who consistently apply themselves. Laughing is good medicine, but it isn't a sufficient substitute for actual exercise.

Exercise is extremely good for your health. It can help treat depression, anxiety, high cholesterol, and obesity as effectively as many prescription medications. Exercise can also increase energy levels, enhance social bonding, reduce stress, and boost self-confidence.

Today's PI

Laugh while you exercise. Why not kill two birds with one stone? Watch something funny while on an exercise machine, or listen to something comedic on headphones. Come up with your own solution, and share it on the website.

DAY 322

Even if I knew that tomorrow the world would go to pieces,
I would still plant my apple tree.

—Martin Luther

Luther illustrates how it's better to light a candle than to curse the darkness. Things might not always happen for the best, but it is always possible to find the best in what happens. We are mortal, so do what you love today. There is really no time to waste!

Be positive. Plant a tree—even one you'll never eat from. Research reveals that happiness is not as related to personal payoffs as much as it is to giveaways. Happiness does cause giving, but giving also leads to happiness. What could be a better coping skill when the future appears most bleak than to help someone else?

Today's PI

If it all fell to pieces tomorrow, would you have done anything differently today? Plan to do something positive, life enhancing, and altruistic in the next seven days. Where in your life can you literally or figuratively plant a tree today for others to enjoy? Reflect and journal on this.

DAY 323

It is better to be loved than feared.

—Senegalese Proverb

Some monarchs ruled by fear. Some tyrants still do. Bullies, from the playground to corporations, often get what they want by brute force. Yet when everything has been said and done and the dust settles, it is far better to achieve through honor, respect, love, and integrity than through fear and intimidation. Love is not a form of manipulation. It requires no justification or special loopholes in the legal and tax codes, and it comes back to the lover tenfold. Insofar as a monetary value can be applied to friendship, each friend adds to happiness more than six times what income adds. (This is in cases where income provides more than one's basic needs.) Nothing else, in terms of happiness-producing monetary value, is quite as robust. Friends are not made through fear; acquiescence is. Since friends and social contacts are in every arena of life, loving others produces the biggest rate of return in the ultimate currency—happiness.

Today's PI

Enhance the happiness in your life by dedicating your energy to showing a close friend or family member that you love him or her. You can express this in any fashion you like—a gift, a letter, spending extra time with that person, practicing empathic listening, etc. Focus on loving that person, and see how you feel at the day's end.

DAY 324

And so we need courage to act, then actually act, hope and faith, and time. Ignoring any one of these ingredients is a forfeiture of odds.

—Henrietta Bargge

Is it possible to see into the future? Perhaps the way to know your future is to start creating it now. You actually begin making the future simply by asking questions about it. Of course, you need to act, have hope and faith in yourself, and take risks. Waiting around might seem easier, more comfortable, familiar, and safe, but to not risk is to not live. Risking failure takes courage. Even with bravery, you can't create everything you envision. Nonetheless, seeing your future now can help you proceed one step closer to making it happen. Waiting and playing it safe—these don't create a future where valuable goals are achieved. Take risks and fall down—often.

Today's PI

Journal about one positive change you hope to see in your future. Look at your current actions (not intentions). Note which align with that future goal and which don't. Reflect on any possible ways you're waiting on your future to happen. Look for evidence from your past that you can be an agent of positive change. After this reflection phase, write down one concrete thing you can begin doing today to enhance the possibility of your desired future. Share your commitment with a trusted ally, and then get busy.

DAY 325

———⊰⊱⊰⊱———

Use what talent you possess: the woods would be very silent if no birds sang except those that sang best.

—Henry Van Dyke

Recovery requires you make some fundamental and profound changes. Taking chances and experiencing new people, places, and things is not easy. However, by virtue of having switched from active addiction to recovery, you've at least demonstrated that you can use curiosity and courage. Keep this in mind. When you use your strengths, you achieve the type of success that can only come from self-actualization. You have a head start, and you can't really fail at being who you are. You're you twenty-four hours a day, seven days a week.

Today's PI

Improve yourself by trying something new. Dance in public, ask someone on a date, schedule a skydiving lesson, ask your boss for a raise, or sample a new type of cuisine. Allow yourself the pleasure of exploring and growing. Afterward, journal about the new thing you did, reflect on any insights you gained from the experience, and share your work on the website.

DAY 326

Happiness...is not a destination: it is a manner of traveling. Happiness is not an end in itself. It is a by-product of working, playing, loving and living.

—Haim Ginott

Happiness and recovery are verbs, and neither is achieved through wishing. Both must be pursued, but not all paths are created equally. Since drugs and addictive behaviors cause intense positive emotions, at least initially, addicts frequently mistake the pursuit of intense happiness for authentic happiness. Research reveals that the frequency (not the intensity) of positive emotions drives happiness. What can make happiness elusive is the manner in which you pursue it. It's important to value happiness, but it's even more crucial to value those behaviors whose side effects contribute to it. As Ginott illustrates, happiness is best pursued indirectly. If you focus too much on it and how you feel, you move from experiencing happiness to evaluating it, and it disappears.

Today's PI

Try not to think about your happiness or about how you feel all day. Of course, attend to crucial events in your life should they arise, but as much as possible, don't worry about your feelings. Attend to meaningful projects and relationships, and be the experiencer all day—not the evaluator.

DAY 327

I cried because I had no shoes. Then I met a man who had no feet.

—Anonymous

If you cry because you don't have enough, try not to berate yourself. You're not a whiner. Your mind is simply a survivor. The human mind wants to survive, so it vigilantly looks for evidence that it has enough, that it belongs to a group, and that it won't be left behind. The mind is adaptive but negatively biased. It is more attuned to what it lacks than what it has.

<u>Today's PI</u>
Instead of making a gratitude list tonight, make two lists. First make an "ingratitude list." Write down ten things you don't have that you cry about. These can be as small as an electric toothbrush or as large as a fleet of fancy cars in a ten-car garage. They can be as personal as the perfect body or that promotion at work. Next to each one, write a small blurb about what you think you would gain if you had it. Think about why you crave that in your life.

Then make a list of what you do have in its place. If you don't have that toothbrush, write that you at least have a toothbrush that works. Instead of a fleet of fancy cars, do you have a jalopy, or can you use the bus? Instead of a perfect body, do you have a heart? When you're finished with both lists, reflect on whether you recognize more blessings than you thought you had, and share your thoughts on the website.

DAY 328

✦

If we only wanted to be happy, it would be easy;
but we want to be happier than other people, which is almost always difficult,
since we think them happier than they are.

—Charles-Louis de Montesquieu

You might think that admitting to others or even yourself that you feel hopeless or helpless is a sign of weakness. Such an honest admission, though, is generally a sign of immense personal power. When you're brave enough to honestly express your deepest fears and yearnings, you allow others to see themselves in you and to connect with your authentic self. Authenticity is power, and it enables you to appreciate that you're not alone and that your self-worth is not a negotiable commodity. Your self-worth is simply your birthright. Nobody is more worthy than anyone else.

Today's PI

Practice mindfulness and self-acceptance. Are you judging your insides according to other people's outsides? Anytime you compare yourself to others, tell yourself, "I am enough just as I am." Allow the judgment to pass.

DAY 329

———❧ ❧———

Love is the emblem of eternity; it confounds all notion of time; effaces all memory of a beginning, all fear of an end.

—Germaine de Stael

Love cannot be seen or touched, but it's incredibly powerful. Love between two people (romantic or platonic) is magical. When each person gives unassumingly to the other, love's power can illuminate and eliminate. Illumination occurs when your line of sight becomes expanded, dynamic, and more creative. What you never dreamed or thought possible becomes a reality. Elimination occurs when your fears and pain melt under love's sweet, enlightening support.

Today's PI

Spend five minutes writing in your journal about what role love plays in your life. Spend some portion of that time journaling about whom you love and who loves you. If you are so moved, share your entry with those you love. Giving the gift of love in this way can be its own reward. Who knows, though? You might be rewarded in other ways.

DAY 330

Life is like playing a violin in public
and learning the instrument as one goes on.

—Samuel Butler

You aren't handed an instruction book upon arrival in the world. You must figure it out as you go along. The organic human growth process requires you make mistakes. Many attempt to avoid the pain and challenge imposed by life's growth opportunities (mistakes) by hiding away from the world—literally or figuratively. If you protect yourself by evading risks, you lose out on experiencing life's greatest joys.

If you aren't failing occasionally, you're not learning, contributing, or fulfilling your potential. It certainly hurts to fail—in love, at work, or in sports—but after a few lessons, you begin to see it's not quite as bad as you feared. The process enables you to develop compassion for yourself and others. You learn everyone is learning how to play the violin—as messy as that might be in public.

Today's PI

This is a visual imagery meditation. Once you've centered yourself on your slow, rhythmic breathing, see yourself and your life as a metaphor for learning to play the violin in public. Visualize getting messy, taking risks, and making mistakes. Imagine you are literally learning how to play the violin in public, and everyone else is doing the same. Everyone sounds poor at first and breaks strings occasionally. However, visualize that everyone simply moves on without shame or judgment and improves with time and practice.

DAY 331

Words are the most powerful drug used by mankind.

—Rudyard Kipling

The words you use are more powerful than you might realize. Words are often stronger and more permanent than steel. Knife wounds heal quickly; word wounds endure. Once released, words cannot be retracted, so exercise prudence.

Your mind hears the words you use to describe yourself, others, and your life experiences. Your words shape your actions, habits, character, and destiny. How you talk about your life is how your life will be. Life reflects the words (both thought and uttered) that everyone uses.

Today's PI

Use the words "get to" in place of "have to": "I get to _____" instead of "I have to _____." This can change irritating obligations into positive privileges, increase gratitude, and decrease stress. Think about how much better "I get to work" sounds than "I have to work," or "I get to go to meetings" sounds than "I have to go to meetings."

DAY 332

——☙ ☙——

*What happens in addiction is that the tools
people use to manage their lives begin to manage them.
This is when the servant becomes the master.*

—Jason Powers

Addiction has an element of choice, but only in the beginning. At some point, that which serves an addict becomes the master. This happens when the addict loses his or her volition and becomes powerless. Strength and the ability to act and make choices are compromised next. Recovery does not mean always being happy, joyous, and free. However, it does generally signify that the addict is free from active addiction's imprisonment. Becoming unhitched from the shackles of addiction's enslavement is the process of regaining strength, resources, freedom, and choice.

Today's PI

Focus on your choices and the freedom you enjoy when you engage intentionally throughout your day. Before each choice today, pause for five reflective seconds on what the next best course of action is. Do you really want to say those words to your significant other? Are you eating that cookie out of hunger or escape? Should you really keep working despite how exhausted you're feeling, or does your body, mind, and soul need a rest? Journal tonight. Where did you enjoy your freedom of choice today? What areas of your life could be improved if you became more mindful of your day-to-day choices?

DAY 333

Emotional intimacy and fearless self-disclosure are mutually inclusive. They feed each other, and one cannot exist without the other.

—Anonymous

Emotional sobriety ("resilience") is a skill everyone can strengthen. Quite frankly, it's the best safeguard against relapse. When you are able to roll with the punches and discover the best in any situation, you are far less likely to try to control things you have no business in. You're less apt to wallow in resentments, and you're more likely to remain humble and grateful and hold on to hope. Emotionally intimate relationships help build emotional sobriety and enhance happiness. But building substantial social bonds takes time and courage. It's frightening to expose our whole selves, warts and all. Coinicidentally, intimacy can be redefined as "into-me-you-see"—the freeing and intensely vulnerable experience of welcoming another to see you for who you truly are. Developing these deep bonds is a worthwhile investment in cultivating resilience. Your support system empowers you to confront turmoil, challenges, and pain head-on.

Today's PI

Enhance the emotional intimacy in one of your primary relationships by engaging in one (or more) of the following:

- *Share five positive recovery PIs, discuss their significance to you, and remain open to feedback.*
- *Ask the person to take the VIA strengths finder, and discuss the results of his or her test and yours. (Feel free to take it again.)*
- *Make a ten-item gratitude list about what you appreciate about that person. Ask that person to do the same for you. Share with each other and discuss.*

DAY 334

—※—

*What I've found that has been consistent for 15 years is, the recovery community is a
place of charity and kindness and optimism and hope and lack of violence. And it's
people who have been in abject misery and now they're struggling to be free.
So lesson number one that I've learned is, it's an incredibly uplifting experience
and an honor to work for the recovering community.*

—General Barry McCaffrey

Recovering addicts are truly a lucky lot! How many diseases have such an
enormous and international network of people who are welcoming, supportive,
kind, and inspiring? Other diseases have support groups, but none have close to
the number or quality of programs and communities that addicts of all shapes
and sizes have. Countless others are willing to love addicts until they can love
themselves. McCaffrey is right on. It's truly a remarkable group.

Today's PI

*Journal about the gratitude you experience for belonging to (or having the ability to belong to) a
community of charity, kindness, optimism, hope, and a lack of violence. Share your appreciation
on the website.*

DAY 335

Sleep is the best meditation.

—Dalai Lama

A well-spent day brings happy sleep.

—Leonardo da Vinci

Too many Americans are work obsessed, sacrificing days and nights in a puritanical devotion to industry. But continual business is neither healthy nor productive. Nothing else can be such a devious nuisance to all of our faculties and our emotional sobriety as sleep deprivation. The brain requires a substantial amount of downtime on a daily basis in order to optimally function. Being well rested restores emotional, physical, and mental balance.

Today's PI
Today's PI has two parts. First, spend your waking hours focusing on "beyond the self." A day well spent is a day helping others, because making a contribution to something greater than the self can increase meaning and purpose in life.

Second, make it a point to sleep one more hour than your normal routine allows. Sleep deprivation increases the chances of relapse, is a risk factor for obesity, and shortens longevity. You might discover that extra sleep is the small change that makes a huge difference.

Altogether, a day well spent fosters purpose and hope, while a night resting well is the best investment in restoring body and mind.

DAY 336

*Think of yourself as on the threshold of unparalleled success.
A whole, clear, glorious life lies before you. Achieve! Achieve!*

—Andrew Carnegie

Andrew Carnegie was right. Thoughts are indeed powerful agents of change. People are not responsible for their first thoughts, but they must be careful about what they actively think afterward. Thoughts can contribute to or hinder goals. Visualizing yourself within a positive, progressive framework is an important step in building confidence and moving closer to your goals. Your thoughts are vital as they translate into actions, and actions are the keys to success. After all, fields do not get tilled in the mind.

Today's PI

Shape positive and progressive thoughts about yourself and your future so your actions (and therefore your destiny) might follow suit. Write continuously for twenty minutes about what your ideal life looks like ten years from now. Be bold. Allow yourself the pleasure of dreaming big while being realistic. Make sure to journal about as many details as possible. Who is by your side? What are your priorities? What are you doing with your career? How is your health and recovery? Allow the words to flow for at least twenty minutes.

DAY 337

The art of living lies not in eliminating but in growing with troubles.

—Bernard M. Baruch

Addiction often starts when drugs or behaviors are used as avoidance strategies, though the only way to truly process a problem is to walk straight through the middle of it. No matter what your problems, using numbing substances or acting out numbing behaviors will only make those problems larger and more perilous. Sometimes you cannot do anything to make things immediately better, but you can certainly worsen any situation. Just as deadly, though subtler, is when you stop working on your recovery program. Growth is not possible without pain or diligence. The minute you stop maintaining your recovery, you start moving toward a relapse. However, even those who recognize this fact too often recoil from change and troubles as if they were poisons. Recovery teaches people that living to avoid pain is not truly living at all.

Today's PI

Reflect on any pain or troubles in your life that you have been trying to avoid. What numbing, addictive, or avoidant behaviors have you been using to circumvent dealing with an issue? Be courageous and explorative, but don't use this exercise as a shaming weapon against yourself. Simply be mindful of any behaviors that are interfering with your growth and well-being.

A reminder for the bold: write continuously for twenty minutes about what your ideal life looks like ten years from now.

DAY 338

You have power over your mind—not outside events.
Realize this, and you will find strength.

—Marcus Aurelius

Perhaps the most common illusion experienced is the one wherein an addict believes he or she has the power to change other people, places, and things. When you try to control what you can't, you waste energy. The only control you really have is in how you think and act. Try as you might to control anything else, you will find yourself enslaved and exhausted. You're truly free when you accept how truly limited you are. Don't confuse acceptance with weakness, though. Acceptance is power. In acceptance you either win or learn. You're not a complete failure by accepting what comes.

Today's PI

Let go. Search your mind and heart for a circumstance outside of yourself that you are trying to control. You might quickly discover an obvious example, or you might have to search deeply for blind spots. Are you trying to manipulate people, places, or things? Next, write that circumstance down on a piece of paper, and either drop it into a bowl of water or, if you can confidently do so safely, create a contained fire to burn it. Utilize this ritual as a symbol of your willingness to release control over this event. You might just find the strength Aurelius spoke of.

A reminder for the bold: write continuously for twenty minutes about what your ideal life looks like ten years from now.

DAY 339

Fame is a vapor, popularity an accident, riches take wing, and only character endures.

—Horace Greeley

Study after study disproves that happiness comes from making buckets of money, enjoying wild popularity, or being famous. These things fail to produce enduring happiness, and they often make the search for happiness more frustrating. People adapt. Good stuff is indeed vaporous and fleeting. Fame and fortune feel great at first, but in a short time, people become immune to their charms. When the house is a mess, when the kids are brats, and when people can't sleep, fame and fortune just don't matter. Character, however, does matter. Character endures. Character is a distinguishing moral and mental nature. It's what sustains a person through the ups and downs in life. Character is the reputation a person earns honestly.

Today's PI
Identify and take pride and joy in the very best parts of your character. Take out your journal, and write down three to six characteristics of yours that are particularly positive and meaningful to you. Think about where these positive characteristics have served you well in your life and recovery. If you struggle to own your strengths, think about what your closest friends or family members would say they love or admire about you and why.

DAY 340

It is almost impossible to find those who admire us entirely lacking in taste.

—J. Petit Senn

Friends are life's sweetest treasure. They join in both our sorrow and success without having to measure. Friendship's language is universal. Meaning over words, imperfect over rehersal. They take us as we are, warts and all, and only get in our way when we are about to fall.

Friends are the family you choose. They're a source of great happiness and assistance when you are about to lose. Friends don't get in your way unless you are falling. They sweeten the good and lessen the appalling.

Like a garden, friendships must be tended to regularly. Otherwise they might wither and decay. With love, though, they will never go away. When you add the right amount of sunlight, attention, devotion, nutrients, and care, you can ensure your friends will always be there.

Today's PI

Plan a social gathering for your friends. After all, they have amazing taste in friends. Look for happiness within the context of your involvement with others and appreciate that you, too, are someone else's friend. The flow of happiness is bidirectional.

DAY 341

There is not a single downside to gratitude—except that it's easy to ignore.

—Phillip White

Do not spoil what you have by desiring what you have not; remember that what you now have was once among the things you only hoped for.

—Epicurus

Gratitude increases health and happiness and improves relationships. Have you overlooked your health, friends, or breathing? Do you take nature for granted? Are you aware of your strengths, freedom, or love? Are you ignoring the "little" blessings in your life, such as electricity, air conditioning, refrigeration, automobiles, planes, trains, police, firefighters, paramedics, teachers, nurses, sanitation, and clean water?

Today's PI

Be grateful. Make a noisy gratitude list. Say it aloud. Include on the list someone you love, and include several reasons you appreciate that person in your life. Don't stop there. At each meal, say grace for the nourishment your body will receive. Compliment someone in public—at work, at play, or on the Internet.

DAY 342

The greatest and most important problems in life are all in a certain sense insoluble. They can never be solved, but only outgrown.

—Carl Jung

Jung said to be patient. People often outgrow their problems, and time allows them to move past their pasts. When you look at your problems and past under a microscope for too long, you can become mired in negative emotions. Apply yourself in useful endeavors. Lead with your strengths, and build upon what you value.

Operate in the flow—the state of being where you lose sense of space, time, and self. To have flow is to be in the groove or zone, and it's where you grow as an individual and a community member. Find your groove, and avoid the trap of suffocating yourself with excessive focus on the negativity of your past and problems.

Today's PI

Make the time to sit in silence and be introspective as you reflect on how the last eleven months of PIs have added to your life. Journal about the specific ways you now live your life. What are you most grateful for? How have you grown? What, if anything, is different now? How do you know? Share your thoughts on the website.

DAY 343

Your own self-realization is the greatest service you can render the world.

—Ramana Maharshi

When you self-realize, you become the best version of yourself. This is a process that unfolds over the course of many years and takes effort. You can become self-realized through meditation because it is this activity, more than any other, that allows you to observe your observer. You are not the stories, thoughts, and emotions that fill your mind. You are much more than a running dialogue and an interpretation of everything. Stories, ideas, thoughts, and emotions can deceive and mislead. Viewing them is like living in a cave of shadows. You can spend your whole life looking at cast shadows on a cave wall and living as if the cave and shadows are the ultimate reality. If breaking free were easy, everyone would be a self-realized gift. It is hard to observe your observer. With time and practice, though, you can rise above the noise and confusion while you become less reactive and more full of joy, happiness, and loving-kindness. You can find increased opportunities to enter a state of flow more easily and thus to thrive in recovery.

Today's PI
Observe the observer. Follow a guided meditation or sit on your own. While meditating for twenty minutes, focus on your breath, and watch your thoughts as they rise like bubbles under the sea. As they come and go, visualize them rising to the surface and disappearing while you float weightlessly in the vast and beautiful ocean.

DAY 344

Anything in life that we don't accept will simply make trouble for us until we make peace with it.

—Shakti Gawain

Accepting yourself and the world around you is vital to living the best life possible. If you do not accept yourself, you will feel empty. Lack of self-acceptance creates a state of lacking——a place where you feel not whole. In turn, you try to fill up externally with power, money, sex, food, drugs, work, shopping, or beauty. These are false doorways to happiness and attempts to fill a void that only acceptance can supply. Acceptance isn't passive; it's active, and it's most often difficult work.

Acceptance is the start of taking courageous action on whatever is in your power to change. Lack of acceptance stimulates you to go to great lengths to cover up or try to change what you do not want to be. Acceptance is an act of humility, perseverance, and strength. Acceptance leads to emotional maturity and ushers in Roger Anderson's wisdom that, "On some days we will be the statue, while on others days we will be the pigeon."

Today's PI
What facade are you trying to maintain today? Practice accepting yourself for who and what you are—a perfectly imperfect human being. Also accept others as they are.

DAY 345

Two kinds of gratitude: The sudden kind we feel for what we take; the larger kind we feel for what we give.

—E. A. Robinson

Let the season of giving be yours and not that of your inheritors.

—Kahlil Gibran

Generous people are rarely mentally ill.

—Karl Menninger

From making kids more popular to improving mental health, kindness is evidence-based medicine. Giving feels better than taking. Generosity fuels the soul and simultaneously nurtures the lives of others. When you're kind, you feel better. Period.

Today's PI

Take the time this week to give once a day for the next seven days. Any giving is valuable, but to make this strategy even more effective, give outside of your usual and customary rituals. Find a homeless shelter, needy people elsewhere, or anything you can give to with your time, talents, and treasures. If possible, give anonymously. Remember that giving is a gift you give to yourself.

DAY 346

We're fools whether we dance or not, so we might as well dance.

—Japanese Proverb

Music expresses that which can't be put into words nor remain silent.

—Victor Hugo

Music and rhythm find their way into the secret places of the soul.

—Plato

Dance first. Think later. It's the natural order.

—Samuel Beckett

I would believe only in a God that knows how to dance.

—Friedrich Nietzsche

Today's PI

We jump, or dance, right into today's PI. Listening to music and dancing are just what the doctor orders for today's PI. Listening to uplifting, positive music can decrease symptoms of depression, improve mood, and decrease the effects of stress on the body. Dancing can improve your coordination, concentration, and self-efficacy. Dancing to your favorite tunes sets your body and mind in hopeful motion.

Don't try dancing in an armory or atop a cactus patch. Pick your environment and your music wisely. Sad music can bring you down. Uplifting music can help you move out of sadness. Dance alone or with others. It's your choice. Just dance!

DAY 347

It is better by noble boldness to run the risk of being subject to half the evils we anticipate than to remain in cowardly listlessness for fear of what might happen.

—Herodotus

What is needed, rather than running away or controlling or suppressing or any other resistance, is understanding fear; that means, watch it, learn about it, come directly into contact with it. We are to learn about fear, not how to escape from it.

—Jiddu Krishnamurti

Fear of failure causes a failure to launch. Indecisiveness can ensnare us before we have even moved a single muscle. Ironically, it is failure that teaches character, and nearly every great success happened on the heels of a previous large failure. Perhaps Salvador Dali put it best when he said, "Have no fear of perfection; you'll never reach it."

Today's PI

If fear overwhelms you and prevents you from engaging in your life, please skip this PI, and see a mental health professional. Identify and focus on your top fear and face it. Sit in quiet reflection for five minutes, and visualize what your life will look like in every way after you have overcome it. Imagine all the rich details of your life, having overcome this fear. How are you living differently? Who are you with? What are you doing? How do you feel?

DAY 348

Most heroes are ordinary people. It's the act that's extraordinary.

—Philip Zimbardo

Exceptional kindness ("heroism") is often misunderstood and misrepresented. Anyone can perform heroic deeds; heroism is a universal human trait. Human nature is what you make of it. Humans are as capable of heroism as they are of heinous acts. You are a potential hero waiting for the right opportunity to be self-sacrificial for your values and enduring ideals. Heroism depends on having and being willing to act on noble meaning and purpose in life.

Heroes understand freedom's responsibility. Everyone is in this together. Be a hero. Be the normal, everyday type who focuses less on "me" and more on "we." Don't sell yourself short. Imagine you are capable of making personal sacrifices for the greater long-term good. "A hero is an ordinary individual who finds the strength to persevere and endure in spite of overwhelming obstacles," said Christopher Reeve.

Today's PI

Throughout the day, look for evidence of everyday heroes in your life. Are there overlooked heroes in your family, workplace, or community? Do you know anyone who was ostracized for having acted heroically? Remember, heroes are ordinary people who nobly help others the best they can. Share your hero stories on the website.

DAY 349

As long as we're persistent in our pursuit of our deepest destiny, we'll continue to grow. We can't choose the day or time when we'll bloom. It happens in its own time.

—Denis Waitley

Are smart, talented people the only ones who can achieve great successes? This might appear true at times when your best doesn't seem to be enough. However, you can accomplish incredible things when you're gritty. Grit, passion, and perseverance can help you achieve more success in life than either talent or IQ.

Isn't it ironic, though, that when you least expect things to change for the better, they often do? What might be even stranger is how frequently these changes occur just precious moments before you are about to completely give up! Perhaps that is why people regret what they didn't do in life more than what they did. For those who called it quits too soon, you will never know what would have happened had you stepped back, practiced patience, and used courage. Since your future materializes on a schedule you do not design, it's best not to quit five minutes before the miracle happens.

Today's PI

Ask yourself, "Am I allowing the universe to unfold as it should, or am I trying to impose my will to make things conform to my timetable or desires?" Reflect and journal.

DAY 350

—⊰⊱—

If I am not for myself, who will be for me? If I am only for myself, what am I? And, if not now, when?

—Hillel HaGadol

While you need other people, you shouldn't make anybody else responsible for your life. You must learn your own lessons and fight your own battles, lest you fail to grow. At work and in relationships, you have to set your own boundaries. Many discover too late that when you put too much on your plate, you suffocate. When business overwhelms you, no one but you can communicate when your limits have been reached or breached. Learn when and how to say no. Hillel's quote, written thousands of years ago, reminds people that they must take responsibility for themselves.

Maintaining recovery requires guarding self-interest, but in moderation. Extreme self-care becomes self-consuming, and you risk shutting yourself off from the power of connection. Hillel's quote also reminds people to seize the day—*carpe diem!* Live as though today is your last day, because tomorrow is promised to no one. If not now, when?

Today's PI
In your journal, answer the three "moral compass" questions Hillel posed. Share them on the website.

DAY 351

—————⟨⟩ ⟨⟩—————

A tree is known by its fruit; a man by his deeds.
A good deed is never lost; he who sows courtesy reaps friendship,
and he who plants kindness gathers love.

—St. Basil

Helping someone else counteracts feelings of hopelessness and despair because hate and loving-kindness cannot coexist. You can't embrace the virtue of good deeds too late.

Good deeds usher in their own personal transformations and their own awakenings. Some virtues, such as kindness, are self-perpetuating. You are made kind by being kind. You might make a living by what you earn, but you make a life by what you give.

Today's PI

Practice five acts of kindness. Make these distinct and novel acts of kindness that you do not normally engage in. There are many ways to give: feed someone, pay for the person behind you in line, volunteer at an animal shelter or retirement home, put money in random parking meters, greet everyone you see with a warm smile, choose only kind words, deliver flowers to someone special in your life (at home or at work), or even just send a sweet, unexpected text message or e-mail to someone letting him or her know you care.

Journal tonight about how you felt. If you did this exercise earlier in the year, compare your two entries.

DAY 352

A coward is incapable of exhibiting love; it is the prerogative of the brave.

—Mohandas Gandhi

Fear is more powerful than reason and stronger than steel. Only one force can overcome fear—love. Love is not for the timid, though. Courage is needed to push a bully like fear aside. Love requires wholehearted commitment and vulnerability.

You can't love without risking the pain of loss. As Gandhi said, though, loving "is the prerogative of the brave." The brave feel love intensely, and they know love is both a duty _and_ an honor. Coincidentally, people who are the hardest to love are generally those who need love the most. Love must be given in order to be felt. It's undeniably boundless and immensely powerful. Love is that energy that empowers you to be patient and kind with those who need the most love.

Today's PI

Love with courage. For the object of this assignment, choose a person who provides you with the greatest opportunity to stretch out of your comfort zone, such as a "difficult person," and give him or her your love. (Realize that today's exercise is among the more challenging PIs throughout the year.) Love them through actions or thoughts.

No act done with love is too small. Be brave and honest. If you feel stuck, ask a trusted friend to assist you with a blind spot or to help process any feelings that impede your ability to love whole-heartedly. Journal tonight about your experience, and share it on the website.

DAY 353

⚜⚜

To describe happiness is to diminish it.

—Henri Stendahl

You spent so much time on happiness-boosting strategies this year. Stendahl's quote, therefore, could be misconstrued as out of place or even counterproductive. However, the single best way to enjoy happy and joyful times is to be fully present while having them. You're not analyzing or describing your experience; you're completely engaged in whatever you're doing.

When you're fully conscious and engaged, you're in the optimal state known as flow. Recall that to experience flow is to be in the zone or groove. Drugs and acting-out behaviors remove analytical thinking, and they impair the mind and thwart full engagement.

Mindfulness can strengthen your ability to quiet your mind's vigilance and analysis. This can increase the chances that you'll enjoy happy and joyful times and be fully present while having them.

Today's PI

Practice mindful meditation. Follow a guided mindful meditation, or sit on your own for ten minutes in silence. Focus only on your breath. Allow the experience to unfold without judgment. As thoughts arise, give them the space to come and go. Focus on your in breath and out breath. As your mind wanders, gently redirect your attention back to your breath.

DAY 354

Those who dream by day are cognizant of many things that escape those who dream only by night.

—Edgar Allen Poe

Dreaming isn't preoccupied with outcomes. Where you direct your mental energy and the degree to which you allow yourself to be open to optimal possibility significantly impact the experience of your life. On the other hand, the degree to which you acknowledge and creatively explore the best of what could be is how you achieve the ~~im~~possible.

Dreaming can remain grounded in reality. You can learn to be a true "possibilitarian" by training your brain to focus your thought processes on positive potentialities. Using your creative mind (rather than relying solely on your analytical/cognitive mind) can enhance your ability to achieve the most distant goals. Creativity expands thought processes and broadens perceptions.

Today's PI

Portray an aspirational dream through a creative medium. This could be a collage, a poem, a painting, a drawing, or any creative form of expression. Think of a dream you currently have. Perhaps it's about a job you hope to attain, a length of sobriety you hope to achieve, or an amazing goal you wish to meet. Reflect and/or meditate on that dream, and allow that reflection to inspire today's creativity project. Consider sharing your project and the dream that inspired it with a loved one or on the website.

DAY 355

❦ ❦

How can you love God whom you have never seen,
and hate your brother you see every day? Or is that why?

—Anonymous

Most recovery fellowships are amazing noncompetitive and nonexclusive spiritual communities. Sadly, it's rare to find other equally inclusive and accepting examples in society. The group members of recovery fellowships are all brothers and sisters. Skin color, religious beliefs, size of homes, hair color, bank accounts, types of clothes, and every other human variable pale in comparison to what the group is—human beings sharing space on a huge rock traveling around the vast unknown expanse of the universe. The members are not what they look like, where they live, or who they know. They are their characters, which are shaped by what they do. Actions, above everything else, define a person. Yet many still struggle with exclusivity, judgment, or intolerance toward some human brothers and sisters based on random criteria.

Today's PI

Take an honest and reflective look at where judgment or intolerance exists within you. Is there an ethnic group you criticize? Do you have negative assumptions about the elderly? The poor? Are you intolerant of "intolerant" people? Practice bravery and humility to look deep within. If you find judgment, turn to whatever your concept of a higher power or spiritual force is. Try asking for assistance in removing it. Try offering a prayer or a positive hope for the individual or group you judge. Opening up your heart to those who challenge the limits of your ability to be loving will enhance your empathy and compassion—two profound contributors to human flourishing.

DAY 356

———◦—◦———

Your time is limited, so don't waste it living someone else's life. Don't let the noise of others' opinions drown out your own inner voice. And most important, have the courage to follow your heart and intuition. They somehow already know what you truly want to become. Everything else is secondary.

—Steve Jobs

In the hustle and bustle of life, it's far too easy to lose sight of one's personal goals. Perhaps you allow other people's demands to keep your dreams hidden from full view. It can be quite disheartening when your goals aren't achieved. However, it's even worse to discover that those unachieved goals weren't even your personal goals to begin with.

Your personal goals are active symbols of your heart and intuition, and they help satisfy your needs for mastery, autonomy, and connection. While achievement can contribute to happiness, it's generally more important to try your best while pursuing personal goals than it is to pursue goals others have for you.

Today's PI

Review your list of goals or write new ones. Take the time to listen to your heart and intuition through quiet mindfulness or reflection. Think back to your most treasured memories. What were you doing? Who was with you? Journal about why that person or people are sacred to you. Perhaps you'll discover a goal or two hidden in the answers you find.

DAY 357

The beginning of atonement is the sense of its necessity.

—Lord Byron

Too often addicts live in shame. Many have regrets and feel remorse about things they've done in the past. Memories haunt some. Unless you address these feelings and reframe the stories you've been hearing, you can suffer unnecessary agony, be disconnected from others, and even relapse. Traditional recovery encourages people to make amends for past wrongdoing. Making meaningful amends is a key step to releasing the chains of guilt, repairing a damaged sense of self, and enhancing overall well-being. In order to access these benefits, though, you must first appreciate the difference between shame and guilt. Guilt is feeling bad about an action. Guilt can be healthy when it shows where you have acted outside your values. It teaches you how to change your behavior. Shame, on the other hand, is a toxic, negative feeling that you are bad. Shame is destructive and unproductive. It informs you that you are inherently "wrong" and "unworthy." It cuts you off from meaningful connections with others.

Today's PI

Seek out any undone amends and make them. If there are none to make, help someone else who is struggling with shame or guilt appreciate that the truly penitent person can have even more righteousness than those who have never fallen. Broaden your perspective. To have both the forces of the "good wolf" and the "bad wolf" inside oneself requires decision making not possible in those blessed only with a good wolf. When you choose wisely, there is more to appreciate about yourself and more estimable qualities than shame would have you believe. In the end, discover that shame is fallacious, useless, and malicious.

DAY 358

*What we have done for ourselves alone dies with us;
what we have done for others and the world remains and is immortal.*

—Albert Pike

Science has added significance to Albert Pike's wise words. Acts of giving can improve your health, assist you in maintaining recovery, and even decrease chronic pain. Furthermore, giving is contagious. When you practice kindness, you infect others with a "giver" bug. People are more likely to act prosocially after witnessing acts of kindness.

Fortunately, giving is not only selfless but self-serving. Beware, though. The line between manipulation and true giving is thin. When kindness motivates giving, you reap the benefits, but giving in order to take doesn't add to your well-being. It actually erodes it.

<u>Today's PI</u>
Add to the goodness of the world. Call someone and ask how he or she is doing, volunteer your time or money, send gifts and thank-you notes to people who have helped you, bring blankets and food to a local shelter, put money in expired parking meters, pay tolls for the car behind you, or do something else. Afterward journal about what you did and how you felt. Share your experience on the website.

DAY 359

*If you find a good solution and become attached to it,
the solution may become your next problem.*

—Robert Anthony

Addicts can relate to Anthony's quote on a more personal level than most people. Drugs, alcohol, and acting-out behaviors initially served as solutions to life's trials and tribulations. At some point these stopped working, though, and started hindering. Ironically, addicts are often the last to know these tools have turned against them. Even though their experiences with drugs and behaviors are in the past, addicts in recovery can still repeat the same mistake in different life arenas if not careful. It's easy to do. Don't become myopic by limiting yourself to solutions that worked at one time or by thinking you know best. You could fail to see that what once worked might not be as successful in the current situation. Everything changes. Change is the only constant. If you're stalled or stuck somewhere, ask yourself if your thinking is fixed ("This is just the way it is") or if you're living in the past ("I've done it this way forever").

Today's PI

Broaden your thinking. Get vulnerable, ask for help, and use a fresh perspective. Today and tomorrow, do all your small day-to-day chores in different ways. Set your alarm five minutes earlier, eat a novel breakfast, lunch, and dinner, drive to work in a new way, and look at your favorite photograph or painting in a new way. For the next two days, unless you're unable, try not to think about goal setting or problem solving. Try not to think, but remain open to listening.

DAY 360

Even a happy life cannot be without a measure of darkness, and the word happy would lose its meaning if it were not balanced by sadness. It is far better to take things as they come along with patience and equanimity.

—Carl Jung

Sadness. Stress. Negativity. At first glance, these words seem out of place in a book aimed at improving human happiness. However, sadness, anger, and anxiety are normal and healthy at times. Even stress can help. While unmitigated and prolonged exposure to stress is very harmful, small amounts of stress can actually be beneficial. They can improve your memory and learning and elicit your body's production of chemicals that boost your immune system. If you accept everything in life as it comes with equal grace and patience, you can actually make things previously labeled "bad," such as stress, work for you. Indeed, stress becomes incapacitating only when you forget about whatever meaning is behind it.

Today's PI

Journal for fifteen minutes about the top current stressor in your life. Recall the meaning behind whatever is stressing you out instead of fighting or fleeing from it. What is the source of stress? Why does it exist? Does it have anything to do with your goals? Is it work or relationship related? Avoid the temptation to find the silver lining. Instead acknowledge that the stress is a real challenge in your life, and use it as fuel.

Heidi Holvorson said, "As it turns out, your mind-set about stress may be the most important predictor of how it affects you."

DAY 361

✦

*If you see the world in black and white,
you're missing important gray matter.*

—Jack Fyock

You're either with us, or you're against us. People are either good or bad. These are two examples of false dilemmas (black-and-white thinking). People often assume there are a limited number of choices or perspectives in life's day-to-day situations. Fear is often the culprit that has us exclude or eliminate a realm of possibility and additional options. Some attempt to compartmentalize and simplify the world and choices by creating such false dichotomies. Believing that something stands for good while anything against that viewpoint is pure evil is an oversimplification. Even differing opinions are not always mutually exclusive.

Black-and-white thinking increases the chances of relapse, especially in challenging times. If you assume your current problems will always cause your life to be bad forever, you might be unresistingly tempted to find a numbing escape from the feelings of helplessness and hopelessness. If you assume people are either "all good" or "all bad," many relationships will dissolve at the first sign of trouble, or the relationships might cause unnecessary agony.

Today's PI
Pay attention to any fallacious black-and-white thinking. How often do you compartmentalize people and events? Make a list of situations (a political party, a religion, etc.) and people you deem "bad." Then reflect on whether you can move them into a more realistic shade of gray.

DAY 362

✦━━⧉❦ ❦⧉━━✦

*Just as a table will topple without the full complement of legs,
so too, must we work to engage the entire spectrum of a full life so that we have enough
legs to remain erect.*

—Mahatma Mohit Khera

Living a life in recovery involves much more than being "dry." Removing the drug or behavior does not eliminate addiction. It does not single-handedly create the best life possible. Recovery is multidimensional. Sobriety does provide the necessary foundation, but it's but one leg under the table. From sobriety's base, you can enrich your life by following your passions, being playful, getting involved in your community, nurturing and developing deep and long-lasting relationships, engaging in satisfying work or physical exercise, helping others, worrying less about yourself, and pursuing more meaning and purpose in your life. Attacking addiction one-dimensionally ignores what it means to live a full life. It's easy to see that if you are sober while smoking cigarettes and gaining excessive weight, you are still killing yourself.

Today's PI

Draw a table representing yourself, with five legs: recovery, health, social connection, meaning, and spiritual connection. Rate each leg on a scale from one to five. One is the least and five is the most involved and fulfilled. Be honest with yourself. Where are you fulfilled today, and where are you lacking? Are you surprised at your results? Is your table erect, or will it fall over? What one thing can you do today in order to better stabilize it?

DAY 363

Turn your face to the sun and the shadows fall behind you.

—Maori Proverb

This Maori proverb is both metaphoric and literal. When you focus on and turn toward the positive, darkness and struggles aren't so frightening. The good stuff allows you to move past obstacles more easily. Nature, though, is the good stuff. Sunlight and the great outdoors have positive emotional and physical effects. Appropriate sun exposure can decrease depression and chronic pain. Many people report feeling happier, more grounded, more spiritually connected, and invigorated by spending time in nature.

Today's PI

Spend at least twenty minutes enjoying nature. Whether you live in a sunny climate or a more frigid zone, decrease the insulation you put between yourself and nature, and the more authentic your experiences can be. Walk barefoot when you can, eat with your hands as they do in other parts of the world, eat a meal outside, hike on a nature trail, or plan a trip to the beach. Be conscientious about your choices. Think about what aspects of nature feel most rewarding for you, and attempt to seek them out. For bonus impact, try bringing along a friend, family member, or pet to enjoy the great outdoors with you.

DAY 364

Through practice we can more deeply realize that happiness is not the result of what we bring into our life, but the consequence of how we choose to experience our life.

—Javy Galindo

Watch your thoughts, for they make your life. Developing self-awareness depends on thought recognition, which is one of the most powerful tools you can develop for optimal wellness. When you recognize that your thinking is creating your experiences, you become less attached to fixed thinking, and you gain control of your experience. You can either entertain thoughts of self-doubt, blame, and victimization, or you can choose more useful thoughts during periods of relative peace to restore your equanimity when faced with challenges. You can't predict the future. So why focus your attention only on adverse prospects when neutral or even positive events are often more useful and likely? Choose gratitude and optimism instead.

Today's PI
Find your anchor in your breath for five minutes, and sit in quiet meditation. Write down three good things that have happened to you so far today, and explain why these good things happened. Then imagine all that could go right for the rest of your day and tomorrow. Anticipate positive occurrences, and become more aware of the precious possibilities that lie before you.

DAY 365

The past is but the beginning of a beginning and all that is and has been is but the twilight of the dawn.

—H. G. Wells

Prepare for tomorrow today, and open up to new beginnings. People learn in recovery that every day is just another day. Addiction does not care if today is a holiday, an anniversary, a Monday, a Saturday, a "good" day, or a "bad" day. Every day is just another day. When it comes right down to it, every moment is just another moment.

At the same time, recovering addicts live in a society with rituals, ceremonies, and meaning. Certain days are certainly unique and special, such as birthdays, holidays, and national celebrations. These days offer unique opportunities to reflect on meaningful times in the present, past, and future. This New Year's Day, symbolically move into a new beginning and set your intentions and hopes for the future. Recovering addicts know a thing or two about turning over a new leaf. Every day in recovery is a new chance and a fresh start. You can put the past years behind you when you choose hope, welcome opportunities to grow, and make room for new starts.

Today's PI

Reflect on how the last year of practicing positive recovery has impacted your life. Reflect on any hardships you faced and blessings you received. How has your life changed from engaging with the PIs in this guide? Share your story on the website.

LEAP YEAR EXTRA DAY—ONLY EVERY FOUR YEARS (DON'T CHEAT)

Today's exercise is more of a game than a PI. Still, it can provide you with surprisingly accurate insight. Open your journal to a new page, and answer the following questions:

1) What is your favorite animal? List three adjectives describing it.
2) What is your favorite color? List three adjectives describing it.
3) What is your favorite body of water (lake, ocean, bath, rain, river, etc.)? List three feelings evoked when thinking about it.
4) Imagine you wake in a white room. The room and all its contents are white. If you see windows, they are whited out as well. Journal about how you feel.

Next, open to a new page in your journal, and describe the following scenario. You are walking through the forest. What do you see? What type of forest is it? What are you walking on? What's the weather like? Do you smell or hear anything? You see a cup. What kind of cup is it? What is it doing there, and what do you do with it? Describe the cup in as much detail as you can. You continue walking through the forest, and you see a key. What kind of key is it, what is it doing there, and what do you do with it? Again, describe the key in detail. You keep walking through the forest, and suddenly an animal of your choosing in the cat family (tiger, lion, Garfield, etc.) jumps out of nowhere. You lock eyes with each other. What kind of cat is it, and what happens next? After that encounter, you come across a body of water. What type of water is it, and what do you do? How do you feel at the edge of this body of water? You keep going and encounter a wall that extends as far in either direction as you can see. What kind of wall is it, and what happens next?

This is a game that can be a fun, completely nonprofessional way to gain some tongue-in-cheek insight into yourself. The guide/key is revealed when you journal about today's PI at PositiveRecovery.com.